CRE**A**TIVE
HOMEOWNER®

D0841804

Midwestern
Inspired Home Designs

CREATIVE HOMEOWNER®, Upper Saddle River, New Jersey

COPYRIGHT © 2005

CRE🏠TIVE
HOMEOWNER®

A Division of Federal Marketing Corp.
Upper Saddle River, NJ

VP/Publisher: Brian H. Toolan
VP/Editorial Director: Timothy O. Bakke
Production Manager: Kimberly H. Vivas

Home Plans Editor: Kenneth D. Stuts
Home Plans Designer Liaison: Maureen Mulligan

Design and Layout: Arrowhead Direct (David Kroha, Cindy DiPierdomenico, Judith Kroha)
Cover Design: 3r1

Current Printing (last digit)
10 9 8 7 6 5 4 3 2 1

Midwestern Inspired Home Designs
Library of Congress Control Number: 2005924175
ISBN: 1-58011-274-9

CREATIVE HOMEOWNER®
A Division of Federal Marketing Corp.
24 Park Way
Upper Saddle River, NJ 07458
www.creativehomeowner.com

Printed in China

Note: The homes as shown in the photographs and renderings in this book may differ from the actual blueprints. When studying the house of your choice, please check the floor plans carefully.

PHOTO CREDITS

Front cover: *top* plan 121044, page 122; *bottom row left to right* plan 401049, pages 244—245; plan 401029, pages 188—189; plan 401029, pages 188—189 **Back cover:** *top* plan 161029, page 272; *center* plan 271002, page 35; *bottom left* plan 391036, page 12; *bottom right* plan 391026, page 9 **page 1:** plan 391023, page 187 **page 3:** *top* plan 211069, page 93; *center* plan 151028, page 207; *bottom* plan 181151, page 181 **pages 4—6:** *all* David Geer **page 7:** plan 131027, page 236 **page 48:** courtesy of Kraftmaid Cabinetry **page 49:** *top* courtesy of Merillat; *bottom* courtesy of Kraftmaid Cabinetry **pages 50—51:** *top right* courtesy of Kraftmaid Cabinetry; *bottom right* courtesy of American Olean; *center* courtesy of Kraftmaid Cabinetry **pages 52—53:** *center* courtesy of Kraftmaid Cabinetry; *bottom right* courtesy of Diamond Cabinets; *top left* courtesy of Wellborn Cabinet **page 54:** *top* courtesy of Wellborn Cabinet; *bottom* courtesy of Diamond Cabinets **page 55:** *top left* courtesy of Iron-A-Way; *top right* courtesy of Rev-A-Shelf; *bottom right* courtesy of Merillat **page 56:** courtesy of Wellborn Cabinet **page 57:** *top* courtesy of Merillat; *bottom* courtesy of Moen **page 58:** *top left* courtesy of Thibaut Wallcoverings; *top right* courtesy of Canac Cabinetry; *bottom right* courtesy of Wellborn Cabinet **page 59:** courtesy of American Olean **pages 104—119:** illustrations by: Warren Cutler **page 144:** *top* courtesy of Thomasville; *both bottom* courtesy of Rubbermaid **page 145:** courtesy of IKEA **page 146:** courtesy of ClosetMaid **page 147:** *top* courtsey of ClosetMaid; *bottom* courtesy of Rubbermaid **pages 148—149:** *all* courtesy of Rubbermaid **page 150:** courtesy of Diamond Cabinets **page 151:** courtesy of Diamond Cabinets **page 166:** courtesy of Mannington Floors **page 167:** courtesy of Congoleum **page 168:** *top* courtesy of Congoleum; *bottom* courtesy of Mannington Floors **page 169:** courtesy of Dal-Tile **page 170:** *left* courtesy of Mannington Floors; *right* courtesy of Congoleum **page 171:** *left* courtesy of Mannington Floors; *right* courtesy of Dal-Tile **page 196:** courtesy of Central Fireplaces **pages 197—199:** courtesy of Aladdin Steel Products **page 201:** George Ross/CH **page 202:** Randall Perry **page 203:** courtesy of Heatilator **page 222—226:** *all* courtesy of Kraftmaid Cabinetry **page 227:** courtesy of IKEA **page 254—255:** *all* courtesy of Sylvania **page 256:** courtesy of Kraftmaid Cabinetry **page 257:** *all* courtesy of Sylvania **page 280:** plan 121029, page 261

Photographers & Manufacturers: Aladdin Steel, Gillespie, IL; 800-637-4455. American Olean, Dallas, TX; 972-991-8904. Central Fireplace, Greenbush, MN 56726. ClosetMaid; 800-874-0008. Congoleum, Mercerville, NJ; 800-274-3266. Dal-Tile, Dallas, TX; 214-398-1411. Diamond Cabinets, Jasper, IN; 812-482-2527. Heatilator, Mt. Pleasant, IA, 800-927-6841. Ikea; www.ikea.com. Iron-A-Way, Morton, IL; 309-266-7232. Kraftmaid Cabinetry, Middlefield, OH; 440-632-5333. Mannington Floors, Salem, NJ; 856-935-3000. Merillat, Adrian, MI; 517-263-0771. Moen, North Olmstead, OH; 800-289-6636. Rev-A-Shelf, Louisville, KY; 800-626-1126. Rubbermaid, Wooster, OH; 888-895-2110. Sylvania, Danvers, MA; 800-544-4828. Thibaut, Newark, NJ; 973-643-3777. Thomasville Furniture, Thomasville, NC; 800-225-0265. Wellborn Cabinet, Ashland, AL; 800-336-8040.

Contents

GETTING STARTED   4

HOME PLANS   8
  800- to 1,500-Square Foot Homes   8

KITCHENS AND BATHS   48

HOME PLANS   60
  1,501- to 1,800-Square Foot Homes   60

PLANNING YOUR LANDSCAPE   104

HOME PLANS   120
  1,801- to 2,100-Square Foot Homes   120

CLUTTER-CUTTING TIPS
FOR YOUR HOME   144

HOME PLANS   152
  1,801- to 2,100-Square Foot Homes   152

FLOORING OPTIONS   166

HOME PLANS   172
  2,101- to 2,500-Square Foot Homes   172

FIREPLACE TECHNOLOGY   196

HOME PLANS   204
  2,101- to 2,500-Square Foot Homes   204

MEDIA ROOMS   222

HOME PLANS   228
  Homes Over 2,500-Square Feet   228

THE RIGHT LIGHT   254

HOME PLANS   258
  Homes Over 2,500-Square Feet   258

HOW TO ORDER   280

PLANS INDEX   286

Getting Started

Maybe you can't wait to bang the first nail. Or you may be just as happy leaving town until the windows are cleaned. The extent of your involvement with the construction phase is up to you. Your time, interests, and abilities can help you decide how to get the project from lines on paper to reality. But building a house requires more than putting pieces together. Whoever is in charge of the process must competently manage people as well as supplies, materials, and construction. He or she will have to

- Make a project schedule to plan the orderly progress of the work. This can be a bar chart that shows the time period of activity by each trade.
- Establish a budget for each category of work, such as foundation, framing, and finish carpentry.
- Arrange for a source of construction financing.
- Get a building permit and post it conspicuously at the construction site.
- Line up supply sources and order materials.
- Find subcontractors and negotiate their contracts.
- Coordinate the work so that it progresses smoothly with the fewest conflicts.
- Notify inspectors at the appropriate milestones.
- Make payments to suppliers and subcontractors.

You as the Builder

You'll have to take care of every logistical detail yourself if you decide to act as your own builder or general contractor. But along with the responsibilities of managing the project, you gain the flexibility to do as much of your own work as you want and subcontract out the rest. Before taking this path, however, be sure you have the time and capabilities. Do you also have the

time and ability to schedule the work, hire and coordinate subs, order materials, and keep ahead of the accounting required to manage the project successfully? If you do, you stand to save the amount that a general contractor would charge to take on these responsibilities, normally 15 to 30 percent of the construction cost. If you take this responsibility on but mismanage the project, the potential savings will erode and may even cost you more than if you had hired a builder in the first place. A subcontractor might charge extra for hav-

Acting as the builder, above, requires the ability to hire and manage subcontractors.

Building a home, opposite, includes the need to schedule building inspections at the appropriate milestones.

ing to return to the site to complete work that was originally scheduled for an earlier date. Or perhaps because you didn't order the windows at the beginning, you now have to pay for a recent cost increase. (If you had hired a builder in the first place he or she would absorb the increase.)

Hiring a Builder to Handle Construction

A builder or general contractor will manage every aspect of the construction process. Your role after signing the construction contract will be to make regular progress payments and ensure that the work for which you are paying has been completed. You will also consult with the builder and agree to any changes that may have to be made along the way.

Leads for finding builders might come from friends or neighbors who have had contractors build, remodel, or add to their homes. Real-estate agents and bankers may have some names handy but are more likely familiar with the builder's ability to complete projects on time and budget than the quality of the work itself.

The next step is to narrow your list of candidates to three or four who you think can do a quality job and work harmoniously with you. Phone each builder to see whether he or she is interested in being considered for your project. If so, invite the

builder to an interview at your home. The meeting will serve two purposes. You'll be able to ask the candidate about his or her experience, and you'll be able to see whether or not your personalities are compatible. Go over the plans with the builder to make certain that he or she understands the scope of the project. Ask if they have constructed similar houses. Get references, and check the builder's standing with the Better Business Bureau. Develop a short list of builders, say three, and ask them to submit bids for the project.

of contract documents. You can enter into a fixed-price contract by negotiating with a single builder on your short list or by obtaining bids from three or four builders. If you go the latter route, give each bidder a set of documents and allow at least two weeks for them to submit their bids. When you get the bids, decide who you want and call the others to thank them for their efforts. You don't have to accept the lowest bid, but it probably makes sense to do so since you have already honed the list to builders you trust. Inform this builder of your intentions to finalize a contract.

Contracts

Lump-Sum Contracts

A lump-sum, or fixed-fee, contract lets you know from the beginning just what the project will cost, barring any changes made because of your requests or unforeseen conditions. This form works well for projects that promise few surprises and are well defined from the outset by a complete set

Cost-Plus-Fee Contracts

Under a cost-plus-fee contract, you agree to pay the builder for the costs of labor and materials, as verified by receipts, plus a fee that represents the builder's overhead and profit. This arrangement is sometimes referred to as "time and materials." The fee can range between 15 and 30 percent of the incurred costs. Because you ultimately pick up the tab—whatever the costs—the contractor is never at risk, as he is with a lump-sum contract. You won't know the final total cost of a cost-plus-fee contract

until the project is built and paid for. If you can live with that uncertainty, there are offsetting advantages. First, this form allows you to accommodate unknown conditions much more easily than does a lump-sum contract. And rather than being tied down by the project documents, you will be free to make changes at any point along the way. This can be a trap, though. Watching the project take shape will spark the desire to add something or do something differently. Each change costs more, and the accumulation can easily exceed your budget. Because of the uncertainty of the final tab and the built-in advantage to the contractor, you should think twice before entering into this form of contract.

Contract Content

The conditions of your agreement should be spelled out thoroughly in writing and signed by both parties, whatever contractual arrangement you make with your builder. Your contract should include provisions for the following:

- The names and addresses of the owner and builder.
- A description of the work to be included ("As described in the plans and specifications dated . . .").
- The date that the work will be completed if time is of the essence.
- The contract price for lump-sum contracts and the builder's allowed profit and overhead costs for changes.
- The builder's fee for cost-plus-fee contracts and the method of accounting and requesting payment.
- The criteria for progress payments (monthly, by project milestones) and the conditions of final payment.
- A list of each drawing and specification section that is to be included as part of the contract.
- Requirements for guarantees. (One year is the standard period for which contractors guarantee the entire project, but you may require specific guarantees on

When submitting bids, all of the builders should base their estimates on the same specifications. Once the work begins, communicate with your builder to keep the work proceeding smoothly.

Inspect your newly built home, if possible, before the builder closes it up and finishes it.

certain parts of the project, such as a 20-year guarantee on the roofing.)
■ Provisions for insurance.
■ A description of how changes in the work orders will be handled.

The builder may have a standard contract that you can tailor to the specifics of your project. These contain complete specific conditions with blanks that you can fill in to fit your project and a set of "general conditions" that cover a host of issues from insurance to termination provisions. It's always a good idea to have an attorney review the draft of your completed contract before signing it.

Working with Your Builder

The construction phase officially begins when you have a signed copy of the contract and copies of any insurance required from the builder. It's not unheard of for a builder to request an initial payment of 10 to 20 percent of the total cost to cover mobilization costs, those costs associated with obtaining permits and getting set up to begin the actual construction. If you agree to this, keep a careful eye on the progress of the work to ensure that the total paid out at any one time doesn't get too far out of sync with the actual work completed.

What about changes? From here on, it's up to you and your builder to proceed in good faith and to keep the channels of communication open. Even so, changes of one sort or another beset every project, and they usually add to its cost.

Light at the End of the Tunnel.

The builder's request for a final inspection marks the end of the construction phase—almost. At the final inspection meeting, you and the builder will inspect the work, noting any defects or incomplete items on a "punch list." When the builder tidies up the punch list items, you should reinspect. Sometimes, builders go on to another job and take forever to clean up the last few details, so only after all items on the list have been completed satisfactorily should you release the final payment, which often accounts for the builder's profit.

Some Final Words

Having a positive attitude is important when undertaking a project as large as building a home. A positive attitude can help you ride out the rigors and stress of the construction process.

Stay Flexible. Expect problems, because they certainly will occur. Weather can upset the schedule you have established for subcontractors. A supplier may get behind on deliveries, which also affects the schedule. An unexpected pipe may surprise you during excavation. Just as certain, every problem that comes along has a solution if you are open to it.

Be Patient. The extra days it may take to resolve a construction problem will be forgotten once the project is completed.

Express Yourself. If what you see isn't exactly what you thought you were getting, don't be afraid to look into changing it. Or you may spot an unforeseen opportunity for an improvement. Changes usually cost more money, though, so don't make frivolous decisions.

Finally, watching your home go up is exciting, so stay upbeat. Get away from your project from time to time. Dine out. Take time to relax. A positive attitude will make for smoother relations with your builder. An optimistic outlook will yield better-quality work if you are doing your own construction. And though the project might seem endless while it is under way, keep in mind that all the planning and construction will fade to a faint memory at some time in the future, and you will be getting a lifetime of pleasure from a home that is just right for you.

Images provided by designer/architect.

Plan #151213

Dimensions: 51' W x 46' D
Levels: 1
Square Footage: 1,231
Bedrooms: 3
Bathrooms: 2
Foundation: Crawl space or slab
Materials List Available: No
Price Category: B

This cute brick ranch home is a great place to live.

Features:

• Foyer: This area welcomes you home with a handy coat closet.

• Great Room: A cozy fireplace and entry to the grilling porch make this gathering area special.

• Kitchen: This fully equipped kitchen is open into the breakfast room with a bay window looking out to the backyard.

• Master Bedroom: This master bedroom has a large walk-in closet and a private bathroom.

• Garage: In addition to two cars, there is room for storage.

Copyright by designer/architect.

Plan #391026

Dimensions: 35' W x 42' D
Levels: 2
Square Footage: 1,470
Main Level Sq. Ft.: 1,035
Upper Level Sq. Ft.: 435
Bedrooms: 3
Bathrooms: 2
Foundation: Crawl space, slab, or basement
Materials List Available: Yes
Price Category: B

Images provided by designer/architect.

A charming front and dormer with arched window are telltale signs this home is the proverbial home sweet home.

Features:

- **Living Room:** The cozy fireplace calls out, "Sit and relax," as this large gathering area welcomes you home.

- **Kitchen:** This island kitchen is open to the breakfast area, which has a sloped ceiling.

- **Master Bedroom:** This secluded room is located upstairs, with easy access to a large bathroom.

- **Bedrooms:** Two almost-equal-sized bedrooms are located on the main floor and share a common full bathroom.

Main Level Floor Plan

Upper Level Floor Plan

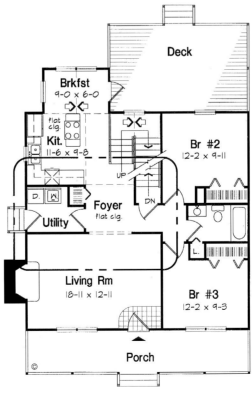

Copyright by designer/architect.

Plan #401043

Dimensions: 38' W x 32' D
Levels: 1
Square Footage: 988
Bedrooms: 3
Bathrooms: 1
Foundation: Basement
Materials List Available: Yes
Price Category: A

This economical, compact home is the ultimate in efficient use of space.

Features:

- **Porch:** The front entry is sheltered by this casual country porch, which also protects the living room windows.

- **Living Room:** This central living room features a cozy fireplace and outdoor access to the front porch.

- **Kitchen:** This U-shaped kitchen serves both a dining area and a breakfast bar. Sliding glass doors lead from here to the rear yard.

- **Master Bedroom:** This room has a walk-in closet and shares a full bathroom with the secondary bedrooms.

- A single or double garage may be built to the side or to the rear of the home.

Right Side Elevation   Rear Elevation   Left Side Elevation

Plan #321025

Dimensions: 28' W x 28' D
Levels: 1
Square Footage: 914
Bedrooms: 2
Bathrooms: 1
Foundation: Basement, walk-out
Materials List Available: Yes
Price Category: A

This cute little home's great layout packs in an abundance of features.

Features:

- Living Room: The cozy fireplace in this open, welcoming room invites you to relax awhile.

- Dining Room: This area has a bay window and is open to the kitchen and the living room.

- Kitchen: This compact kitchen has everything you'll need, including a built-in pantry.

- Master Bedroom: Generously sized, with a large closet, this room has a private door into the common bathroom.

- Bedroom: This secondary bedroom can also be used as a home office.

Images provided by designer/architect.

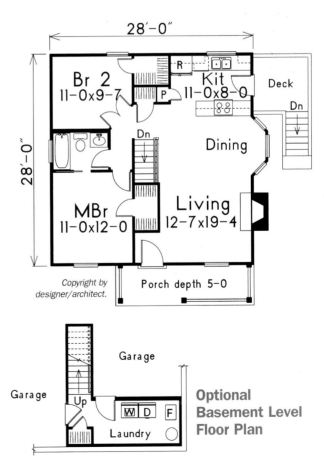

Copyright by designer/architect.

**Optional
Basement Level
Floor Plan**

Plan #391036

Dimensions: 28' W x 32' D
Levels: 2
Square Footage: 1,301
Main Level Sq. Ft.: 728
Upper Level Sq. Ft.: 573
Bedrooms: 3
Bathrooms: 2
Foundation: Basement
Materials List Available: Yes
Price Category: B

This home, as shown in the photograph, may differ from the actual blueprints. For more detailed information, please check the floor plans carefully.

Images provided by designer/architect.

This home is a vacation haven, with views from every room, whether it is situated on a lake or a mountaintop.

Features:

• Main Floor: A fireplace splits the living and dining rooms in this area.

• Kitchen: This kitchen flows into the dining room and is gracefully separated by a bar.

• Master Suite: A large walk-in closet, full bathroom, and deck make this private area special.

• Bedroom or Loft: The second floor has this bedroom or library loft, with clerestory windows, which opens above the living room.

• Lower Level: This lower floor has a large recreation room with a whirlpool tub, bar, laundry room, and garage.

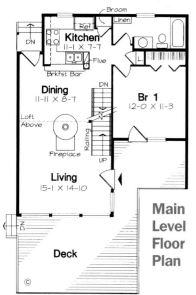

Main Level Floor Plan

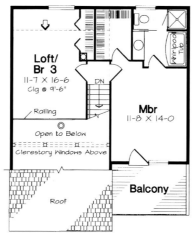

Upper Level Floor Plan

Copyright by designer/architect.

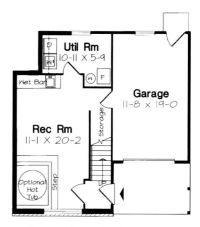

Lower Level Floor Plan

Plan #181219

Dimensions: 30' W x 26' D
Levels: 2
Square Footage: 1,311
Main Level Sq. Ft.: 791
Upper Level Sq. Ft.: 520
Bedrooms: 2
Bathrooms: 1½
Foundation: Basement
Materials List Available: Yes
Price Category: B

Images provided by designer/architect.

The double bay windows and arched entry with a fanlight window play up the classic cottage look and feel of this home.

Features:

• Home Office: Work-from-home professionals will appreciate this smart work space located near the front entrance.

• Family Room: This family room opens to the dining room and kitchen to share its hearty fireplace.

• Kitchen: This kitchen, with it built-in lunch counters, partners with the dining area for a wide-open look.

• Laundry Room: This large laundry room with exterior side entry is positioned beside the centralized kitchen for convenience.

• Bedrooms: Upstairs, two bedrooms with ample closets and one full bathroom provide plenty of personal space and comfort.

Main Level Floor Plan

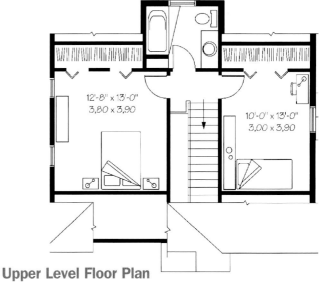

Upper Level Floor Plan

Copyright by designer/architect.

Plan #181215

Dimensions: 30' W x 32' D
Levels: 1
Square Footage: 929
Bedrooms: 2
Bathrooms: 1
Foundation: Basement
Materials List Available: Yes
Price Category: A

Whether just starting out or wrapping it up for the Golden Years, this generous one-level is perfect for two-plus. A peaked roofline, Palladian window, and covered front porch are a visual delight.

Features:

- Entry: An open interior branches out from the entry hall to the family room, where a cathedral ceiling soars to 10'-6¾".

- Dining Room: This room, which adjoins the family room, also embraces openness.

- Kitchen: This cordial kitchen features a breakfast counter for two and sprawling space for food preparation.

- Bedrooms: A full bathroom is nestled between two large bedrooms. Bedroom 1 enjoys a front and side view. Bedroom 2 has an intimate backyard vista.

Images provided by designer/architect.

Copyright by designer/architect.

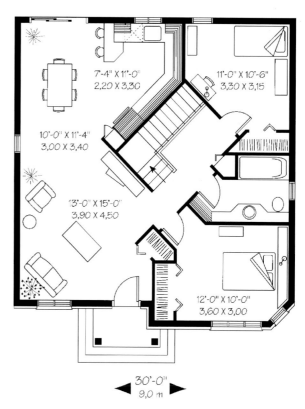

32'-0"
9,6 m

30'-0"
9,0 m

Plan #391008

Dimensions: 50' W x 40' D

Levels: 1

Square Footage: 1,312

Bedrooms: 3

Bathrooms: 2

Foundation: Crawl space, slab, or basement

Materials List Available: Yes

Price Category: B

Images provided by designer/architect.

Here's the sum of brains and beauty, which will please all types of families, from starters and nearly empty nesters to those going golden.

Features:

• **Entry:** This restful fresh-air porch and formal foyer bring you graciously toward the great room, with its fireplace and vaulted ceiling.

• **Dining Room:** This adjacent dining room features sliding doors to the deck and smooth open access to the U-shaped kitchen.

• **Laundry Room:** The laundry area has its own separate landing from the garage, so it's conveniently out of the way.

• **Master Suite:** This master suite with tray ceilings features nearly "limitless" closet space, a private bath, and large hall linen closet.

• **Bedrooms:** The two secondary bedrooms, also with roomy closets, share a full bath. Bedroom 3 easily becomes a home office with direct foyer access and a window overlooking the porch.

Plan #151220

Dimensions: 48' W x 56'2" D
Levels: 1
Square Footage: 1,325
Bedrooms: 3
Bathrooms: 2
Foundation: Crawl space or slab
Materials List Available: No
Price Category: B

Images provided by designer/architect.

This charming home, great for a narrow lot, is perfect for first-time homeowners. Welcome friends and family on the front porch before entering the living room.

Features:

- Living Room: This large room has a raised ceiling and a clever bay window.

- Kitchen: This kitchen, with a raised bar for additional seating, is open to the dining room.

- Master Suite: This space features a large walk-in closet and a private bathroom.

- Bedrooms: Two secondary bedrooms have large closets and share a hall bathroom.

- Garage: This garage has room for two cars, plus there is a storage area.

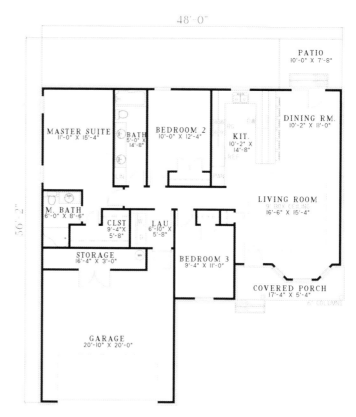

Copyright by designer/architect.

Plan #151218

Dimensions: 48' W x 30'6" D
Levels: 1
Square Footage: 1,008
Bedrooms: 2
Bathrooms: 2
Foundation: Crawl space or slab
Materials List Available: No
Price Category: B

This economical home may be just what you're looking for!

Features:

- Great Room: This gathering room has a vaulted ceiling.

- Kitchen: This kitchen boasts an abundant amount of cabinets, and counter space is open to the dining room.

- Master Suite: This retreat area features a large walk-in closet and a private bathroom.

- Bedroom: The second bedroom has its own door into the hall bathroom.

- Carport: This area has room for one car, plus there is a storage area.

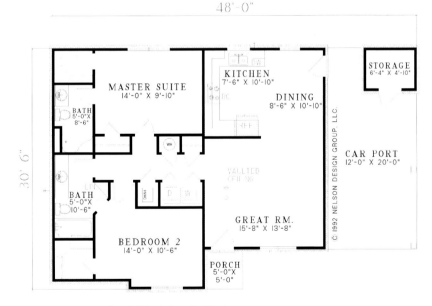

48'-0"

30'-6"

MASTER SUITE
14'-0" X 9'-10"

BATH
5'-0" X 8'-6"

BATH
5'-0" X 10'-6"

BEDROOM 2
14'-0" X 10'-6"

KITCHEN
7'-6" X 10'-10"

DINING
8'-6" X 10'-10"

VAULTED CEILING

GREAT RM.
15'-8" X 13'-8"

PORCH
5'-0" X 5'-0"

STORAGE
6'-4" X 4'-10"

CAR PORT
12'-0" X 20'-0"

© 1992 NELSON DESIGN GROUP, LLC.

Plan #401047

Dimensions: 38' W x 34' D
Levels: 1
Square Footage: 1,064
Bedrooms: 2
Bathrooms: 1
Foundation: Basement
Materials List Available: Yes
Price Category: B

Images provided by designer/architect.

This farmhouse design squeezes space-efficient features into its compact design. Twin dormer windows flood the vaulted interior with natural light and accentuate the high ceilings.

Features:

- Porch: This cozy front porch opens into a vaulted great room and its adjoining dining room.

- Great Room: A warm hearth in this gathering place for the family adds to its coziness.

- Kitchen: This U-shaped kitchen has a breakfast bar open to the dining room and a sink overlooking a flower box. Nearby side-door access is found in the handy laundry room.

- Bedrooms: Vaulted bedrooms are positioned along the back of the plan. They contain wall closets and share a full bathroom with a soaking tub.

- Future Expansion: An open-rail staircase leads to the basement, which can be developed into living or sleeping space at a later time, if needed.

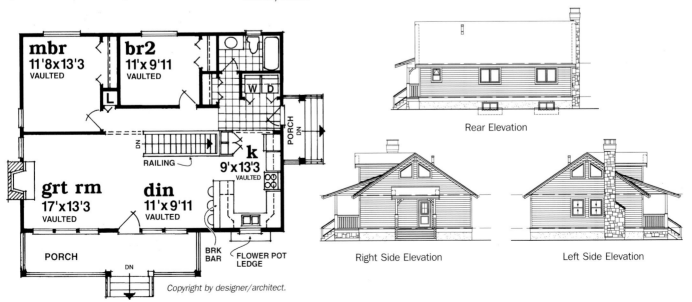

Copyright by designer/architect.

Plan #401005

Dimensions: 24' W x 36' D
Levels: 2
Square Footage: 1,073
Main Level Sq. Ft.: 672
Upper Level Sq. Ft.: 401
Bedrooms: 3
Bathrooms: 1½
Foundation: Basement
Materials List Available: Yes
Price Category: B

Scalloped fascia boards in the steep gable roof and the fieldstone chimney detail enhance this chalet.

Features:

- Outdoor Living: The front-facing deck and covered balcony are ideal outdoor living spaces.

- Living Room: The fireplace is the main focus in this living room, separating it from the dining room.

- Bedrooms: One bedroom is found on the first floor; two additional bedrooms and a full bath are upstairs.

- Storage: You'll find three large storage areas on the second floor.

Images provided by designer/architect.

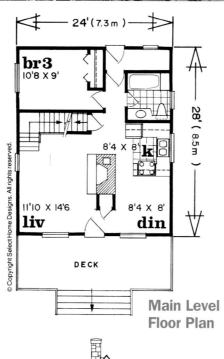

Main Level Floor Plan

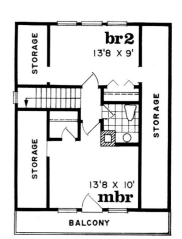

Upper Level Floor Plan

Copyright by designer/architect.

Rear Elevation

Left Side Elevation

Plan #181235

Dimensions: 22' W x 26'4" D
Levels: 2
Square Footage: 1,077
Main Level Sq. Ft.: 550
Upper Level Sq. Ft.: 527
Bedrooms: 3
Bathrooms: 1
Foundation: Basement
Materials List Available: Yes
Price Category: B

Everything about this design is made for sharing, from the wraparound porch and balcony to the interior.

Features:

- Main Level: This level showcases the family room with fireplace and the generous eat-in island kitchen.

- Second Level: This level provides three spacious bedrooms, a perfect setup for a vacation home.

- Master Bedroom: This room enjoys lots of space, natural light. and a private balcony.

- Bedrooms: The two secondary bedrooms enjoy backyard views and just the right amount of closets.

Images provided by designer/architect.

Main Level Floor Plan

11'-8" X 11'-0"
3,50 X 3,30

26'-4"
7,9 m

15'-4" X 14'-0"
4,60 X 4,20

22'-0"
6,6 m

Upper Level Floor Plan

8'-10" X 10'-10"
2,65 X 3,25

9'-10" X 8'-6" / 10'-10"
2,95 X 2,55 / 3,25

11'-11" X 13'-10"
3,58 X 4,15

Copyright by designer/architect.

Plan #401041

Dimensions: 38' W x 31' D
Levels: 1
Square Footage: 1,108
Bedrooms: 3
Bathrooms: 2
Foundation: Basement
Materials List Available: Yes
Price Category: B

Craftsman styling and a welcoming porch create marvelous curb appeal for this design. A compact footprint allows economy in construction.

Features:

- High Ceiling: This volume ceiling in the living and dining rooms and the kitchen make the home live larger than its modest square footage suggests.

- Kitchen: This area features generous cabinet space and flows directly into the dining room to create a casual country feeling. (Note the optional buffet.)

- Master Bedroom: This room offers a walk-in closet, a full bath, and a bumped-out window overlooking the rear yard.

- Expansion: The lower level provides room for an additional bedroom, den, family room, and full bath.

Images provided by designer/architect.

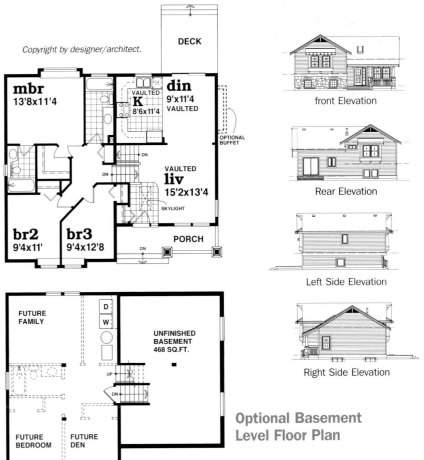

Optional Basement Level Floor Plan

Plan #351018

Dimensions: 40'8" W x 38'6" D

Levels: 1

Square Footage: 1,251

Bedrooms: 3

Bathrooms: 2

Foundation: Crawl space or slab

Materials List Available: Yes

Price Category: B

Images provided by designer/architect.

Covered Porch
17-0 x 7-0

Dining Room
12-0 x 10-0
9' CLG.

Future Storage/
Shop
14-0 x 6-0

Bedroom #3
12-0 x 13-8
9' CLG.

Gas
Logs

Clos.

Great Room
17-0 x 22-0
12' CLG.

Kitchen
12-0 x 13-0

Future Garage
22-0 x 24-0

**GARAGE PLANS
ARE INCLUDED**

Tub/ Shr.

Bath

Hall

Clos.

Foyer
12' CLG. HT

Bath

Tub/ Shr.

Bedroom #2
12-0 x 12-0

VAULT

Clos.

Covered Porch
14-4 x 5-0

Bedroom #1
12-0 x 10-6

VAULT

VAULT

Copyright by designer/architect.

Plan #371009

Dimensions: 51'5½" W x 52' D

Levels: 1

Square Footage: 1,223

Bedrooms: 3

Bathrooms: 2

Foundation: Slab

Materials List Available: No

Price Category: B

Images provided by designer/architect.

51'-5½"

PORCH

FIRE
PLACE
HEARTH

VANITY

B.1

MEDIA
CENTER

DINING RM.
11'-0" X 10'-0"

SLOPE CLG. UP TO 10'-0"

MASTER
SUITE
12'-4" x 13'-4"

LIN.

VAN.

B.2

SLOPE CLG. UP TO 10'-0"

LIVING RM.
14'-0" X 17'-0"

RAISED
BAR

KITCH.
11'-0" x 9'-0"

52'-0"

STOR.

BOOKS

SLOPE CLG. UP TO 10'-0"

BED RM.2
10'-0" x 10'-0"

BED RM.3
10'-0" x 10'-5"

ENT

W/H

STORAGE

PANT.

UTIL.

W.
D.

STOR.

PORCH

GARAGE
20'-0" x 20'-0"

Copyright by designer/architect.

Plan #291005

Dimensions: 16' W x 28' D

Levels: 2

Square Footage: 896

Main Level Sq. Ft.: 448

Upper Level Sq. Ft.: 448

Bedrooms: 2

Bathrooms: 1½

Foundation: Crawl space

Materials List Available: No

Price Category: A

Images provided by designer/architect.

Copyright by designer/architect.

16'-0"

28'-0"

KITCHEN

W/D

F

UP

LAV

LIVING ROOM
15'-4" x 11'-4"

PORCH

BEDROOM 2
13'-0" x 9'-0"

LIN

BATH

DN

BEDROOM 1
13'-0" x 11'-4"

**Main Level
Floor Plan**

**Upper Level
Floor Plan**

Plan #181216

Dimensions: 31'8" W x 30' D

Levels: 1

Square Footage: 910

Bedrooms: 2

Bathrooms: 1

Foundation: Basement

Materials List Available: Yes

Price Category: A

Images provided by designer/architect.

Copyright by designer/architect.

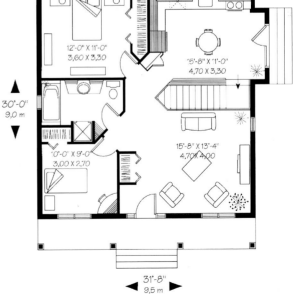

12'-0" X 11'-0"
3,60 X 3,30

'5'-8" X 1'-0"
4,70 X 3,30

'0'-0" X 9'-0"
3,00 X 2,70

15'-8" X 13'-4"
4,70 X 4,00

30'-0"
9,0 m

31'-8"
9,5 m

Plan #101026

Dimensions: 50' W x 57'4" D

Levels: 1

Square Footage: 1,420

Bedrooms: 3

Bathrooms: 2

Foundation: Crawl space

Materials List Available: No

Price Category: B

Excellent looks and a great personality make this home a perfect match for your family.

Features:

- Family Room: Large windows look onto the front yard in this large all-purpose area, which is open to the dining area.

- Kitchen: This U-shaped kitchen has a raised bar and is open into the dining and family rooms.

- Master Suite: This area features large bay windows looking onto the backyard. The luxurious private bath has a double vanity and a walk-in closet.

- Bedrooms: The two secondary bedrooms have large closets and share a hall bathroom.

- Laundry Area: Conveniently located near the bedrooms, this room has bifold doors to keep utility area out of view.

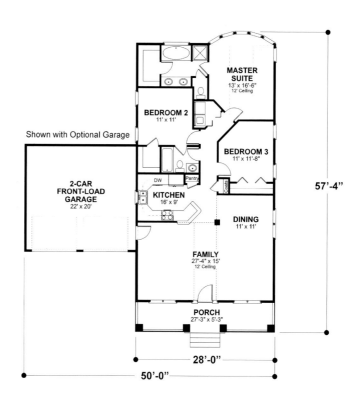

Plan #371010

Dimensions: 56' W x 43'1" D

Levels: 1

Square Footage: 1,429

Bedrooms: 3

Bathrooms: 2

Foundation: Slab

Materials List Available: No

Price Category: B

Images provided by designer/architect.

This warm American Traditional home has all the conveniences.

Features:

- **Living Room:** This large room has 10-ft.-high ceilings, a media center, and a fireplace.

- **Kitchen:** This kitchen boasts a built-in pantry and is open to the dining area, which has a built-in hutch.

- **Master Suite:** This suite boasts a media center, a sitting area, two walk-in closets, and a private bath.

- **Bedrooms:** These two additional bedrooms share a private bathroom.

Copyright by designer/architect.

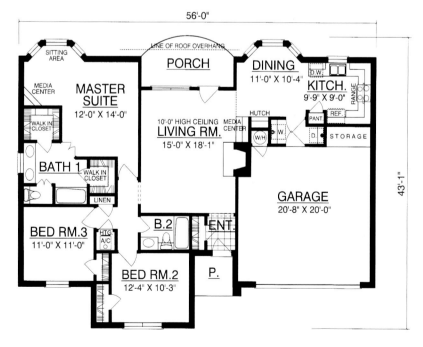

Plan #371030

Dimensions: 38'10" W x 64'4" D
Levels: 1
Square Footage: 1,434
Bedrooms: 3
Bathrooms: 2
Foundation: Slab
Materials List Available: No
Price Category: B

The stylish front of this country home conceals a charming floor plan. This is the perfect home for a young family.

Features:

- Living Room: Entertaining is a snap in this large, open room with a bookcase and a fireplace.

- Kitchen: This kitchen has a raised bar, a pantry, and breakfast nook.

- Master Suite: This large suite has a luxurious master bathroom with two walk-in closets.

- Bedrooms: The two additional bedrooms share a convenient bathroom with a dressing room.

Images provided by designer/architect.

Copyright by designer/architect.

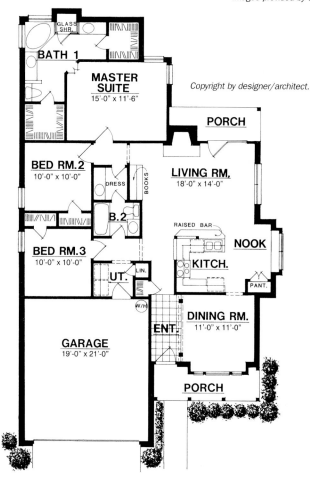

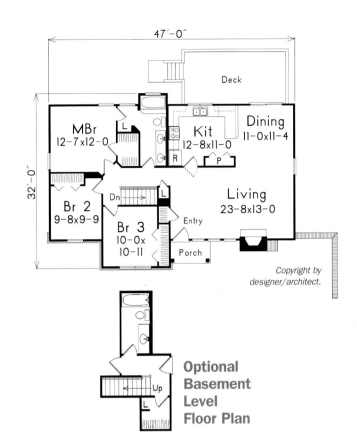

47'-0"

Deck

MBr
12-7x12-0

Kit
12-8x11-0

Dining
11-0x11-4

32'-0"

Br 2
9-8x9-9

Dn

Br 3
10-0x
10-11

Entry

Living
23-8x13-0

Porch

Copyright by designer/architect.

Plan #321024

Images provided by designer/architect.

Dimensions: 47' W x 32' D
Levels: 1
Square Footage: 1,403
Bedrooms: 3
Bathrooms: 1-2
Foundation: Daylight basement
Materials List Available: Yes
Price Category: B

Up

Optional Basement Level Floor Plan

Bfst.
10⁰ x 9⁰

Grt. rm.
14⁰ x 17⁴

Mbr.
12⁰ x 14⁰

SNACK BAR

Kit.
10⁰ x 10⁴

10'-0" CEILING

9'-0" CLG.

WHIRLPOOL

46'-0"

STORAGE

W. D.

Gar.
19⁴ x 25⁸

COVERED STOOP

Br. 2
10⁰ x 10⁰

Br. 3
10⁰ x 10⁰

50'-0"

Copyright by designer/architect.

Plan #121060

Images provided by designer/architect.

Dimensions: 50' W x 46' D
Levels: 1
Square Footage: 1,339
Bedrooms: 3
Full Bathrooms: 2
Foundation: Basement
Materials List Available: Yes
Price Category: B

Plan #391060

Dimensions: 58' W x 34'4" D

Levels: 1

Square Footage: 1,359

Bedrooms: 3

Bathrooms: 2

Foundation: Crawl space, slab or basement

Materials List Available: Yes

Price Category: B

Images provided by designer/architect.

Big bay windows and one-story styling make this home irresistible.

Features:

- Living Room: This great-sized living room winds its way to a formal dining room and kitchen.

- Master Suite: This area (with luxury bath room) shows off a tray ceiling and a window seat with a front-yard view.

- Bedroom 2: This room has a spacious closet and a personal view of the backyard, plus a full bath.

- Den: This room with double doors can become bedroom 3 if necessary.

Deck

Dining
11-0 x 11-2

Br #2
10-10 x 11-10

Den/Br #3
10-0 x 11-10

Optional Door Location

Decor. Ceiling

Kit
10-0 x 11-2

Ldry

Rolling

Solid Wall w/ Opt. Door Location

DN

Ref.

Pan.

Decor. Ceiling

Plant Ledge

Living Rm
14-10 x 17-0

Garage
20-4 x 21-8

MBr #1
11-7 x 13-0

10' clg

Seat

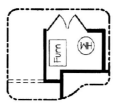

Furn

WH

Plan #371049

Dimensions: 52' W x 45' D
Levels: 1
Square Footage: 1,440
Bedrooms: 3
Bathrooms: 2
Foundation: Slab
Materials List Available: No
Price Category: B

Images provided by designer/architect.

This country classic is sure to please. It has three bedrooms and is perfect for any-size family.

Features:

- Living Room: This large room with 10-foot-high ceiling is just off the entry. Bookcases surround the inviting fireplace here.

- Dining Room: The living room flows into this large room, which features a beautiful bay window.

- Kitchen: This fully functional kitchen is perfect for any chef. The garage is accessible through the adjoining utility room.

- Master Suite: This private area boasts a luxurious master bath with a marble tub, glass shower, and his and her walk-in closets.

- Bedrooms: The two large additional bedrooms share a convenient bath.

Copyright by designer/architect.

Plan #181233

Dimensions: 38' W x 36' D

Levels: 2

Square Footage: 1,482

Main Level Sq. Ft.: 895

Upper Level Sq. Ft.: 587

Bedrooms: 2

Bathrooms: 1½

Foundation: Basement or walk-out

Materials List Available: Yes

Price Category: B

Images provided by designer/architect.

An airy screened porch and front deck endow this all-season home with the aura of a resort.

Features:

- Open Living: A feel-at-home layout brings together both the family room, with its fireplace, and the dining area.

- Family Room: This versatile room opens onto the front porch for fresh air and a view.

- Kitchen: This bountiful food-preparation space expands to a lunch counter that also serves the dining area.

- Bedrooms: Upstairs, there are two bedrooms: one overlooks the backyard, and the other oversees the front. A full bathroom with separate shower and tub commands a generous area between the two bedrooms.

Main Level Floor Plan

8'-0" X 13'-6"
2,40 X 4,05

14'-4" X 8'-6"
4,30 X 2,55

24'-8" X 12'-8"
7,40 X 3,80

11'-4" X 13'-8"
3,40 X 4,10

36'-0"
10,8 m

38'-0"
11,4 m

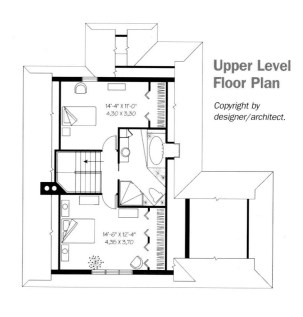

Upper Level Floor Plan

Copyright by designer/architect.

14'-4" X 11'-0"
4,30 X 3,30

14'-6" X 12'-4"
4,35 X 3,70

33'-0"

BED RM.2
10'-0" X 10'-0"

WALK IN
CLOSET

MASTER
SUITE
11'-4"X 15'-0"

WALK IN
CLOSET

LINEN

BED RM.3
10'-0"X 10'-0"

WALK IN
CLOSET

BATH 1

MARBLE
TUB

B.2

SHOWER

DINING RM.
13'-8"x 12'-0"

MEDIA
CENTER

65'-0"

STORAGE

LIVING RM.
12'-0"x 17'-10"

RAISED
BAR

D.W.

KITCH.
13'-0"X 9'-0"

REF

ENT.

UT.

WALK IN
PANTRY

D.
W.

P.

GARAGE
19'-0" x 19'-7"

Images provided by designer/architect.

Plan #371069

Dimensions: 33' W x 65' D
Levels: 1
Square Footage: 1,484
Bedrooms: 3
Bathrooms: 2
Foundation: Crawl space or slab
Materials List Available: No
Price Category: B

Copyright by designer/architect.

10'-4" X 13'-4"
3,10 X 4,00

9'-8" X 10'-0"
2,90 X 3,00

12'-8" X 14'-8"
3,80 X 4,40

Images provided by designer/architect.

Plan #181226

Dimensions: 28' W x 29'8" D
Levels: 2
Square Footage: 1,485
Main Level Sq. Ft.: 735
Upper Level Sq. Ft.: 750
Bedrooms: 3
Bathrooms: 1½
Foundation: Basement
Materials List Available: Yes
Price Category: B

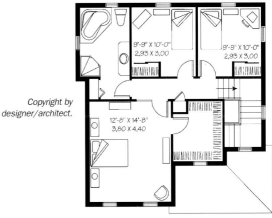

9'-9" X 10'-0"
2,93 X 3,00

9'-9" X 10'-0"
2,93 X 3,00

12'-8" X 14'-8"
3,80 X 4,40

Copyright by designer/architect.

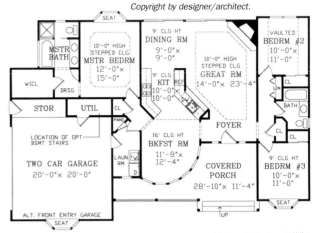

Images provided by designer/architect.

Plan #131003

Dimensions: 60' W x 39'10" D

Levels: 1

Square Footage: 1,466

Bedrooms: 3

Bathrooms: 2

Foundation: Crawl space, slab, or basement

Materials List Available: Yes

Price Category: B

Breakfast Room

Plan #131017

Dimensions: 69'8" W x 39'4" D

Levels: 1

Square Footage: 1,480

Bedrooms: 3

Bathrooms: 2

Foundation: Crawl space, slab, or basement

Materials List Available: Yes

Price Category: C

Images provided by designer/architect.

Alternate Floor Plan

Part Plan with Optional Basement

Rear Elevation

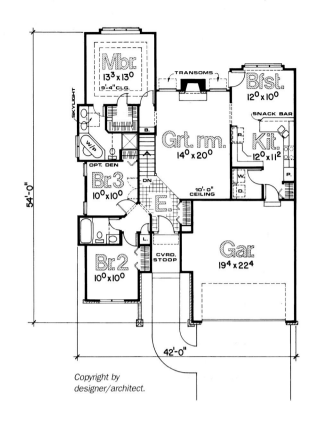

Plan #121002

Dimensions: 42' W x 54' D

Levels: 1

Square Footage: 1,347

Bedrooms: 3

Bathrooms: 2

Foundation: Basement

Materials List Available: Yes

Price Category: B

Images provided by designer/architect.

This home, as shown in the photograph, may differ from the actual blueprints. For more detailed information, please check the floor plans carefully.

Copyright by
designer/architect.

Plan #151010

Dimensions: 38'4" W x 68'6" D

Levels: 1

Square Footage: 1,379

Bedrooms: 3

Bathrooms: 2

Foundation: Crawl space, slab

Materials List Available: No

Price Category: B

Images provided by designer/architect.

Copyright by
designer/architect.

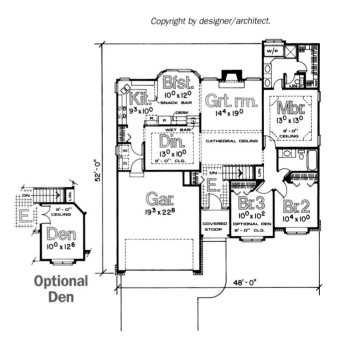

Copyright by designer/architect.

Deck

Master Br
15-4x11

Great
Room
16-8x19

Dining

Kitchen/
Brkfst
13-8x12-8

Bar

dn

Den/Br 3
11-4x12-4

Garage
19-4x19-4

Br 2
11x10

35'-4"

52'-8"

Plan #271001

Dimensions: 52'8" W x 35'4" D

Levels: 1

Square Footage: 1,400

Bedrooms: 3

Bathrooms: 2

Foundation: Basement

Materials List Available: Yes

Price Category: B

Images provided by designer/architect.

Copyright by designer/architect.

w/p

Kit.
9³x10⁰

Bfst.
10⁰x12⁰
SNACK BAR

Grt. rm.
14⁴x19⁰

Mbr.
13⁰x13⁰
9'-0"
CEILING

WET BAR

Din.
13⁰x10⁰
9'-0" CLG.

CATHEDRAL CEILING

DN

Gar.
19³x22⁸

Br.3
10⁰x10²
OPTIONAL DEN
9'-0" CLG.

Br.2
10⁴x10⁰

COVERED
STOOP

52'-0"

DN

9'-0"
CEILING

Den
10⁰x12⁶

**Optional
Den**

48'-0"

Plan #121005

Dimensions: 48' W x 52' D

Levels: 1

Square Footage: 1,496

Bedrooms: 3

Bathrooms: 2

Foundation: Basement

Materials List Available: Yes

Price Category: B

Images provided by designer/architect.

This home, as shown in the photograph, may differ from the actual blueprints. For more detailed information, please check the floor plans carefully.

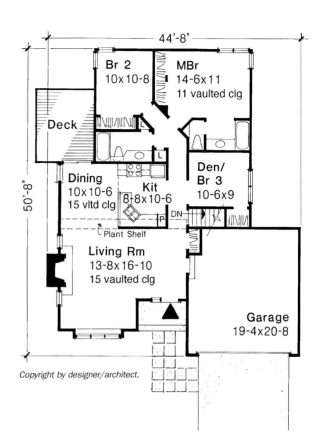

Images provided by designer/architect.

Plan #271002

Dimensions: 44'8" W x 50'8" D

Levels: 1

Square Footage: 1,252

Bedrooms: 3

Bathrooms: 2

Foundation: Basement

Materials List Available: Yes

Price Category: B

Copyright by designer/architect.

Copyright by designer/architect.

Plan #131014

Dimensions: 48' W x 43'4" D

Levels: 1

Square Footage: 1,380

Bedrooms: 3

Bathrooms: 2

Foundation: Crawl space, slab, or basement

Materials List Available: Yes

Price Category: B

Images provided by designer/architect.

Rear Elevation

Bonus Room

FUTURE EXPANSION
20'-0" x 15'-4"

Plan #351021

Dimensions: 61' W x 47'4" D

Levels: 1

Square Footage: 1,500

Bedrooms: 3

Bathrooms: 2

Foundation: Crawl space, slab, or basement

Materials List Available: Yes

Price Category: C

Images provided by designer/architect.

This lovely home provides a functional split-floor-plan layout with many of the features that your family desires.

Features:

- Great Room: This large gathering area, with a vaulted ceiling, has a gas log fireplace.

- Kitchen: This open kitchen layout has plenty of counter space for that growing family.

- Master Suite: This expansive master bedroom and bath has plenty of storage space in its separate walk-in closets.

- Garage: This two-car garage has a storage area.

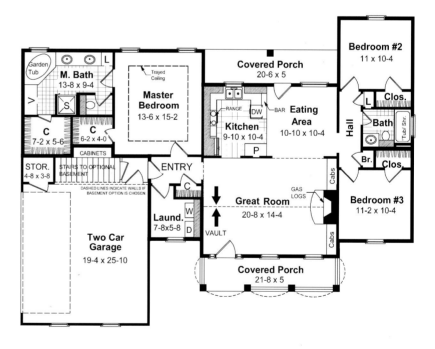

Copyright by designer/architect.

Plan #151212

Dimensions: 47' W x 63'6" D
Levels: 1
Square Footage: 1,462
Bedrooms: 3
Bathrooms: 2
Foundation: Crawl space or slab
Materials List Available: No
Price Category: B

Images provided by designer/architect.

This brick home has charm and elegance.

Features:

- Great Room: You'll love the vaulted ceiling in this gathering area, with its cozy fireplace and access to the optional covered grilling deck.

- Kitchen: This efficient peninsula kitchen has a breakfast bar and is open to the dining room.

- Master Suite: Located on the opposite side of the home from the secondary bedrooms, this area boasts a large sleeping area and a luxurious bathroom.

- Bedrooms: The two secondary bedrooms share a common hall bathroom.

- Garage: This two-car garage has an additional storage area.

Copyright by designer/architect.

Plan #181223

Dimensions: 27'8" W x 26' D

Levels: 2

Square Footage: 1,440

Main Level Sq. Ft.: 720

Upper Level Sq. Ft.: 720

Bedrooms: 3

Bathrooms: 2

Foundation: Basement

Materials List Available: Yes

Price Category: B

Images provided by designer/architect.

This home has a beautiful style, with its wraparound covered porch at the front and the right.

Features:

• **Entry:** This entry welcomes you home and has a coat closet. Just to the left is a full bathroom.

• **Living Room:** You'll have great view of the backyard in this relaxing area, which is open to the dining area.

• **Kitchen:** This large kitchen has everything you'll need: lots of cabinets and counter space.

• **Upper Level:** Three good-size bedrooms and a full bathroom occupy this section of the home.

Main Level Floor Plan

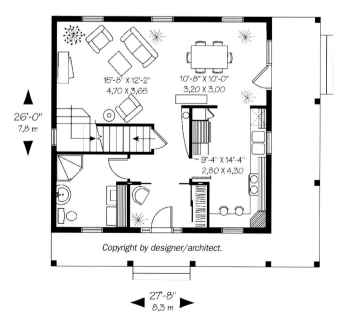

Copyright by designer/architect.

Upper Level Floor Plan

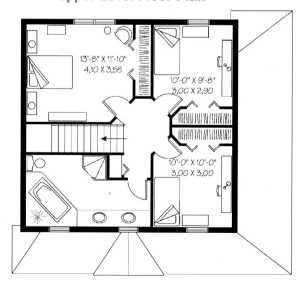

Plan #391006

Dimensions: 50' W x 45'4" D
Levels: 1
Square Footage: 1,456
Bedrooms: 3
Bathrooms: 2
Foundation: Crawl space, slab, or basement
Materials List Available: Yes
Price Category: B

Images provided by designer/architect.

Celebrating the union of beauty and function, this single-level layout makes a large appearance, with its peaked rooflines, elongated windowing, and sloping ceilings in the living room and bedroom #3 (or home office).

Features:

- Foyer: Soft angles define the space in the house, beginning with this foyer entry that curves to all the important rooms.

- Master Suite: Private rooms gather on the opposite side of the plan, with this master suite owning special windowing, an enormous walk-in closet, and a highly specialized bathroom with compartments that maintain privacy as two people use the various facilities at once.

- Bedroom: This other secondary bedroom enjoys a full bath and plenty of closet space.

- Utility Areas: Laundry facilities are easy to access, and a two-car garage has convenient front entry.

Copyright by designer/architect.

Rear View

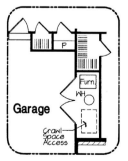

Crawl Space/ Slab Option

Plan #101036

Dimensions: 50' W x 60' D

Levels: 1

Square Footage: 1,343

Bedrooms: 3

Bathrooms: 2

Foundation: Basement

Materials List Available: No

Price Category: B

Images provided by designer/architect.

This lovely three-bedroom brick home with an attached two-car garage is perfect for any family.

Features:

- Family Room: This room with 12-ft.-high ceiling is open to the dining room.

- Kitchen: This kitchen boasts a built-in pantry, access to the garage, and a peninsula reaching into the family room.

- Master Bedroom: This main bedroom features a 12-ft.-high ceiling and its own private screened in porch.

- Master Bath: This bath features a walk-in closet, double vanity, and separate shower area.

- Bedrooms: Two additional bedrooms share a full bathroom located in the hallway.

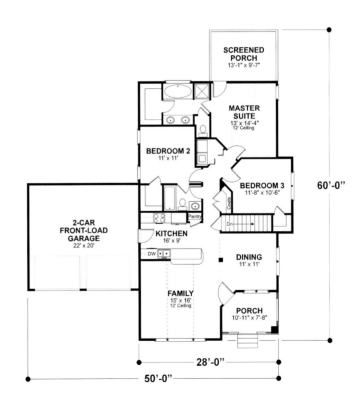

Copyright by designer/architect.

Plan #371006

Dimensions: 49'7" W x 48'6" D

Levels: 1

Square Footage: 1,374

Bedrooms: 3

Bathrooms: 2

Foundation: Crawl space, slab, or basement

Materials List Available: No

Price Category: B

This elegant brick-and-siding country home brings affordable living to a new level. The three bedrooms and two baths makes the most of the floor space.

Features:

• Master Suite: This large master suite has a large master bath with two walk-in closets.

• Dining Room: This formal room is located just off the entry.

• Living Room: This large but comfortable room has a cozy fireplace.

• Kitchen: This spacious kitchen with a breakfast nook has a view of the backyard.

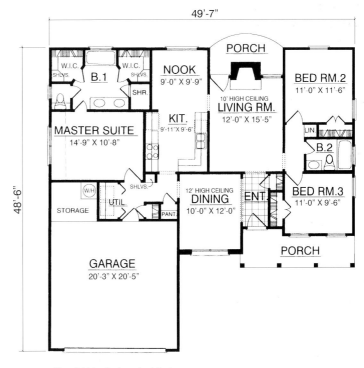

Plan #371028

Dimensions: 50'2" W x 47' D

Levels: 1

Square Footage: 1,376

Bedrooms: 3

Bathrooms: 2

Foundation: Slab

Materials List Available: No

Price Category: B

Images provided by designer/architect.

An efficient and affordable floor plan comes to life in this traditional brick home. This is the perfect home for anyone just starting out or for the "empty-nester."

Features:

- Living Room: This open room boasts a media center and cozy fireplace.

- Dining Room: The living room leads to this spacious room with a beautiful bay window that looks out into the backyard.

- Kitchen: This kitchen has a raised bar and a pantry.

- Bedrooms: The two other bedrooms share a convenient bath.

Copyright by designer/architect.

Plan #391064

Dimensions: 54' W x 28' D

Levels: 1

Square Footage: 988

Bedrooms: 3

Bathrooms: 2

Foundation: Crawl space, basement

Materials List Available: Yes

Price Category: A

Wishing for a sweet place of your own? Here's one that generates more comfort and style than many of its larger relatives.

Features:

- **Facade:** Gabled roofs, arched windows, and a covered patio charm the exterior.

- **Dining Room:** This curvaceous room is open to both the kitchen and living room for a big, bright feeling.

- **Master Bedroom:** This sanctuary features a bedroom and private bath.

- **Bedrooms:** Two secondary bedrooms share a full bath.

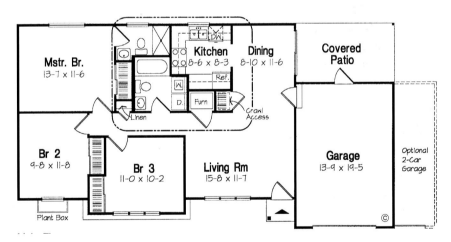

Copyright by designer/architect.

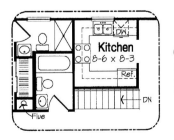

Optional Basement Level Floor Plan

Plan #401007

Dimensions: 25' W x 36'6" D
Levels: 2
Square Footage: 1,286
Main Level Sq. Ft.: 725
Upper Level Sq. Ft.: 561
Bedrooms: 3
Bathrooms: 2
Foundation: Crawl space
Materials List Available: Yes
Price Category: B

This cozy chalet design begins with a railed veranda opening to a living room with a warm fireplace.

Features:

• Dining Room: This formal room also has a snack-bar counter that opens to the kitchen.

• Master Bedroom: Located on the second floor with a private balcony, this room has its own full bath.

• Bedrooms: One bedroom with a roomy wall closet is on the first floor. The second one is on the upper floor.

• Storage: Additional storage is found on the second floor.

Images provided by designer/architect.

Main Level Floor Plan

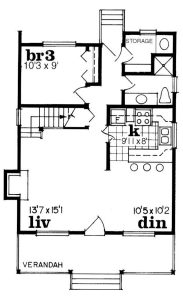

Upper Level Floor Plan

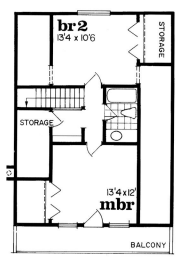

Copyright by designer/architect.

Right Side Elevation

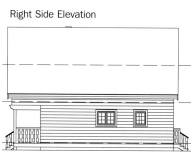

Left Side Elevation

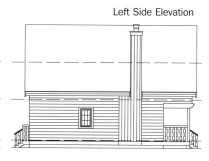

Rear Elevation

Plan #181227

Dimensions: 24' W x 29' D

Levels: 2

Square Footage: 1,248

Main Level Sq. Ft.: 624

Upper Level Sq. Ft.: 624

Bedrooms: 3

Bathrooms: 1½

Foundation: Basement

Materials List Available: Yes

Price Category: B

Images provided by designer/architect.

Architecturally rich, this striking design boasts ribbon and Palladian windows as well as a pavilion effect.

Features:

- Open Layout: A central staircase divides this otherwise fully open and contemporary layout.

- Kitchen: This large kitchen, with ample counter and cabinetry, keeps the laundry facilities and powder room close at hand.

- Casual living: An open living and dining room celebrates casual living and personal style.

- Master Bedroom: This bedroom, with its wall-length closet, overlooks the front porch through wide ribbon windows.

- Bedrooms: The two secondary bedrooms and a bright full bathroom are also nestled comfortably on the second level.

Main Level Floor Plan

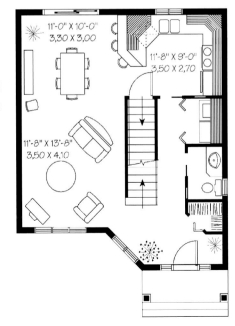

Upper Level Floor Plan

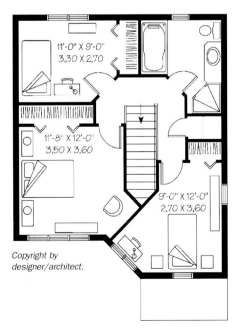

Copyright by designer/architect.

Plan #371005

Dimensions: 52'6" W x 45'8" D

Levels: 1½

Square Footage: 1,250

Bedrooms: 2

Bathrooms: 2

Foundation: Crawl space, slab, or basement

Materials List Available: No

Price Category: B

This quaint country home feels much larger because of the cathedral ceiling in the living room and an upstairs loft. This is the perfect vacation getaway or a home for a small family.

Features:

- Front Porch: This large front porch is perfect for relaxing and entertaining.

- Living Room: This room is an open area and is great for having guests over.

- Loft: This area overlooks the living room and has an optional bath.

- Master Suite: This area has a large walk-in closet and its own private bath.

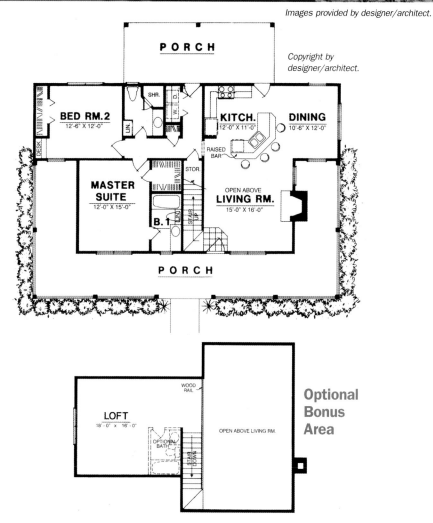

Plan #401019

Dimensions: 34' W x 32' D
Levels: 1½
Square Footage: 1,256
Main Level Sq. Ft.: 898
Upper Level Sq. Ft.: 358
Bedrooms: 3
Bathrooms: 1½
Foundation: Crawl space
Materials List Available: Yes
Price Category: B

Images provided by designer/architect.

A surrounding sun deck and expansive window wall capitalize on vacation-home views in this design. The full-height windows flood the living and dining rooms with abundant natural light and bring attention to the high vaulted ceilings.

Features:

- **Living Room:** A woodstove in this room warms cold winter nights.

- **Kitchen:** This efficient U-shaped kitchen has ample counter and cupboard space. Behind it is a laundry room and rear entrance.

- **Master Bedroom:** Located on the first floor, this main bedroom has a large wall closet.

- **Bedrooms:** Two family bedrooms are on the second floor and have use of a half-bath.

Main Level Floor Plan

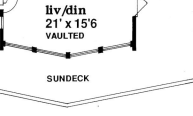

Upper Level Floor Plan

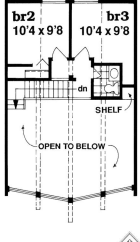

Copyright by designer/architect.

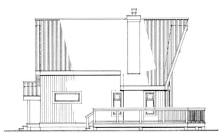

Left Side Elevation

Rear Elevation

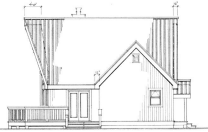

Right Side Elevation

Kitchens and Baths

Of all the rooms in a house, kitchens present unique decorating challenges because so much tends to happen in these spaces. In addition to preparing meals, most families use kitchens as gathering and entertaining areas. Kitchens need to be functional, comfortable, and inviting.

Who can't relate to this scenario: you turn on the oven to preheat it, but wait, did you take out the large roasting pan first?

How about the lasagna dish, muffin tins, pizza stone, and cookie sheets that are in there, too? Now where can you put everything that was in the oven while the casserole is baking and the countertop is laden with the rest of tonight's dinner ingredients? Good cabinetry outfitted with an assortment of organizing options can help you there. It can make your kitchen more efficient and a whole lot neater while establishing a style, or "look," for the room.

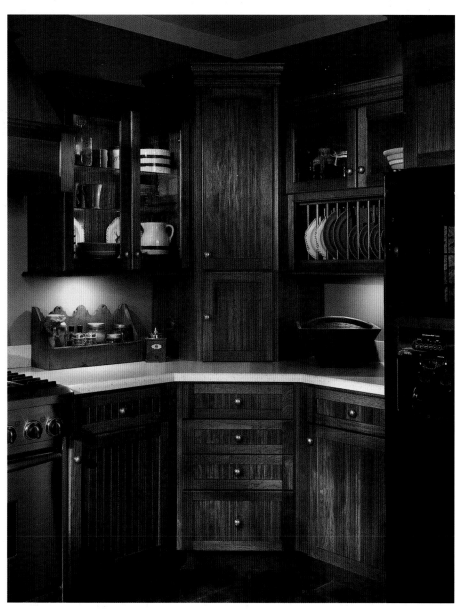

Cabinet Construction

Basically, cabinets are constructed in one of two ways: framed or frameless. Framed cabinets have a traditional look, with a full frame across the face of the cabinet box that may show between closed doors. This secures adjacent cabinets and strengthens wider cabinet boxes with a center rail. Hinges on framed cabinets may or may not be visible around doors when they are closed. The door's face may be ornamented with raised or recessed panels, trimmed or framed panels, or a framed-glass panel with or without muntins (the narrow vertical and horizontal strips of wood that divide panes of glass).

Frameless Cabinets. Also known as European-style cabinets, although American manufacturers also make them, frameless cabinets are built without a face frame and sport a clean, contemporary look, often not befitting a Southern or Country style. There's no trim or molding with this simple design. Close-fitting doors cover the entire front of the box, no ornamentation appears on the face of the doors, and hinges are typically hidden inside the cabinet box.

Selecting Cabinets

Choosing one type over another is generally a matter of taste, although framed units offer slightly less interior space. But the quality of construction is a factor that should always be taken into consideration. How do you judge it? Solid wood is too expensive for most of today's budgets, but it might be used on just the doors and frames. More typical is plywood box construction, which offers good structural support and solid wood on the doors and frames. To save money, cabinetmakers sometimes use strong plywood for support elements, such as the box and frame, and medium-density fiberboard for other parts,

such as doors and drawer fronts. In yet another alternative, good-quality laminate cabinets can be made with high-quality, thick particleboard underneath the laminate finish.

Quality Points. There are other things to look for in cabinet construction. They include dovetail or mortise-and-tenon joinery and solidly mortised hinges. Also, make sure that the interior of every cabinet is well finished, with adjustable shelves that are a minimum ⅜ inch thick to prevent bowing.

Bead-board paneled doors, opposite, are at home in Southern-style kitchens.

Framed cabinets, above, offer a traditional look to an otherwise modern kitchen.

Country-style designs have many attributes of Cottage decor, right.

Unless you have the time and skill to build the cabinets yourself or can hire someone else to do it, you'll have to purchase them in one of four ways. **Knockdown cabinetry** (also known as RTA, ready to assemble) is shipped flat and, sometimes, unfinished because you put the pieces together. **Stock cabinetry** comes in standard sizes but limited styles and colors; it is often available on the spot or can be delivered quickly. Like stock, **semicustom cabinetry** comes in standard styles, but it is manufactured to fit a homeowner's specific size and finish needs. **Custom cabinetry** is not limited in terms of style or size because it is built to the designer's specifications.

The Decorative Role of Cabinets

The look you create in your kitchen will be largely influenced by the cabinetry you select. Finding a style that suits you and how you will use your new kitchen is similar to shopping for furniture. In fact, don't be surprised to see many furniture details dressing up the cabinets on view in showrooms and home centers today.

Details That Stand Out. Besides architectural elements such as fluted pilasters, corbels, moldings, and bull's-eye panels, look for details such as fretwork, rope motifs, gingerbread trim, balusters, composition ornamentation (it looks like carving), even footed cabinets that mimic separate furniture pieces. If your taste runs toward less fussy design, you'll also find handsome door and drawer styles that feature minimal decoration, if any. Woods and finishes are just as varied, and range from informal looks in birch, oak, ash, and maple to rich mahogany and cherry. Laminate finishes, though less popular than they were a decade ago, haven't completely disappeared from the marketplace, but an array of colors has replaced the once-ubiquitous almond and white finishes.

Color

Color is coming on strong on wood cabinetry, too. Accents in one, two, or more hues are pairing with natural wood tones. White-painted cabinets take on a warmer glow with tinted shades of this always popular neutral. Special "vintage" finishes, such as translucent color glazes, continue to grow in popularity, as do distressed finishing techniques such as wire brushing and rubbed-through color that add both another dimension and the appeal of handcraftmanship, even on mass-produced items.

If you're shy about using color on such a high-ticket item as cabinetry, try it as an accent on molding, door trim, or island cabinetry. Just as matched furniture suites have become passé in other rooms of the house, the same is true for the kitchen, where mixing several looks can add sophistication and visual interest.

Cabinet Hardware

Another way to emphasize your kitchen's style is with hardware. From exquisite reproductions in brass, pewter, wrought iron, or ceramic to handsome bronze, chrome, nickel, glass, steel, plastic, rubber, wood, or stone creations, a smorgasbord of shapes and designs is available. Some pieces are highly polished; others are matte-finished, smooth, or hammered. Some are abstract or geometrical; others are simple,

elegant shapes. Whimsical designs take on the forms of animals or teapots, vegetables or flowers. Even just one or two great-looking door or drawer pulls can be showstoppers in a kitchen that may otherwise be devoid of much personality. Like mixing cabinet finishes, a combination of two hardware styles—perhaps picked up from other materials in the room—makes a big design statement. As the famed architect Mies Van der Rohe once stated, "God is in the details," and the most perfect detail in your new kitchen may be the artistic hardware that you select.

Cabinet style will set the tone for the design of the entire kitchen. The simple door styles keeps the room at left airy and casual.

The rustic look of the cabinets above is tailor-made for any Country style kitchen.

Color accents, such as the splash of color on the kitchen island shown right, can customize any simple cabinet design.

Cabinet hardware should complement the cabinet door and drawer designs, but it should also be easy for everyone in the household to grasp, above.

Kitchen storage comes in a variety of forms, including cabinets, drawers, pullout extensions, and the glass-front bins shown to the right.

Besides looks, consider the function of a pull or knob. You have to be able to grip it easily and comfortably. If your fingers or hands get stiff easily, or if you have arthritis, select C- or U-shaped pulls. If you like a knob, try it out in the showroom to make sure it isn't slippery or awkward when you grab it. Knobs and pulls can be inexpensive if you can stick to unfinished ones that you can paint in an accent color picked up from the tile or wallpaper. If you don't plan to buy new cabinets, changing the hardware on old ones can redefine their style. The right knob or pull can suggest any one of a number of vintage looks or decorative styles, from Colonial to Victorian, and reinforce your decor.

Types of Storage

Storage facilities can make or break a kitchen, so choose the places you'll put things with care. Here's a look at a few alternatives:

Pantries. How often you shop and how many groceries you typically bring home determine the amount of food storage space your family needs. If you like to stock up or take advantage of sales, add a pantry

to your kitchen. To maximize a pantry's convenience, plan shallow, 6-inch-deep shelves so that cans and packages will never be stored more than two deep. This way, you'll easily be able to see what you've got on hand. Pantries range in size from floor-to-ceiling models to narrow units designed to fit between two standard-size cabinets.

Appliance Garages. Appliance garages make use of dead space in a corner, but they can be installed anywhere in the vertical space between wall-mounted cabinets and the countertop. A tambour (rolltop) door hides small appliances like a food processor or anything else you want within reach but hidden from view.

Lazy Susans and Carousel Shelves. Rotating shelves like lazy Susans and carousels maximize dead corner storage and put items like dishes or pots and pans within easy reach. A lazy Susan rotates 360 degrees, so just spin it to find what you're looking for. Carousel shelves, which attach to two right-angled doors, rotate 270 degrees; open the doors, and the shelves swing out allowing you to reach items easily.

Pivoting Shelves. Door-mounted shelves and in-cabinet swiveling shelf units offer easy access to kitchen supplies. Taller units serve as pantries that hold a great deal in minimal space.

Pullout Tables and Trays. In tight kitchens, pullout tables and trays are excellent ways to gain eating space or an extra work surface. Pullout cutting boards come in handy near cooktops, microwaves, and food prep areas. Pullout tea carts are also available.

Customized Organizers. If you decide to use value-priced cabinets or choose to forego the storage accessories offered by manufacturers, consider refitting their interiors with cabinet organizers you purchase yourself. These plastic, plastic-coated wire, or enameled-steel racks and hangers are widely available at department stores, hardware stores, and home centers.

Some of these units slide in and out of base cabinets, similar to the racks in a dishwasher. Others let you mount shallow drawers to the undersides of wall cabinets.

Still others consist of stackable plastic bins with plenty of room to hold kitchen sundries.

Beware of the temptation to over-specialize your kitchen storage facilities. Sizes and needs for certain items change, so be sure to allot at least 50 percent of your kitchen's storage to standard cabinets with one or more movable shelves. And don't forget to allow for storing recyclable items.

Today's cabinets can be customized with storage accessories, right.

Full-height pantries, above, provide a number of different types of storage near where you need the items. This pantry is next to the food-prep area.

Base cabinets can be outfitted with accessories for kitchen storage or for wet bar storage as shown in the cabinet below.

Storage Checklist

Here's a guide to help you get your storage needs in order.

■ **Do you like kitchen gadgets?**
Plan drawer space, countertop sorters, wall magnets, or hooks to keep these items handy near where you often use them.

■ **Do you own a food processor, blender, mixer, toaster oven, electric can opener, knife sharpener, juicer, coffee maker, or coffee mill?**
If you're particularly tidy, you may want small appliances like these tucked away in an appliance garage or cupboard to be taken out only when needed. If you pre-fer to have frequently used machines sitting on the counter, ready to go, plan enough space, along with conveniently located electrical outlets.

■ **Do you plan to store large quantities of food?**
Be sure to allow plenty of freezer, bin, and shelf space for the kind of food shopping you do.

■ **Do you intend to do a lot of freezing or canning?**
Allow a work space and place to stow equipment. Also plan adequate storage for the fruits of your labor—an extra stand-alone freezer, a good-sized food safe in the kitchen, or a separate pantry or cellar.

■ **Do you bake often?**
Consider a baking center that can house your equipment and serve as a separate baking-ingredients pantry.

■ **Do you collect pottery, tinware, or anything else that might be displayed in the kitchen?**
Soffits provide an obvious place to hang small objects like collectible plates. Eliminating soffits provides a shelf on top of the wall cabinets for larger light-weight objects like baskets. Open shelving, glass-front cupboards, and display cabinets are other options.

■ **Do you collect cookbooks?**
If so, you'll need expandable shelf space and perhaps a bookstand.

Personal Profile of You and Your Family

■ **How tall are you and everyone else who will use your kitchen?**
Adjust your counter and wall-cabinet heights to suit. Multilevel work surfaces for special tasks are a necessity for good kitchen design.

■ **Do you or any of your family members use a walker, leg braces, or a wheelchair?**
Plan a good work height, knee space, grab bars, secure seating, slide-out work

Fold-down ironing boards, above left, are a true luxury. If you have the space, install one near the kitchen or laundry room.

Corner cabinets often contain storage space you can't reach. Make it accessible by installing swing-out shelves, above right, or a lazy Susan.

Glass doors put your kitchen items on display. The owners of the kitchen below chose distinctive pottery and glassware for their glass-door cabinets.

boards, and other convenience features to make your kitchen comfortable for all who will use it.

■ **Are you left- or right-handed?**
Think about your natural motion when you choose whether to open cupboards or refrigerator doors from the left or right side, whether to locate your dishwasher to the left or right of the sink, and so on.

■ **How high can you comfortably reach?**
If you're tall, hang your wall cabinets high. If you're petite, you may want to hang the cabinets lower and plan a spot to keep a step stool handy.

■ **Can you comfortably bend and reach for something in a base cabinet?**
Can you lift heavy objects easily and without strain or pain?
If your range is limited in these areas, be sure to plan roll-out shelving on both upper and lower tiers of your base cabinets. Also, look into spring-up shelves designed to lift mixer bases or other heavy appliances to counter height.

■ **Do you frequently share cooking tasks with another family member?**
If so, you may each prefer to have your own work area.

ous plan demands this kind of attention. Even if you are designing a modest bath, you can greatly increase its performance and your ultimate comfort by thoughtfully planning out every square inch of floor and wall space. In fact, small spaces require more attention to details than larger spaces.

Types of bathrooms

The most-common-size American bathroom measures 60 x 84 inches or 60 x 96 inches. The most common complaint about it is the lack of space. The arrangement may have suited families 50 years ago, but times and habits have changed. If it's the only bathroom in the house, making it work better becomes even more important.

When planning the layout, try angling a sink or shower unit in a corner to free up some floor space. Unlike a traditional door, which swings into the room and takes up wall space when it is open, a pocket door slides into the wall. Another smart way to add function to a small bathroom is to remove the drywall and install shelves between the studs.

The Importance of Lighting. You can also make a small bathroom feel roomier by bringing in natural light with a skylight or roof window or by replacing one small standard window with several small casement units that can be installed high on the wall to maintain privacy while admitting light.

Bath Design

Many professionals believe that bathrooms may be the most difficult rooms in the house to design properly. The space is often small, yet it must be able to accommodate a variety of large fixtures. In addition, many homeowners tend to focus, at least initially, on the way the bathroom looks. They fall in love with the whirlpool tub that is really too large for the space or the exquisite hand-painted sink that, while beautiful, demands too much effort to keep it

looking that way. Design your bath to be functional as well as beautiful.

Architect Louis Sullivan said, "Form follows function." That does not mean that style has to be subservient to function, but there must be a balance between the two. So even if you have a clear picture about how you want the new bathroom to look, put that thought on hold—temporarily—and think about how it will work.

Thorough Planning. Don't mislead yourself into believing that only a luxuri-

The Master Bath

The concept of the master bath has come of age in the past decade. It is one of the most popular rooms for splurging on high-end items and gives one of the highest returns on investment upon resale. It's where you can create that sought-after getaway—the home version of a European spa.

Latest Trends. Some popular amenities to include in your plan are a sauna, greenhouse, exercise studio, fireplace, audio and video systems, faucets and sprayers with full massaging options, steam room,

Windows placed high on the wall let in light while maintaining privacy, opposite.

Master baths, above, often contain an attached dressing area.

Traditional designs do not prevent you from using the latest shower products, right.

Cottage baths tend to be bright and airy, such as the one shown to the left.

A simple floral design decorates the border of the medicine cabinet above.

Traditional bathroom cabinetry should be simple in design, below.

whirlpool tub, and dressing table. You are only limited by size and imagination.

Planning for Extras. Extras can be tempting but may require special planning. For example, you may need additional support in the floor, as well as supplemental heating and ventilation. You would not want to slip into a tub and have it fall two floors to the middle of the living room.

Some of the best floor plans for the modern adult bath also include a separate room for the toilet and bidet, a detached tub and shower, and dual sinks on opposite sides of the room with adjacent dressing rooms and walk-in closets. Modern couples

want to share a master bed and bath, but they also want to have privacy and the ease of getting ready in the morning without tripping over their mates. The only way to do this harmoniously is to mingle the parts of the room that invite sharing and separate those elements that are always private. Such items as a sauna, exercise area, and a whirlpool tub would be part of shared space. Dressing tables and clothes closets would be private spaces.

The Powder Room

The guest bath. The half bath. It has a lot of names, and it may be the most efficient room in the house, providing just what you

need often in tight quarters. A powder room normally includes nothing more than a lavatory and a toilet. You can find small-scale fixtures specifically designed for the powder room, from the tiniest lavs to unusually narrow toilets.

Keep a small powder room as light and open as possible. Plan to install good lighting because the powder room is often used for touching up makeup.

Focal Points. In the powder room, the vanity is often the focal point. The room offers the best opportunity to showcase a decorative piece, such as a hand-painted pedestal sink or a custom-made vanity.

Because the powder room is often for guests and is normally located on the ground floor near the living area, take extra care to ensure privacy. If possible, the best location is in a hallway, away from the living room, kitchen, and dining area. This room can also handle stronger wall colors—either dark or bright ones—as well as larger, bolder wallpaper patterns because it is a short-stay room.

The Family Bath

Compartmentalizing is the best way to start planning the family bath. But remember, when you separate the bathroom into smaller, distinct areas, you run the risk of making the room feel cramped. Try to alleviate this with extra natural light, good artificial lighting, and translucent partitions made of glass blocks or etched glass. Anything that divides with privacy while also allowing light to enter will help ease the closed-in feeling.

Separate Areas. If separating the fixtures is not possible because of the size of the room, include a sink in the dressing area within the master bedroom to provide a second place for applying makeup or shaving. It will help relieve bottlenecks when everyone is dressing in the morning.

Investigate building a back-to-back bath in lieu of one large shared room. Another popular option is to locate the bathing fixtures, both the tub and separate shower, in the center of the room; install the bidet, a toilet, and sink on either side in their own separate areas. To make the arrangement work, keep each side of the room accessible to the door.

There are other options you can use. It is important to remember that you don't need to do them all at once; you can do some remodeling once you've moved into your house.

Ceramic-tile counters for bathroom vanities are easy to clean and can stand up to abuse.

Plan #131007

Dimensions: 59'10" W x 47'8" D

Levels: 1

Square Footage: 1,595

Bedrooms: 3

Bathrooms: 2

Foundation: Crawl space, slab, basement, or walkout

Materials List Available: Yes

Price Category: D

Images provided by designer/architect.

Imagine living in this home, with its traditional country comfort and individual brand of charm.

Features:

• Exterior elements: The mixture of a front porch with a cameo front door, decorative posts, bay windows, and dormers will delight you.

• Great Room: A tray ceiling gives distinction to this large room, and a wet bar eases entertaining.

• Screened Porch: At dusk and dawn, this porch is sure to be your favorite outdoor spot.

• Kitchen: Eat any meal in this large kitchen for a touch of homey charm.

• Dining Room: Perfect for hosting a formal dinner, this bayed dining room can increase your enjoyment of simple family meals.

• Master Bedroom: For the sake of privacy, this room is somewhat secluded. Decorate to emphasize the elegant tray ceiling.

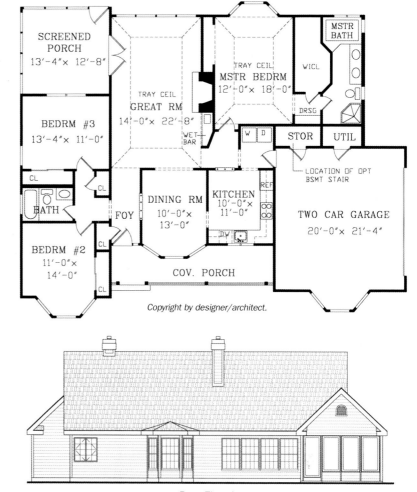

Copyright by designer/architect.

Rear Elevation

Alternate Front View

Foyer / Dining Room

Add the Extras

Simple or plain, it's the little conveniences and miscellaneous touches that push the dining experience to perfection. Here are some extra things to think about.

- You can never have too many serving trays when you entertain outside. For carrying food or drinks from the kitchen or the grill, trays are indispensable.

- A serving cart on wheels makes a perfect movable outdoor bar and provides an additional serving surface. Look for one at yard sales or buy one new.

- Chances are you won't have a sideboard, but a few small tables to hold excess items are great substitutes for one. They're also easier to position in the different places where you need them.

- For cooler weather or even a summer's evening with a bit of nip in the air, nothing beats an outdoor fireplace for comfort. You could build one into the house, but various types of stand-alone units are sold in home centers. To add a Southwest ambiance, consider a chiminea, a clay fireplace. Try burning some piñon pine, and you'll feel as if you're in Santa Fe. Be sure to follow manufacturers' instructions when using these fireplaces. You might also have to store them during the winter.

- Pots of fragrant plants—lavender, scented geraniums, flowering tobacco, or jasmine—provide a sensual aroma. Flowers such as roses climbing up an arbor or trellis are beautiful, evoke a romantic feeling, and lend a delicate scent to the atmosphere as well.

Nothing adds romance and intrigue to an evening soiree as candlelight does. Include just a few candles for an intimate dinner. Use more for a larger gathering, placing one or more on each table. Scatter luminaries around the yard. As the beautiful evening dusk begins, light candles, a few at a time, so your eyes can adjust to the dimming light. Not only do the candles illuminate the night in a magical way but they can also keep bugs at bay.

Great Room

Plan #351005

Dimensions: 61' W x 47'4" D

Levels: 1

Square Footage: 1,501

Bedrooms: 3

Bathrooms: 2

Foundation: Crawl space, slab, or basement

Materials List Available: Yes

Price Category: C

Images provided by designer/architect.

This home provides a very functional split-floor-plan layout with many of the features that your family desires.

Features:

- Porches: Enjoy the beautiful weather on one of your porches, front and rear.

- Great Room: This large room, with its vaulted ceiling and gas log fireplace, is perfect for entertaining.

- Kitchen: With plenty of counter space for that growing family, this kitchen has an open layout.

- Master Suite: This expansive master bedroom and bathroom area has plenty of storage space in the separate walk-in closets.

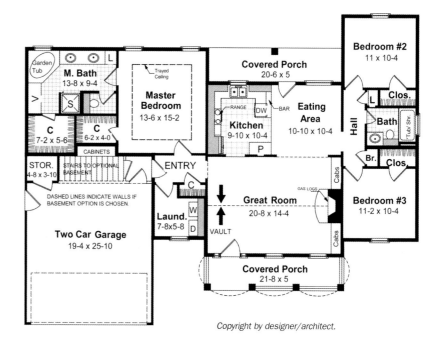

Copyright by designer/architect.

Plan #151215

Dimensions: 53' W x 56'6" D
Levels: 1
Square Footage: 1,519
Bedrooms: 3
Bathrooms: 2
Foundation: Crawl space or slab
Materials List Available: No
Price Category: C

Images provided by designer/architect.

This brick home, with a front-loading garage, is the perfect home for a young family.

Features:

- Great Room: This large entertainment area has a corner fireplace and entry to the grilling porch.

- Kitchen: Designed with a walk-through layout, this kitchen is open to the breakfast room.

- Master Suite: This private area, located on the opposite side of the home from the secondary bedrooms, features a master bathroom with large his and her walk-in closets.

- Bedrooms: The two secondary bedrooms share a common bathroom.

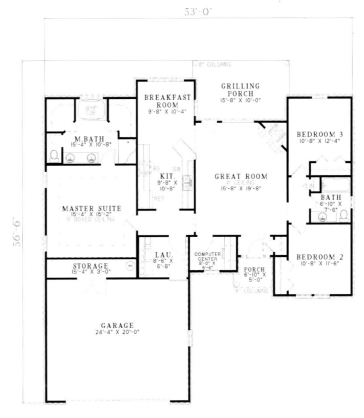

Copyright by designer/architect.

Plan #391039

Dimensions: 50' W x 45'4" D

Levels: 1

Square Footage: 1,539

Bedrooms: 3

Bathrooms: 2

Foundation: Crawl space, slab, or basement

Materials List Available: Yes

Price Category: C

Images provided by designer/architect.

A gabled roofline and easy-going front porch charm the exterior. Practical and pretty touches dramatize the interior.

Features:

- Foyer: This entry hall has a large walk-in closet.

- Kitchen: This kitchen's creative horizontal shape invites plenty of amenities. There is abundant cabinet space and a close-at-hand laundry facility.

- Dining Room: The kitchen's breakfast bar looks cheerfully into this formal room.

- Master Bedroom: A tray ceiling adds to the appeal of this room. The bump-out window seat invites breaks for daydreaming; a large walk-in closet handles wardrobes for two.

- Master Bath: This lavish master bathroom features a window over the tub.

- Bedrooms: The two additional bedrooms have their own unique styling, including excellent closet space and charming windows.

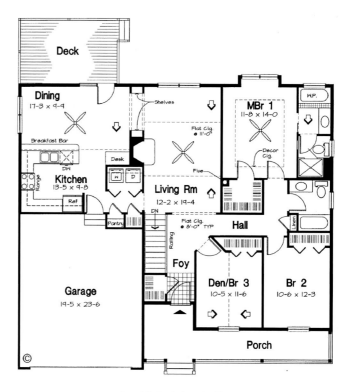

Copyright by designer/architect.

Plan #401008

Dimensions: 87' W x 44' D
Levels: 1
Square Footage: 1,541
Bedrooms: 3
Bathrooms: 2
Foundation: Basement
Materials List Available: Yes
Price Category: C

This popular design begins with a wraparound covered porch made even more charming by turned wood spindles.

Features:

• **Great Room:** The entry opens directly into this great room, which is warmed by a woodstove.

• **Dining Room:** This room offers access to a screened porch for outdoor after-dinner leisure.

• **Kitchen:** This country kitchen features a center island and a breakfast bay for casual meals.

• **Bedrooms:** Family bedrooms share a full bath that includes a soaking tub.

Images provided by designer/architect.

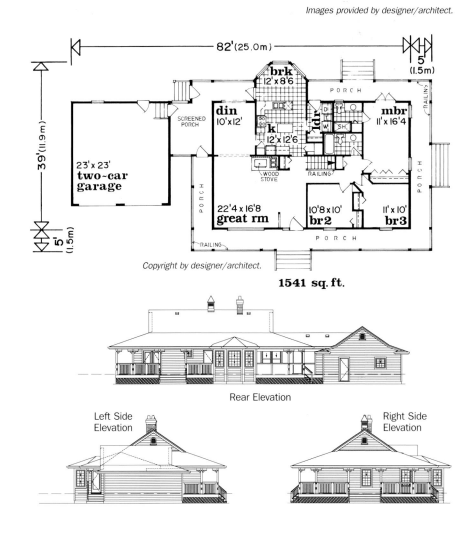

Copyright by designer/architect.

1541 sq. ft.

Rear Elevation

Left Side Elevation

Right Side Elevation

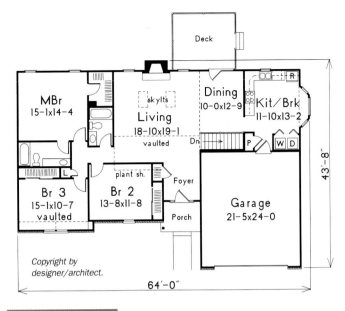

Copyright by
designer/architect.

Plan #321014

Dimensions: 64' W x 43'8" D
Levels: 1
Square Footage: 1,676
Bedrooms: 3
Bathrooms: 2
Foundation: Basement
Materials List Available: Yes
Price Category: C

Images provided by designer/architect.

SMARTtip

Blending Architecture

An easy way to blend the new deck with the architecture of a house is with railings. Precut railings and caps come in many styles and sizes.

Plan #151026

Dimensions: 34' W x 66'8" D
Levels: 2
Square Footage: 1,574
Main Level Sq. Ft.: 1,131
Upper Level Sq. Ft.: 443
Bedrooms: 3
Bathrooms: 2½
Foundation: Crawl space, slab;
optional full basement plan available
for extra fee
Materials List Available: No
Price Category: C

Main Level Floor Plan

Upper Level Floor Plan

Images provided by designer/architect.

Copyright by designer/architect.

Plan #151009

Dimensions: 44' W x 86'2" D

Levels: 1

Square Footage: 1,601

Bedrooms: 3

Bathrooms: 2

Foundation: Crawl space or slab

Materials List Available: No

Price Category: C

Images provided by designer/architect.

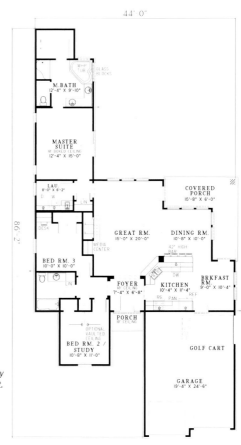

Copyright by designer/architect.

Plan #321021

Dimensions: 80' W x 42' D

Levels: 1

Square Footage: 1,708

Bedrooms: 3

Bathrooms: 2

Foundation: Crawl space or basement

Materials List Available: Yes

Price Category: C

Images provided by designer/architect.

SMARTtip

Planning a Safe Children's Room

Keep safety in mind when planning a child's room. Make sure that there are covers on electrical outlets, guard rails on high windows, sturdy screens in front of radiators, and gates blocking any steps. Other suggestions include safety hinges for chests and nonskid backing for rugs.

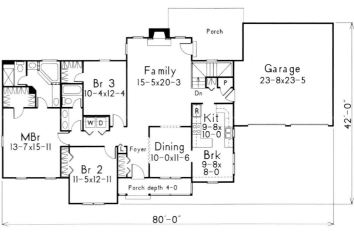

Copyright by designer/architect.

Plan #401021

Dimensions: 28' W x 39'9" D
Levels: 1½
Square Footage: 1,543
Main Level Sq. Ft.: 1,061
Upper Level Sq. Ft.: 482
Bedrooms: 3
Bathrooms: 2
Foundation: Crawl space
Materials List Available: Yes
Price Category: C

A sun deck makes this design popular, and it is even more enhanced by views through an expansive glass wall in the living and dining rooms. These rooms are warmed by a woodstove and enjoy vaulted ceilings.

Images provided by designer/architect.

Features:

- Kitchen: This area has a vaulted ceiling, plus a food-preparation island and breakfast bar.
- Laundry Room: Behind the kitchen is this utility room with side-deck access.

- Master Suite: A skylighted staircase leads up to this area and has a walk-in closet and private bath.
- Bedrooms: You'll find two bedrooms and a full bath on the first floor.

Main Level Floor Plan

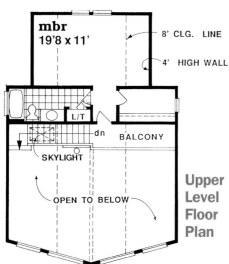

Upper Level Floor Plan

Copyright by designer/architect.

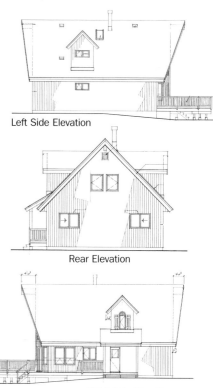

Left Side Elevation

Rear Elevation

Right Side Elevation

Plan #401044

Dimensions: 34' W x 48' D
Levels: 2
Square Footage: 1,568
Main Level Sq. Ft.: 1,012
Upper Level Sq. Ft.: 556
Bedrooms: 3
Bathrooms: 2½
Foundation: Basement
Materials List Available: Yes
Price Category: C

Country comes home to this plan with details such as a metal roof, horizontal siding, multi-pane double-hung windows, and front and rear porches.

Features:

- Entry: This recessed front entry leads to the great room, flanked by a breakfast bar and formal dining room with access to both the front and rear porches.

- Great Room: This room is warmed by a fireplace and features a two-story ceiling.

- Master Suite: Located the first level, this sweet retreat has a private bath and walk-in closet.

- Bedrooms: Upstairs, two more bedrooms and a full bathroom complete the plan.

Main Level Floor Plan

PORCH

mbr 12'4x12'8

din 12'x10'

k 8'4x10'

W D

CABINETS

BREAKFAST BAR

DN UP

great rm 17'x13'6

PORCH

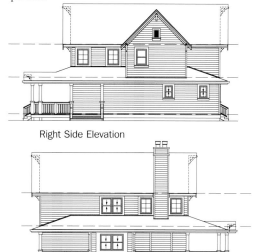

Right Side Elevation

Left Side Elevation

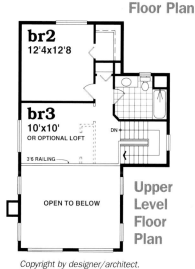

br2 12'4x12'8

br3 10'x10' OR OPTIONAL LOFT

DN

3'6 RAILING

OPEN TO BELOW

Upper Level Floor Plan

Rear Elevation

Plan #391021

Dimensions: 54' W x 48'4" D

Levels: 1

Square Footage: 1,568

Bedrooms: 3

Bathrooms: 2

Foundation: Crawl space, slab, or basement

Materials List Available: Yes

Price Category: C

Images provided by designer/architect.

A peaked porch roof and luminous Palladian window play up the exterior appeal of this ranch home, while other architectural components dramatize the interior.

Features:

- **Living Room:** There is a soaring ceiling in this living room, where a corner fireplace and built-in bookshelves provide cozy comfort.

- **Dining Room:** Open to the living room, this room features sliders to the wood deck, which makes it conducive to both casual and formal entertaining.

- **Kitchen:** This well-planned kitchen seems to have it all—a built-in pantry, a double sink, and a breakfast bar that feeds into the dining room. The bar provides additional serving space when needed.

- **Master Suite:** This private retreat is situated far from the public areas. A large walk-in closet with a private bath and double vanity add to the suite's intimate appeal.

- **Bedrooms:** The two additional bedrooms boast large closets and bright windows. The generous hall bathroom is located conveniently nearby.

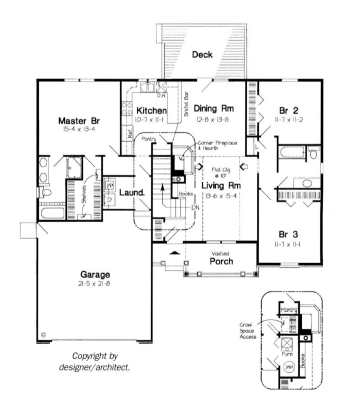

Copyright by designer/architect.

Plan #371031

Dimensions: 67'2½" W x 40'6" D

Levels: 1

Square Footage: 1,599

Bedrooms: 3

Bathrooms: 2

Foundation: Slab

Materials List Available: No

Price Category: C

The beautiful brick-and-stone detail of this traditional home sets it apart from the rest.

Features:

- **Family Room:** With its 10-ft.-high ceiling, media center, and cozy fireplace, this large room is great for entertaining.

- **Dining Room:** Although it is open to the kitchen and family room, wooden columns set this room apart.

- **Kitchen:** This functional kitchen has a breakfast bar and is open to the dining and family rooms, bringing these three rooms together.

- **Master Suite:** This suite, with its stepped-up ceiling, boasts a luxurious bathroom with his and her vanities and a marble tub, glass shower, and walk-in closet.

- **Bedrooms:** The two additional large bedrooms share a convenient hall bathroom.

Images provided by designer/architect.

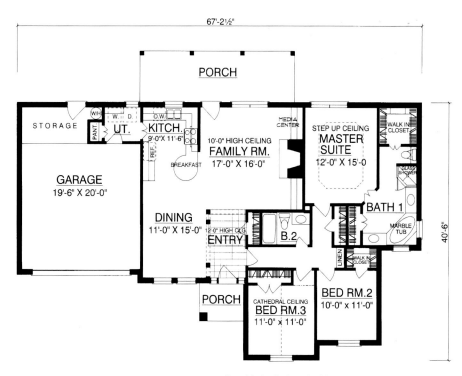

Copyright by designer/architect.

Plan #351023

Dimensions: 61'8" W x 45'8" D

Levels: 1

Square Footage: 1,600

Bedrooms: 3

Bathrooms: 2

Foundation: Crawl space, slab, or basement

Materials List Available: Yes

Price Category: C

Images provided by designer/architect.

This beautiful three-bedroom home has everything your family needs to live the comfortable life.

Features:

- **Great Room:** Just off the foyer is this large room. It features a cozy fireplace and access to the rear covered porch.

- **Dining Room:** This formal room has large windows with a view of the backyard.

- **Kitchen:** This kitchen has an abundance of cabinets and counter space. It is open to the dining room.

- **Master Suite:** This isolated suite, with its jetted tub, separate shower, large closet, and dual vanities, is a perfect retreat.

- **Bedrooms:** The two secondary bedrooms have large closets and share a hall bathroom.

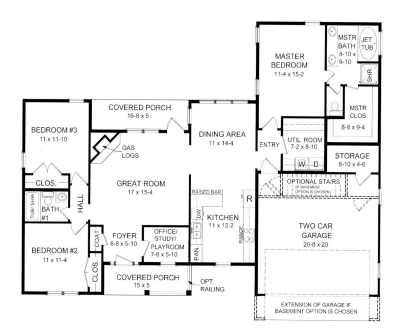

Copyright by designer/architect.

Plan #401027

Dimensions: 44'8" W x 41'4" D
Levels: 2
Square Footage: 1,634
Main Level Sq. Ft.: 1,099
Upper Level Sq. Ft.: 535
Bedrooms: 3
Bathrooms: 2
Foundation: Basement
Materials List Available: Yes
Price Category: C

Features:

- Vaulted Ceilings: Inside, the open plan includes a vaulted great room with fireplace, a vaulted dining room, and a vaulted kitchen.
- Kitchen: This area has a pass-through to the dining room and large pantry for the ultimate in convenience and functionality.
- Master Suite: Located on the first floor for privacy this retreat contains a walk-in closet with dressing room, a sitting area, and full skylighted bath.
- Bedrooms: Two family bedrooms are on the second floor.

This design offers several different options to make the floor plan exactly as you like it. The exterior is graced by a wrapping veranda, round columns, stone facing with cedar-shingled accents, and a trio of dormers.

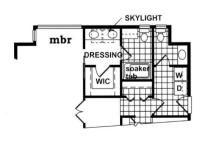

Optional Lower Level Floor Plan

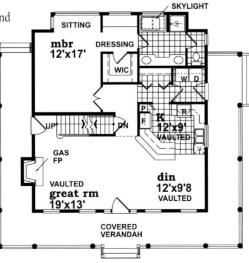

Main Level Floor Plan

Upper Level Floor Plan

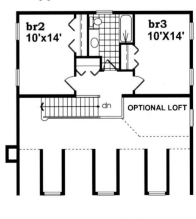

Plan #391038

Dimensions: 59' W x 44' D
Levels: 1
Square Footage: 1,642
Bedrooms: 3
Bathrooms: 2
Foundation: Crawl space, slab, or basement
Materials List Available: Yes
Price Category: C

This home features triple arches trimming a restful exterior front porch, great arched windows with shutters, and a complex classic roofline that steals the eye.

Features:

- Dining Room: A formal parlor sits across the hall from this spectacular room with decorative tray ceiling and built-in cabinetry.

- Kitchen: This kitchen is the heart of the home, with an island and peninsula counter/snack bar that opens into the great room.

- Great Room: This expansive room boasts a big, open layout with a corner fireplace.

- Master Suite: This super-private suite has a large walk-in closet and a sunny bath with a tub beneath a window.

- Bedrooms: These two additional bedrooms flank a full bathroom.

- Garage: This two-car garage makes all the difference for families with more than one automobile.

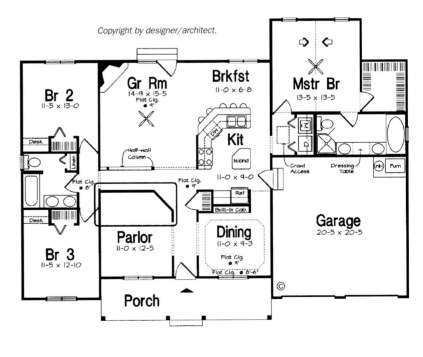

Optional Basement Stairs

Plan #351032

Dimensions: 64' W x 39' D
Levels: 1
Square Footage: 1,650
Bedrooms: 3
Bathrooms: 2
Foundation: Crawl space or slab
Materials List Available: Yes
Price Category: C

This home has many features you would find in a larger house.

Features:

- Great Room: A tray ceiling and a built-in entertainment center accentuate this expansive room, which has easy access to the dining room and kitchen.

- Master Suite: This isolated suite has a jetted tub, a separate shower, a large walk-in closet, and dual vanities.

- Utility Room: You'll have plenty of space for storing/folding clothing and other goods in this room.

- Flexible Space: This flexible space is a useful addition as a much-needed home office, storage, or other family space.

Plan #371053

Dimensions: 51'2" W x 66'7" D
Levels: 1
Square Footage: 1,654
Bedrooms: 3
Bathrooms: 2
Foundation: Slab
Materials List Available: No
Price Category: C

Images provided by designer/architect.

A cozy country porch and large inviting windows are the perfect way to say, "I'm home." This country charmer has everything you need.

Features:

- Kitchen: This large kitchen boasts a cathedral ceiling and a raised bar.

- Dining Room: This room has a cathedral ceiling and is open to the living room and kitchen.

- Living Room: The fireplace and cathedral ceiling give this room an inviting feeling.

- Master Suite: This private retreat features two walk-in closets. The old-fashioned bath with an antique tub is perfect for relaxing.

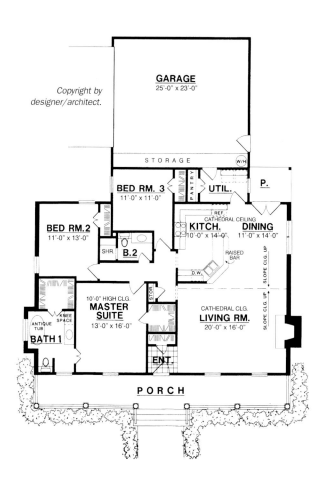

Plan #351033

Dimensions: 62'2" W x 45'8" D

Levels: 1

Square Footage: 1,654

Bedrooms: 3

Bathrooms: 2

Foundation: Crawl space, slab, or basement

Materials List Available: Yes

Price Category: C

Images provided by designer/architect.

This gorgeous three-bedroom brick home would be the perfect place to raise your family.

Features:

• Great Room: This terrific room has a gas fireplace with built-in cabinets on either side.

• Kitchen: This island kitchen with breakfast area is open to the great room.

• Master Bedroom: This private room features a vaulted ceiling and a large walk-in closet.

• Master Bath: This private area has a walk-in closet, jetted tub, and double vanities.

• Bedrooms: The two additional bedrooms share a bathroom located in the hall.

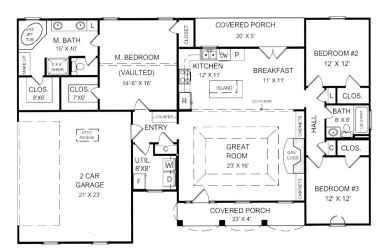

Copyright by designer/architect.

Plan #371032

Dimensions: 55'6" W x 46' D

Levels: 1

Square Footage: 1,659

Bedrooms: 3

Bathrooms: 2

Foundation: Slab

Materials List Available: No

Price Category: C

Images provided by designer/architect.

This charming country home has an impressive look that is all its own. This is the perfect home for any size family.

Features:

- Living Room: This massive room boasts a stepped ceiling, built in bookshelves and a media center.

- Kitchen: This large kitchen with walk-in pantry opens into the dining room.

- Master Suite: This area also has a high stepped ceiling and a sitting area with a view of the backyard. The large master bath has two walk-in closets and a marble tub.

- Bedrooms: The two large additional bedrooms share a convenient bath.

- Bonus Room: Located above the garage, this area can be a playroom.

Copyright by designer/architect.

Bonus Area Floor Plan

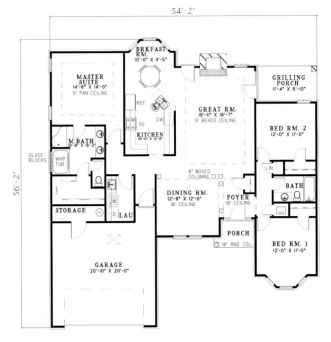

Plan #151007

Dimensions: 54'2" W x 56'2" D

Levels: 1

Square Footage: 1,787

Bedrooms: 3

Bathrooms: 2

Foundation: Crawl space, slab, basement, or walkout

Materials List Available: No

Price Category: C

Images provided by designer/architect.

Copyright by designer/architect.

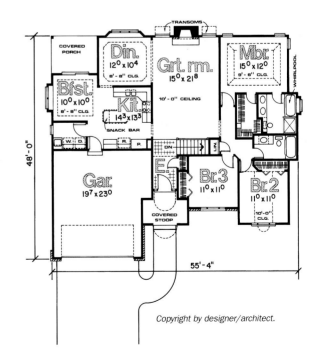

Plan #121004

Dimensions: 55'4" W x 48' D

Levels: 1

Square Footage: 1,666

Bedrooms: 3

Bathrooms: 2

Foundation: Basement

Materials List Available: Yes

Price Category: C

Images provided by designer/architect.

Copyright by designer/architect.

Plan #351026

Dimensions: 50' W x 65' D

Levels: 1

Square Footage: 1,603

Bedrooms: 3

Bathrooms: 2

Foundation: Crawl space or slab

Materials List Available: Yes

Price Category: C

The "open" nature of this home's floor plan is designed to meet the needs of many homeowners and builders who are looking to build on a relatively narrow lot.

Features:

- **Great Room:** The focal point of this room is the entertainment center. The area is open and inviting.

- **Kitchen:** This kitchen boasts a raised bar for conversations with family and friends while isolating them from the work triangle.

- **Master Suite:** The great amenities in this suite include a tray ceiling, large garden tub, over sized shower, linen closet, and large wardrobe closet.

- **Flex Space:** Located next to the master suite, this flex space may serve as an office, nursery, or hobby room.

- **Patio:** This spacious patio lends itself to grilling out, sunbathing, and visiting with friends.

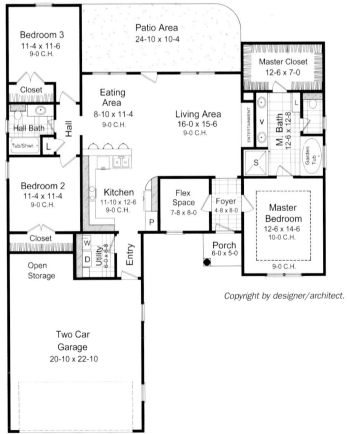

Plan #151219

Dimensions: 48' W x 74'4" D
Levels: 1
Square Footage: 1,712
Bedrooms: 2
Bathrooms: 2
Foundation: Crawl space or slab
Materials List Available: No
Price Category: C

This country home has a friendly open floor plan and a bonus room above.

Features:

- Great Room: This area has a cozy fireplace and is open into the dining area.

- Dining Area: With enough room for a family-sized table, this area is great for a large household and is open to the kitchen and great room.

- Kitchen: This U-shaped kitchen has a breakfast bar and is close to the garage.

- Master Suite: This large retreat has a private bathroom with a large walk-in closet.

Images provided by designer/architect.

Copyright by designer/architect.

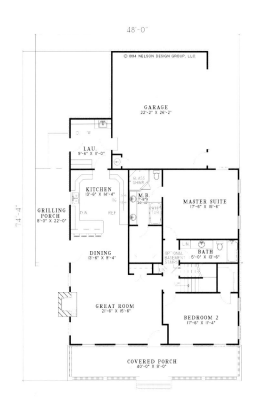

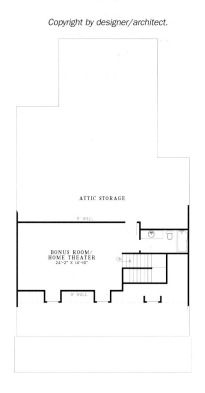

Bonus Area Floor Plan

Plan #151210

Dimensions: 70' W x 50' D
Levels: 1
Square Footage: 1,716
Bedrooms: 3
Bathrooms: 2
Foundation: Crawl space or slab
Materials List Available: No
Price Category: C

This traditional three-bedroom brick home will be the envy of the neighborhood.

Features:

- **Great Room:** This large gathering room, with a cozy fireplace, has access to the rear porch.

- **Dining Room:** This room with a view of the front yard is located just of the entry.

- **Kitchen:** This kitchen boasts an abundant amount of cabinets, and counter space is open to the breakfast area and the great room.

- **Master Suite:** This suite features a private bathroom with double vanities and a whirlpool tub.

- **Bedrooms:** Two secondary bedrooms have large closets and share a hall bathroom.

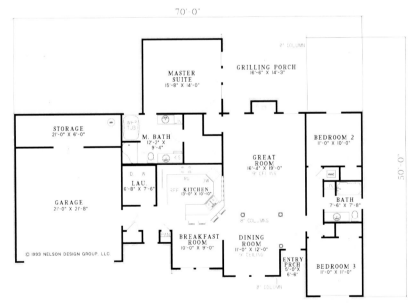

Plan #371012

Dimensions: 56'4" W x 52'10" D

Levels: 1

Square Footage: 1,720

Bedrooms: 3

Bathrooms: 2

Foundation: Slab

Materials List Available: No

Price Category: C

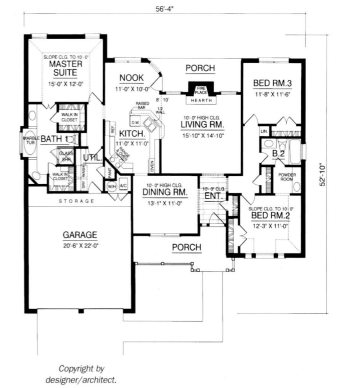

Images provided by designer/architect.

Copyright by designer/architect.

Plan #351003

Dimensions: 64' W x 45'10" D

Levels: 1

Square Footage: 1,751

Bedrooms: 3

Bathrooms: 2

Foundation: Crawl space, slab, or basement

Materials List Available: Yes

Price Category: C

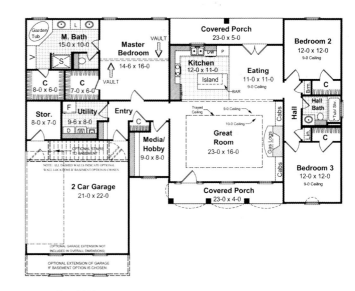

Images provided by designer/architect.

Copyright by designer/architect.

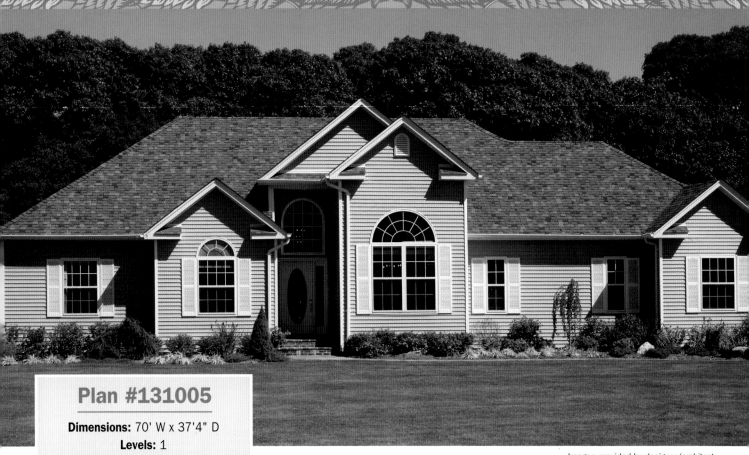

Plan #131005

Dimensions: 70' W x 37'4" D
Levels: 1
Square Footage: 1,595
Bedrooms: 3
Bathrooms: 2
Foundation: Crawl space, slab, or basement
Materials List Available: Yes
Price Category: C

With the finest features of an open design in the main living areas, this home gives privacy where you need it. Best of all, it's wheelchair accessible.

Features:

• Foyer: A high ceiling gives this area real presence and serves to blend it seamlessly with the great room and the dining room.

• Great Room: The open design allows you to use this room as an extension of the dining room or, if you wish, furnish it to create a private reading nook or visually separate media center.

• Breakfast Room: Both this room and the adjacent well-appointed kitchen flow into the rest of the living area. However, access to the rear porch, where you can sit out and enjoy the weather while you eat, distinguishes this room.

• Master Suite: Located in the same wing as the other bedrooms, this suite has a separate entrance and features a vaulted ceiling, three closets, and a compartmented bath.

SMARTtip

Create a Courtyard

Create a private walled-garden retreat with fences covered by climbing vines. Add height with trellises, and divide spaces with clipped boxwood hedges. Include an (almost) instant patio by digging away an area of sod and then covering it with a layer of sand and landscaping mesh to discourage weeds. Then cover it with pea gravel, and add a garden bench, statuary, and perhaps an antique or two. The result? European ambiance for even the most nondescript suburban yard.

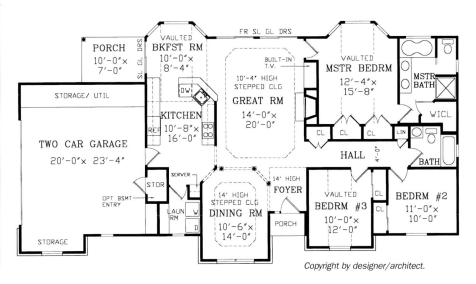

Foyer

Dining Room

Living Room

Great Room

SMARTtip

Natural Trellis

Create a natural rustic trellis that might even, if growing conditions are right, produce its own pretty blooms. Cut and place saplings in the ground as uprights. Then weave old grapevines with smaller saplings for the lattice.

Plan #371034

Dimensions: 49'2" W x 53'2" D

Levels: 1

Square Footage: 1,753

Bedrooms: 3

Bathrooms: 2

Foundation: Slab

Materials List Available: No

Price Category: C

Images provided by designer/architect.

Copyright by designer/architect.

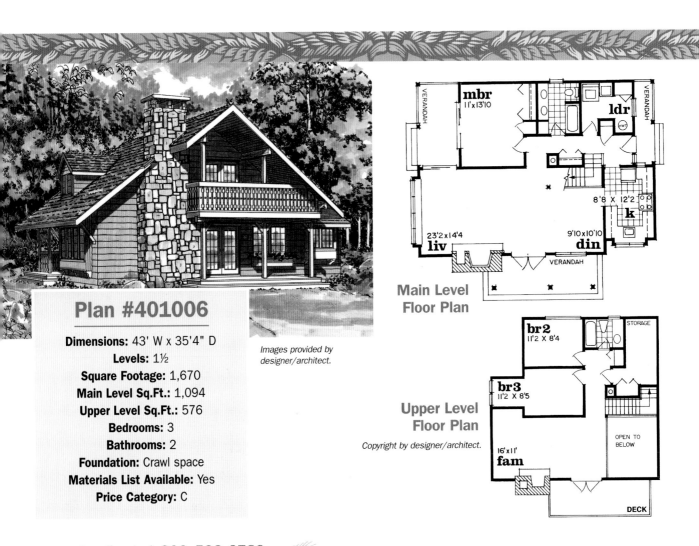

Plan #401006

Dimensions: 43' W x 35'4" D

Levels: 1½

Square Footage: 1,670

Main Level Sq.Ft.: 1,094

Upper Level Sq.Ft.: 576

Bedrooms: 3

Bathrooms: 2

Foundation: Crawl space

Materials List Available: Yes

Price Category: C

Images provided by designer/architect.

Main Level Floor Plan

Upper Level Floor Plan

Copyright by designer/architect.

Plan #371011

Dimensions: 55'4" W x 49'10" D
Levels: 1
Square Footage: 1,681
Bedrooms: 3
Bathrooms: 2½
Foundation: Slab
Materials List Available: No
Price Category: C

Images provided by designer/architect.

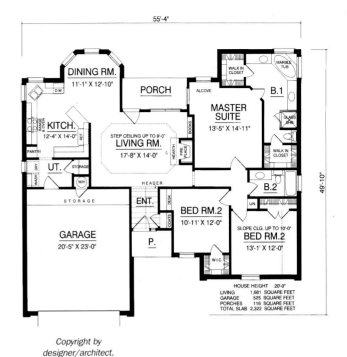

Copyright by designer/architect.

Plan #101027

Dimensions: 50' W x 48'8" D
Levels: 2
Square Footage: 1,695
Main Level Sq. Ft.: 880
Upper Level Sq. Ft.: 815
Bedrooms: 3
Bathrooms: 2½
Foundation: Basement
Materials List Available: No
Price Category: C

Images provided by designer/architect.

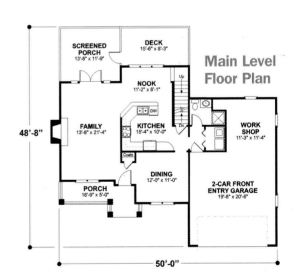

Copyright by designer/architect.

**Main Level
Floor Plan**

Copyright by designer/architect.

Plan #391005

Dimensions: 60' W x 40'4" D

Levels: 1

Main Level Sq. Ft.: 1,575

Bedrooms: 3

Bathrooms: 2

Foundation: Crawl space, slab, or basement

Materials List Available: Yes

Price Category: C

Images provided by designer/architect.

Front View

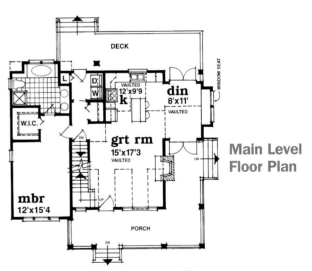

**Main Level
Floor Plan**

Plan #401036

Dimensions: 42' W x 38' D

Levels: 2

Square Footage: 1,583

Main Level Sq. Ft.: 1,050

Upper Level Sq. Ft.: 533

Bedrooms: 3

Bathrooms: 2

Foundation: Basement

Materials List Available: Yes

Price Category: C

Images provided by designer/architect.

**Upper Level
Floor Plan**

Copyright by designer/architect.

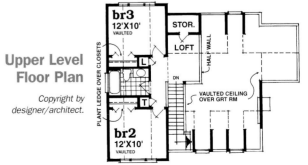

Images provided by designer/architect.

Plan #371033

Dimensions: 73' W x 33' 4" D
Levels: 1
Square Footage: 1,724
Bedrooms: 3
Bathrooms: 2
Foundation: Slab
Materials List Available: No
Price Category: C

This beautiful brick-and-stone country home will be the envy of the neighborhood.

Features:

- Front Porch: This charming yet functional porch welcomes you home.

- Family Room: This large room, with its cathedral ceiling and cozy fireplace, is ideal for entertaining.

- Kitchen: This gourmet kitchen has all the necessities you will ever need, including a raised bar area.

- Master Suite: This cozy area features a stepped ceiling. The luxurious bath boasts a marble tub and two walk-in closets.

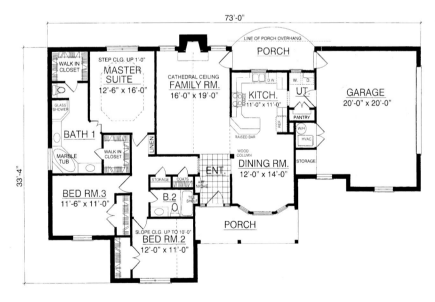

Copyright by designer/architect.

Plan #371071

Dimensions: 73' W x 47'4" D

Levels: 1

Square Footage: 1,729

Bedrooms: 3

Bathrooms: 2

Foundation: Crawl space, slab

Materials List Available: No

Price Category: C

Images provided by designer/architect.

Copyright by designer/architect.

Plan #181225

Dimensions: 31' W x 31' D

Levels: 2

Square Footage: 1,746

Main Level Sq. Ft.: 873

Upper Level Sq. Ft.: 873

Bedrooms: 3

Bathrooms: 1½

Foundation: Basement

Materials List Available: Yes

Price Category: C

Images provided by designer/architect.

Main Level Floor Plan

Upper Level Floor Plan

Copyright by designer/architect.

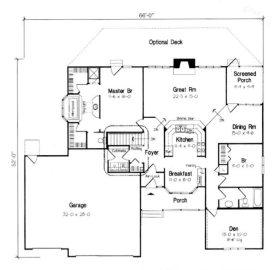

Images provided by designer/architect.

Copyright by designer/architect.

Rear View

Crawl Space/Slab Option

Plan #391004

Dimensions: 66' W x 52' D

Levels: 1

Square Footage: 1,750

Bedrooms: 2

Bathrooms: 2

Foundation: Crawl space, slab, or basement

Materials List Available: Yes

Price Category: C

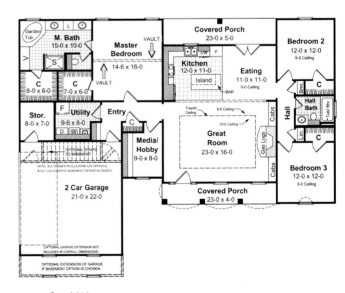

Images provided by designer/architect.

Copyright by designer/architect.

Plan #351002

Dimensions: 64' W x 45'10" D

Levels: 1

Square Footage: 1,751

Bedrooms: 3

Bathrooms: 2

Foundation: Crawl space, slab, or basement

Materials List Available: Yes

Price Category: C

Plan #321003

Dimensions: 67'4" W x 48' D

Levels: 1

Square Footage: 1,791

Bedrooms: 4

Bathrooms: 2

Foundation: Basement

Materials List Available: Yes

Price Category: C

Images provided by designer/architect.

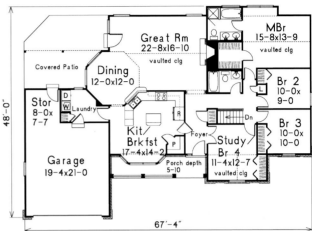

Great Rm
22-8x16-10
vaulted clg

MBr
15-8x13-9
vaulted clg

Covered Patio

Dining
12-0x12-0

Br 2
10-0x
9-0

Stor
8-0x
7-7

D
W
Laundry

Kit
Brkfst
17-4x14-2

R

P

Foyer

Dn

Br 3
10-0x
10-0

Study
Br 4
11-4x12-7
vaulted clg

Garage
19-4x21-0

Porch depth
5-10

48'-0"

67'-4"

Plan #321001

Dimensions: 83' W x 42' D

Levels: 1

Square Footage: 1,721

Bedrooms: 3

Bathrooms: 2

Foundation: Crawl space, slab, or basement

Materials List Available: Yes

Price Category: C

Images provided by designer/architect.

83'-0"

Atrium Below
Dn

Brk
11-5x12-0

Great Rm
16-0x16-10
vaulted

MBr
16-0x14-0
vaulted

Covered
Porch

Kit
11-5x
12-0

vaulted

L

Garage
29-4x21-4

P

R

U
D

Dining
11-0x11-6

Br 3
11-1x13-3

Br 2
11-0x12-9

Porch
27-8x5-0

42'-0"

Rear View

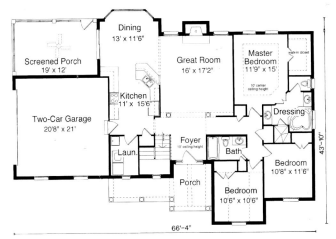

Copyright by designer/architect.

Rear Elevation

Plan #161007

Dimensions: 66'4" W x 43'10" D

Levels: 1

Square Footage: 1,611

Bedrooms: 3

Bathrooms: 2

Foundation: Basement

Materials List Available: Yes

Price Category: C

Images provided by designer/architect.

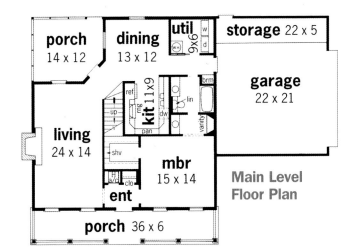

Main Level Floor Plan

Images provided by designer/architect.

Copyright by designer/architect.

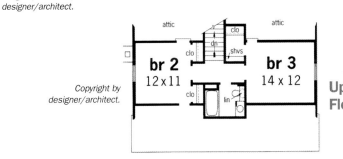

Upper Level Floor Plan

Plan #211069

Dimensions: 58' W x 42' D

Levels: 1½

Square Footage: 1,600

Main Level Sq. Ft.: 1,136

Upper Level Sq. Ft.: 464

Bedrooms: 3

Bathrooms: 2

Foundation: Crawl space

Materials List Available: Yes

Price Category: C

Images provided by
designer/architect.

Copyright by designer/architect.

Plan #371036

Dimensions: 60' W x 58'5" D

Levels: 1

Square Footage: 1,764

Bedrooms: 4

Bathrooms: 2

Foundation: Slab

Materials List Available: No

Price Category: C

Copyright by designer/architect.

Images provided by
designer/architect.

Plan #371072

Dimensions: 75'10" W x 38'8" D

Levels: 1

Square Footage: 1,772

Bedrooms: 3

Bathrooms: 2

Foundation: Crawl space, slab

Materials List Available: No

Price Category: C

Rear Elevation

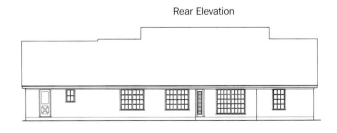

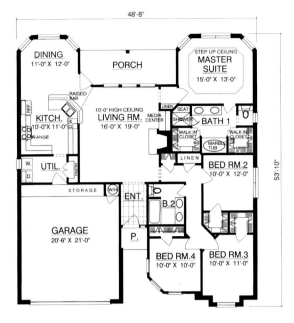

Plan #371037

Dimensions: 48'8" W x 53'10" D

Levels: 1

Square Footage: 1,774

Bedrooms: 4

Bathrooms: 2

Foundation: Slab

Materials List Available: No

Price Category: C

Images provided by designer/architect.

Copyright by designer/architect.

Main Level Floor Plan

Upper Level Floor Plan

Copyright by designer/architect.

Plan #391016

Dimensions: 45'8" W x 35'8" D

Levels: 2

Square Footage: 1,785

Main Level Sq. Ft.: 891

Upper Level Sq. Ft.: 894

Bedrooms: 3

Bathrooms: 2½

Foundation: Crawl space, slab, or basement

Materials List Available: Yes

Price Category: C

Images provided by designer/architect.

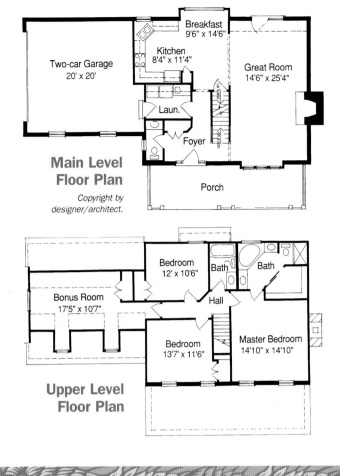

Main Level Floor Plan

Copyright by designer/architect.

Two-car Garage 20' x 20'

Kitchen 8'4" x 11'4"

Breakfast 9'6" x 14'6"

Great Room 14'6" x 25'4"

Laun.

Foyer

Porch

Plan #161024

Dimensions: 54'4" W x 26'8" D

Levels: 2

Square Footage: 1,698

Main Level Sq. Ft.: 868

Upper Level Sq. Ft.: 830

Bonus Space Sq. Ft.: 269

Bedrooms: 3

Bathrooms: 2½

Foundation: Basement

Materials List Available: No

Price Category: C

Images provided by designer/architect.

This home, as shown in the photograph, may differ from the actual blueprints. For more detailed information, please check the floor plans carefully.

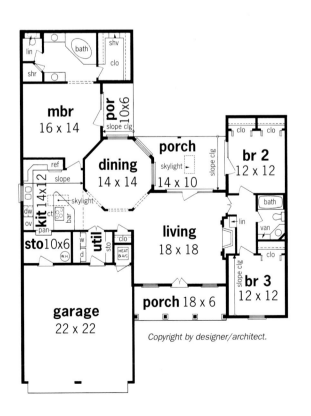

Bedroom 12' x 10'6"

Bath

Bath

Bonus Room 17'5" x 10'7"

Hall

Bedroom 13'7" x 11'6"

Master Bedroom 14'10" x 14'10"

Upper Level Floor Plan

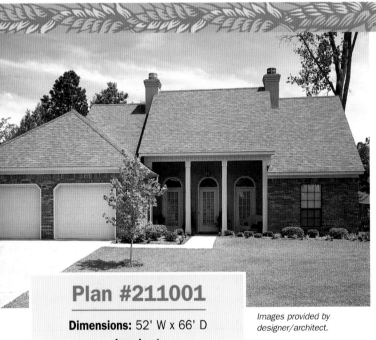

Plan #211001

Dimensions: 52' W x 66' D

Levels: 1

Square Footage: 1,655

Bedrooms: 3

Bathrooms: 2

Foundation: Slab

Materials List Available: Yes

Price Category: C

Images provided by designer/architect.

mbr 16 x 14

lin

bath

shv clo

shr

por 10x6 slope clg

ref

kit 14x12

slope

skylight

dw ov

bar

pan

sto 10x6

util

dining 14 x 14

skylight

porch 14 x 10

slope clg

living 18 x 18

clo clo

br 2 12 x 12

bath

van

lin

clo

garage 22 x 22

porch 18 x 6

br 3 12 x 12

slope clg

Copyright by designer/architect.

Plan #401030

Dimensions: 36' W x 40' D
Levels: 1½
Square Footage: 1,795
Main Level Sq. Ft.: 1,157
Upper Level Sq. Ft.: 638
Bedrooms: 3
Bathrooms: 2½
Foundation: Crawl space
Materials List Available: Yes
Price Category: C

A sun deck is what makes this design so popular, but it is enhanced by views through an expansive wall of glass in the living and dining rooms.

Features:

• **Living Room:** Both this room and the dining room are warmed by a woodstove and enjoy vaulted ceilings.

• **Kitchen:** This area has a vaulted ceiling and a food-preparation island and breakfast bar. Behind the kitchen is a laundry room with side access.

Images provided by designer/architect.

• **Master Bedroom:** This master bedroom and its walk-in closet and private bath are conveniently located on the first floor.

• **Bedrooms:** Two bedrooms and a full bath room are found on the first floor.

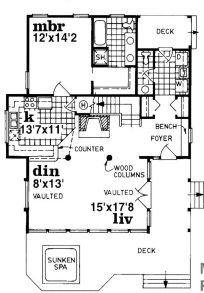

Main Level Floor Plan

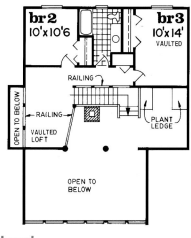

Upper Level Floor Plan

Copyright by designer/architect.

Plan #151211

Dimensions: 58' W x 71'8" D

Levels: 1

Square Footage: 1,797

Bedrooms: 3

Bathrooms: 2

Foundation: Crawl space or slab (basement for fee)

Materials List Available: No

Price Category: C

This three-bedroom brick home was designed with the family in mind.

Features:

- Great Room: This large space, with a fireplace, will provide the perfect setting for movie night.

- Kitchen: Enjoy meals in your breakfast or dining room—or quick snacks at the bar in this kitchen.

- Master Suite: Retiring to this suite is truly a luxury in itself. A 10-ft. boxed ceiling enhances the generous bedroom, while the bathroom includes a glass shower and whirlpool tub.

- Bedrooms: These two additional bedrooms, which share a full bathroom, round out the lovely design.

Plan #351040

Dimensions: 63'4" W x 53' D

Levels: 1

Square Footage: 1,800

Bedrooms: 3

Bathrooms: 2½

Foundation: Crawl space, slab, or basement

Materials List Available: Yes

Price Category: D

This home is a fine example of a great open plan with a split bedroom layout.

Features:

- Gathering Areas: The home has a lovely covered front porch, a screened porch, and a patio for small groups to gather.

- Great Room: Enjoy the vaulted ceiling, gas log fireplace, and built-ins in this room.

- Master Suite: This master suite has a tray ceiling, large his and her closet, a jetted tub, an oversized shower, and a large vanity next to one of the closets.

- Bedrooms: All bedrooms feature walk-in closets with their own private bath. Bedroom 2 could be used as an in-law suite.

- Flex Space: This area is provided for uses such as an office, media center, half bath, hobby room, or winter-wear closet.

Images provided by designer/architect.

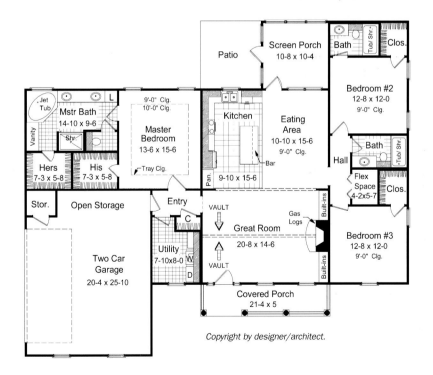

Copyright by designer/architect.

Plan #371013

Dimensions: 58'4" W x 49'6" D

Levels: 1

Square Footage: 1,791

Bedrooms: 3

Bathrooms: 2

Foundation: Slab

Materials List Available: No

Price Category: C

The beautiful brick-and-cast-stone detail of this traditional home sets it apart from the rest.

Features:

- Family Room: This massive family room opens into the spacious dining room.

- Kitchen: Fully functional, this kitchen has a breakfast bar and a nook, which connect it with the family room.

- Master Suite: This large suite with step-up ceiling has a large master bathroom with two walk-in closets.

- Bedrooms: The two secondary bedrooms have ample closet space and share a convenient bathroom.

Copyright by
designer/architect.

Plan #131047

Dimensions: 69'10" W x 51'8" D
Levels: 1
Square Footage: 1,793
Bedrooms: 3
Bathrooms: 2
Foundation: Crawl space, slab, or basement
Materials List Available: Yes
Price Category: C

Images provided by designer/architect.

The country charm of this well-designed home is mixed with the convenience and luxury normally reserved for more contemporary plans.

Features:

- **Great Room:** The spaciousness of this great room is enhanced by the 11-ft. stepped ceiling. A fireplace makes it cozy on cool evenings or on chilly winter days, and two sets of French sliding glass doors open to the back porch.

- **Kitchen:** In addition to the convenient layout of this design, you'll also love its bright, airy position. It includes an old-fashioned pantry,

a sink under a window, and a sunny breakfast area that opens to the wraparound porch.

- **Master Suite:** You'll find 11-ft. ceilings in both the master bedroom and the bayed sitting area that the suite includes. In the bath, the circular spa tub is surrounded by a glass-block wall.

- **Bonus Space:** A permanent staircase leads to an unfinished bonus space on the upper level.

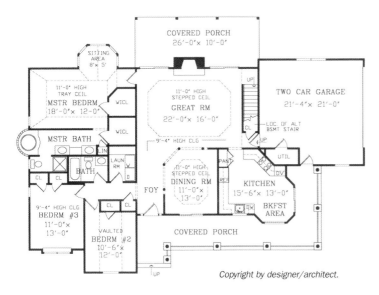

Copyright by designer/architect.

Rear Elevation

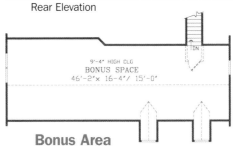

Bonus Area

Plan #321008

Dimensions: 57' W x 52'2" D
Levels: 1
Square Footage: 1,761
Bedrooms: 4
Bathrooms: 2
Foundation: Basement
Materials List Available: Yes
Price Category: C

One look at the roof dormers and planter boxes that grace the outside of this ranch, and you'll know that the interior is planned for comfortable family living.

Features:

• Great Room: A vaulted ceiling in this room points up its generous dimensions. Put a grouping of chairs near the fireplace to take advantage of the cozy spot it creates in chilly weather.

• Kitchen: Open to the great room, this kitchen has been planned for convenience. It features a pass-through to the dining area for easy serving when you've got a crowd to feed.

• Master Bedroom: A vaulted ceiling here makes you feel especially pampered, and the walk-in closet and amenity-filled bath add to that feeling.

• Additional Bedrooms: Great closet space characterizes all the rooms in this home, making it easy for children of any age to keep it organized and tidy.

Images provided by designer/architect.

Copyright by designer/architect.

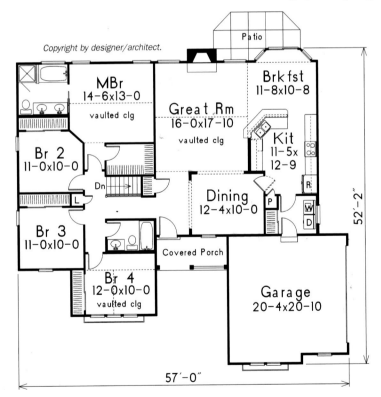

SMARTtip

Hanging Wallpaper

Use liner paper to smooth out a damaged wall and to provide uniform support for expensive paper.

Plan #271077

Dimensions: 69'6" W x 53' D
Levels: 1
Square Footage: 1,786
Bedrooms: 1
Bathrooms: 1½
Foundation: Basement or daylight basement
Materials List Available: No
Price Category: C

This wonderful home has an optional finished basement plan to add three more bedrooms—ideal for a growing family.

Features:

- Great Room: This large gathering room has a fireplace with built-in cabinets on either side.

- Kitchen: This island kitchen, with dinette area, is open to the great room.

- Master Bedroom: This luxurious room provides a view of the backyard.

- Master Bath: This private bathroom has a walk-in closet and double vanities.

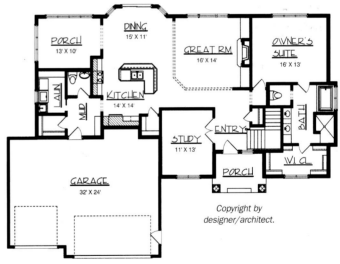

Optional Basement Level Floor Plan

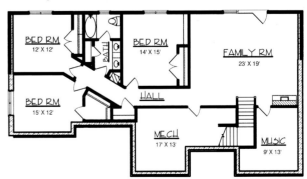

Plans for Your Landscape

L andscapes change over the years. As plants grow, the overall look evolves from sparse to lush. Trees cast cool shade where the sun used to shine. Shrubs and hedges grow tall and dense enough to provide privacy. Perennials and ground covers spread to form colorful patches of foliage and flowers. Meanwhile, paths, arbors, fences, and other structures gain the comfortable patina of age.

Constant change over the years—sometimes rapid and dramatic, sometimes slow and subtle—is one of the joys of landscaping. It is also one of the challenges. Anticipating how fast plants will grow and how big they will eventually get is difficult, even for professional designers, and was a major concern in formulating the designs for this book.

To illustrate the kinds of changes to expect in a planting, these pages show one of the designs at three different "ages." Even though a new planting may look sparse at first, it will soon fill in. And because of careful spacing, the planting will look as good in 10 to 15 years as it does after 3 to 5. It will, of course, look different, but that's part of the fun.

At Planting

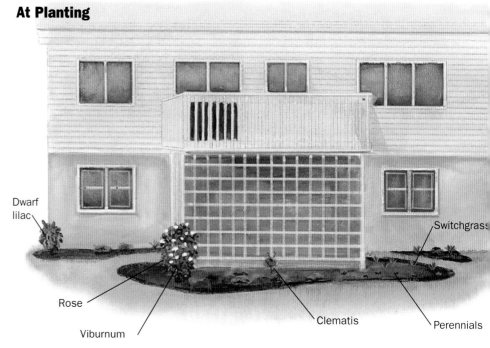

Dwarf lilac · Rose · Viburnum · Clematis · Switchgrass · Perennials

Three to Five Years

Rose · Dwarf lilac · Juniper · Viburnum · Juniper · Clematis · Switchgrass · Perennials

At Planting—Here's how the deck planting might appear in late spring immediately after planting. The rose and clematis haven't begun to climb the new lattice trellis. The viburnum and lilac, usually sold in 2- to 5-gal. cans, start blooming as young plants and may have flowers when you buy them, but there will be enough space that you may want to plant some short annuals around them for the first few growing seasons. You can put short annuals between the new little junipers, too. The switchgrass and perennials, transplanted from quart- or gallon-size containers, are just low tufts of foliage now, but they grow fast enough to produce a few flowers the first summer.

Three to Five Years—As shown here in midsummer, the rose and clematis now reach most of the way up the supports. Although they aren't mature yet, the lilac, viburnum, and junipers look nice and bushy, and they're big enough that you don't need to fill around them with annuals. So far, the vines and shrubs have needed only minimal pruning. Most grasses and perennials reach full size about three to five years after planting; after that, they need to be divided and replanted in freshly amended soil to keep them healthy and vigorous.

Ten to Fifteen Years—Shown again in summer, the rose and clematis now cover their supports, and the lilac and viburnum are as tall as they'll get. To maintain all of these plants, you'll need to start pruning out some of the older stems every year in early spring. The junipers have spread sideways to form a solid mass; prune them as needed along the edge of the lawn and pathways. When the junipers crowd them out, move the daylilies to another part of your property, or move them to the front of the bed to replace the other perennials, as shown here.

Ten to Fifteen Years

Rose

Clematis

Juniper

Dwarf lilac

Viburnum

Juniper

Daylily

First Impressions

Make a Pleasant Passage to Your Front Door

Why wait until a visitor reaches the front door to extend a cordial greeting? Well-chosen plants and a revamped walkway not only make the short journey a pleasant one, they can also enhance your home's most public face and help settle it comfortably in its surroundings.

The curved walk in this design offers visitors a friendly welcome and a helpful "Please come this way." The first stage of the journey passes between two clipped shrub roses into a handsome garden "room" with larger shrubs near the house and smaller, colorful perennials by the walk. An opening in a hedge of long-blooming shrub roses then leads to a wider paved area that functions as an outdoor foyer. There you can greet guests or relax on the bench and enjoy the plantings that open out onto the lawn. A double course of pavers intersects the walk and an adjacent planting bed, and the circle it describes contrasts nicely with the rectilinear lines of the house and hedge.

Site: Sunny

Season: Summer

Concept: A distinctive walkway and colorful plantings make an enticing entry to your home.

C 'Frau Dagmar Hartop' rose

J Walk

'Frau Dagmar Hartop' C rose

Plants and Projects

Mixing shrubs and perennials, this planting offers colorful flowers and attractive foliage from spring through fall. The shrubs provide structure through the winter and are handsome when covered with new snow. The perennials are dormant in winter; cut them to the ground to make room for snow shoveled off the walk. Maintenance involves pruning the shrubs and clipping spent flowers to keep everything tidy.

Ⓐ **'Sea Green'** *Juniperus chinensis* (use 3 plants)
This rugged evergreen shrub anchors a corner of the first garden "room" with arching branches that provide year-round pale green color.

House

Window

Stoop

Drive

Lawn

1 square = 1 ft.

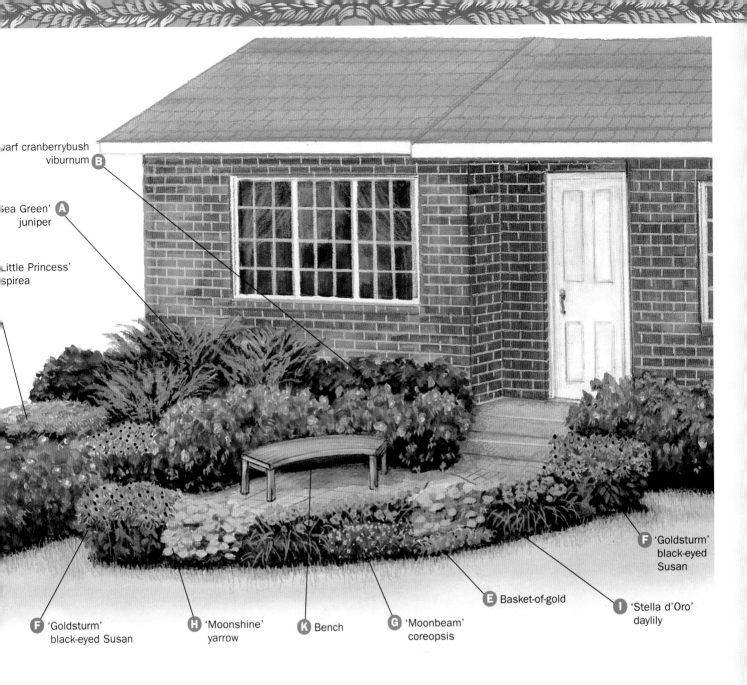

Dwarf cranberrybush viburnum **B**

'Sea Green' juniper **A**

'Little Princess' spirea

F 'Goldsturm' black-eyed Susan

E Basket-of-gold

I 'Stella d'Oro' daylily

F 'Goldsturm' black-eyed Susan

H 'Moonshine' yarrow

K Bench

G 'Moonbeam' coreopsis

Note: All plants are appropriate for USDA Hardiness *Zones 3, 4, 5, and 6.*

Dwarf cranberrybush
Viburnum opulus 'Nanum'
(use 5)
This small deciduous shrub has a dense, bushy habit and dark green, maplelike leaves that turn shades of red in fall. It won't outgrow its place beneath the windows.
'Frau Dagmar Hartop' *Rosa*
(use 18 or more)
With its crinkly bright green leaves, fragrant single pink flowers, and colorful red hips from autumn into winter, this easy-to-grow deciduous shrub puts on quite a show. Flowers all summer; forms a dense "natural-looking" hedge. Extend the planting along the house as needed.

D **'Little Princess'** *Spiraea japonica*
(use 7)
Another compact deciduous shrub, with dainty twigs and leaves. Bears clear pink flowers in June and July.
E **Basket-of-gold** *Aurinia saxatilis*
(use 4)
The planting's first flowers appear on this perennial in spring. After the fragrant yellow blooms fade, the low mounds of gray leaves look good through late fall.
F **'Goldsturm'** *Rudbeckia fulgida*
(use 20) A popular prairie perennial, this bears large golden yellow flowers (each with a dark "eye" in the center) that are a cheerful sight in late summer.
G **'Moonbeam'**
Coreopsis verticillata (use 22)
For months during the summer, this perennial features masses of tiny pale yellow flowers on neat mounds of lacy dark green foliage.
H **'Moonshine'** *Achillea* (use 17)
A perennial offering flat heads of sulphur yellow flowers for much of the summer. The fine gray-green leaves contrast nicely with surrounding foliage.
I **'Stella d'Oro' daylily**
Hemerocallis (use 30)
Distinctive golden yellow flowers hover over this perennial's attrac-

tive grassy foliage from mid-June until fall.
J **Walk**
Made of precast concrete pavers, the walk and decorative edgings require careful layout and installation. Consider renting a mason's saw to ensure accuracy when cutting pavers.
K **Bench**
A nursery or garden center can usually order a simple curved bench like the one shown here, although a straight, simple bench will do, too.

A Step Up

Plant a Foundation Garden

Homes on raised foundations are seldom without foundation plantings. These simple skirtings of greenery hide unattractive concrete-block underpinnings and help overcome the impression that the house is hovering a few feet above the ground. Useful as these plantings are, they are too often just monochromatic expanses of clipped junipers, dull as dishwater. But as this design shows, a durable, low-maintenance foundation planting can be more varied, more colorful, and more fun.

This design makes a front porch an even more welcome haven on a hot summer's day. Chosen for a shady site, the plants include evergreen shrubs and perennials that combine handsome foliage and pretty flowers. Hanging planters filled with annuals extend the garden right onto the porch.

The plants are arranged to provide interest when viewed from the porch as well as from the street or entry walk. The bed sweeps out in a graceful curve to connect with the steps and entry walk, making an attractive setting for visitors.

Site: Shady

Season: Summer

Concept: A planting to be enjoyed from the street or while sitting on the cool shady porch.

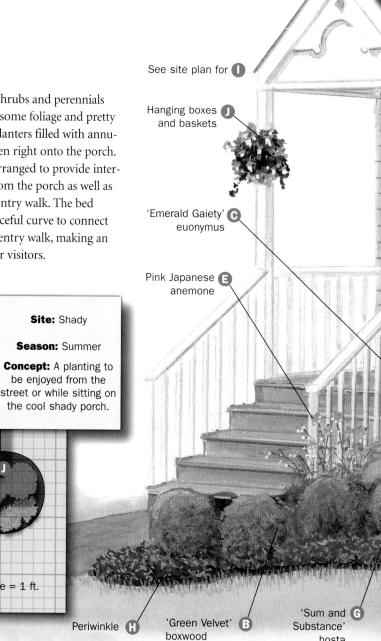

See site plan for **I**

Hanging boxes and baskets **J**

'Emerald Gaiety' **C** euonymus

Pink Japanese **E** anemone

Periwinkle **H**

'Green Velvet' **B** boxwood

'Sum and **G** Substance' hosta

1 square = 1 ft.

Plants and Projects

A foundation planting should look good in each season. Rhododendron blossoms in spring give way to a summer display of hosta, astilbe, and anemone flowers in shades of pink and white. Once the perennials have died back, they reveal the vining euonymus covering the base of the porch. Along with the other evergreens, it carries the planting through fall and winter. Other than tending the planters, care involves a minimum of seasonal cleanup. The shrubs' natural forms are tidy, so pruning is an infrequent chore.

A 'Olga Mezitt' *Rhododendron* (use 3 plants)
An evergreen shrub with striking clusters of pink flowers in early spring and dark green foliage that turns maroon in color in winter.

B 'Green Velvet' *Buxus* (use 10)
These tidy little evergreen shrubs will form an informal hedge (with minimal pruning) at the front of the planting. The foliage stays green through the winter.

C 'Emerald Gaiety'
Euonymus fortunei (use 6)
This evergreen vine quickly covers lattice panels beneath the porch.

Dark green leaves are edged with white and may turn pink in the winter.

D 'Ostrich Plume'
Astilbe × arendsii (use 5)
The cascading, pink plumes of th[e] perennial are eye-catching from the porch or the street. Shiny, dar[k] green, divided foliage looks good long after the midsummer bloom has faded.

D 'Ostrich Plume' astilbe

H Periwinkle

F 'Royal Standard' hosta

G 'Sum and Substance' hosta

A 'Olga Mezitt' rhododendron

Note: All plants are appropriate for USDA Hardiness *Zones 3, 4, 5, and 6.*

Pink Japanese
Anemone vitifolia (use 1)
Lovely mauve-pink flowers rise above the dark green lobed leaves of this perennial in late summer and fall.

'Royal Standard' *Hosta* (use 3)
This perennial's fragrant white flowers rise above a mound of big green leaves in late summer, perfuming the porch with a sweet scent.

G 'Sum and Substance' *Hosta* (use 8)
Huge, glossy gold, textured leaves form large showy mounds at each end of the planting. Although it bears lavender flowers in late summer, some people remove them to showcase the foliage.

H Periwinkle *Vinca minor* (use 18)
Dark green shiny leaves and blue spring flowers of this perennial

ground cover form a clean, ever-green edge in front of the box-woods.

I Sweet woodruff *odoratum* (use 5)
Tucked between a boxwood and the anemone, this perennial ground cover is a pleasant surprise to visitors approaching the steps. Bears tiny white flowers in spring.

J Hanging boxes and baskets (as desired)

Hang window boxes from the railing and baskets from the porch roof and plant them with shade-tolerant annuals, such as the trailing ivy, impatiens, begonias, coleus, and vinca vine we've shown here.

Up Front and Formal

Garden Geometry Transforms a Small Front Yard

Formal gardens have a special appeal. Their simple geometry is soothing in a hectic world, and their look is timeless, never going out of style. Traditional two-story homes with symmetrical facades are especially suited to the clean lines and balanced features shown here.

The design creates a small courtyard at the center of four rectangular beds defined by evergreen hedges and flagstone walkways. Inside the hedges, carefree perennial catmint makes a colorful floral carpet during the summer. The flagstone paving reinforces the design's geometry, while providing access to the front door from the sidewalk. (If a driveway runs along one side of the property, the crosswalk could extend to it through an opening in the hedge.) At

the center of the composition, the paving widens to accommodate a planter filled with annuals, a pleasant setting for greetings or good-byes. A bench at one end of the crosswalk provides a spot for longer chats or restful moments enjoying the plantings or, perhaps, contemplating a garden ornament at the other end.

Loose, informal hedges soften the rigid geometry. Deciduous shrubs change with the seasons, offering flowers in the spring and brilliant fall foliage, while the evergreens are a dependably colorful presence year round.

Note: All plants are appropriate for USDA Hardiness *Zones 3, 4, 5, and 6.*

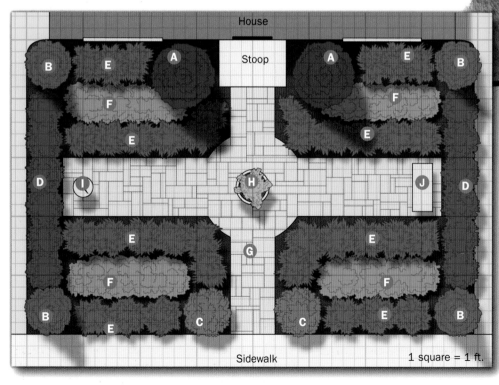

'Nigra' arborvitae **A**

'Techny' **B** arborvitae

Garden **I** ornament

'Blue Wonder' **F** catmint

House

Stoop

Sidewalk — 1 square = 1 ft.

Plants and Projects

Precise layout is important in a simple design such as this. Start with the flagstone walks; they aren't difficult to build but require some time and muscle. The hedge shrubs are chosen for their compact forms. You'll need to clip the lilacs annually to maintain their shape, but the junipers will require little pruning over the years.

A **'Nigra'** *Thuja occidentalis* (use 2 plants)
These upright, pyramidal evergreen trees stand like sentinels at the front door, where their scented foliage greets visitors. Prune to

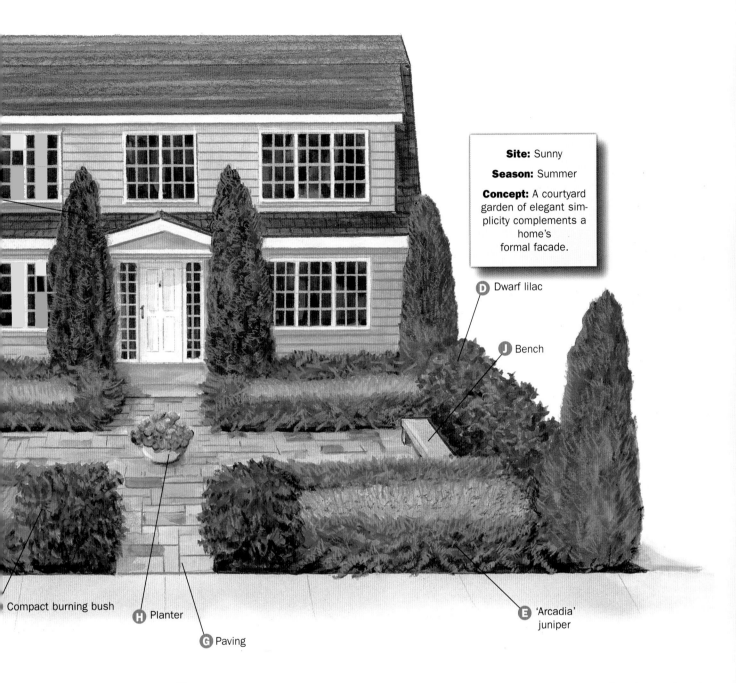

Site: Sunny

Season: Summer

Concept: A courtyard garden of elegant simplicity complements a home's formal facade.

D Dwarf lilac

J Bench

E 'Arcadia' juniper

D Dwarf lilac

J Bench

Compact burning bush

H Planter

G Paving

keep their height in scale with the house.

'Techny' arborvitae *Thuja occidentalis* (use 4)
Marking the corners of the design, this evergreen tree forms a shorter, broader cone than its cousin by the door.

Compact burning bush
Euonymus alatus 'Compactus' (use 2)
A deciduous shrub forming a neat globe of green foliage, it turns an attention-grabbing crimson in fall. An excellent choice to mark the property's entrance.

D **Dwarf lilac** *Syringa meyeri* '*Palibin*' (use 12)
This compact deciduous shrub makes an attractive loose hedge offering fragrant springtime flowers and glossy green foliage that has a purplish cast in fall.

E **'Arcadia' juniper** *Juniperus sabina* (use 36)
The arching branches of this spreading evergreen shrub line the walks with bright green color through four seasons.

F **'Blue Wonder' catmint** *Nepeta × faassenii* (use 40)
Loose spikes of misty blue flowers

rise above the silvery, aromatic foliage of this perennial in June, filling the beds with color. Blooms continue or repeat through the summer.

G **Paving**
Rectangular flagstones in random sizes suit the style of this house; brick or precast pavers work with other house styles.

H **Planter**
Nurseries and garden centers offer a range of planters that are suitable for formal settings. Choose one that complements the style of your house and fill it with colorful

annuals such as the geraniums in the round stone planter shown here. If you're ambitious, change the plantings with the seasons.

I **Garden ornament**
Place a sundial (shown here), reflecting ball, statue, or other ornament as a focal point at the end of the crosswalk.

J **Bench**
A stone bench is a nice companion for the planter and sundial here, but wood or metal benches can also work well in formal garden settings.

Angle of Repose

Make a Back-door Garden in a Sheltered Niche

Many homes offer the opportunity to tuck a garden into a protected corner. In the front yard, such spots are ideal for an entry garden or a landscaping display that enhances the view of your house from the sidewalk or the street. If the niche is in the backyard, like the site shown here, the planting can be more intimate, part of a comfortable outdoor room you can stroll through at leisure or enjoy from a nearby terrace or window.

This planting has been specially designed with spring in mind, so we're showing that season here. During the summer, perennials and shrubs will take over the show. Dozens of spring bulbs light up the corner from February through May, assisted by the spring blossoms on the rho-

dodendrons and Korean spice viburnum.

Early flowers aren't the only pleasures of spring, though. Step along the path to appreciate the magic of spring at closer range. Watch buds burst into leaf on the burning bush and cotoneaster, and mark the progress of the season as new, succulent shoots of summer perennials emerge.

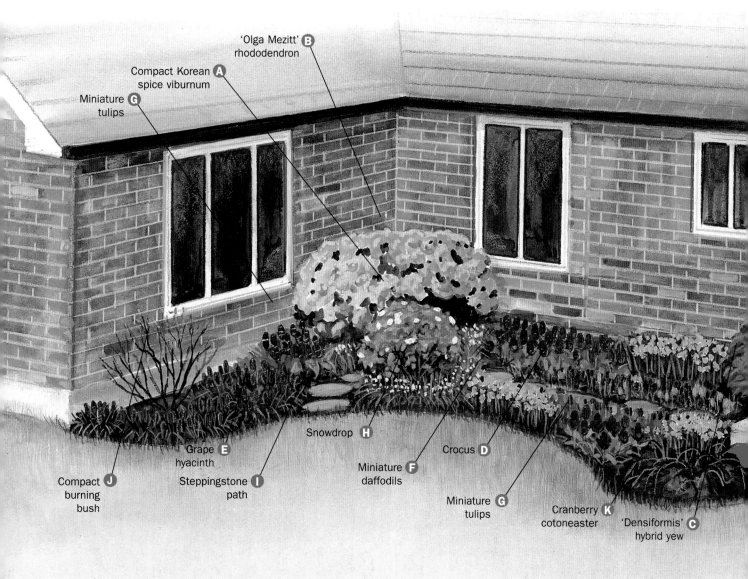

Plants and Projects

terplant generous drifts and clumps
bulbs among the perennials. Once
anted, bulbs require little care
yond clipping off spent flowers.
ter they bloom, their foliage is hid-
n by the emerging perennials.
vide the bulbs every few years if
e patches become crowded or if
u want to plant some elsewhere.

Compact Korean spice *Viburnum carlesii 'Compactum'* (use 1 plant)
The fragrant white flower clusters of this spring-blooming deciduous shrub invite you down the path. Foliage is attractive in summer and fall.

B **'Olga Mezitt'** *Rhododendron* (use 3)
This evergreen shrub is covered with clear pink flowers for weeks from early spring. The small dark green leaves (which turn maroon in fall) make a fine backdrop for the perennials.

C **'Densiformis'** *hybrid yew Taxus ¥ media* (use 1)
An evergreen shrub, it makes a low, spreading mound of fine-textured dark green foliage.

D **Crocus** *Crocus* (use 50)
Cup-shaped flowers on short stalks in early spring. Plant 6 or 8

per square foot along the path. A mix of purple- and gold-flowered types will go well with the other bulbs.

E **Grape hyacinth**
Muscari armeniacum (use 25)
Grassy foliage and fragrant purple flowers resembling grape clusters make a pretty spring carpet beneath the burning bush.

F **Miniature daffodils**
Narcissus (use 25)
A spring planting isn't complete without these cheerful favorites. 'February Gold', 'Baby Moon', and 'Tête-à-Tête' offer small, early yellow flowers and low foliage that is easily covered later by the perennials.

G **Miniature tulips** *Tulipa* (use 20)
Shorter than "ordinary" tulips, but just as colorful, 'Red Riding Hood' and 'Lilac Wonder' are good choices here.

H **Snowdrop** *Galanthus nivalis* (use 25)
One of the first flowers of spring, the nodding, snowy white blooms beckon above slender, grassy foliage at the bend in the path.

I **Steppingstone path**
Precast pavers, 2 ft. in diameter, can be installed after you've prepared the planting bed. Tamp down the soil along the path, set the pavers in place, and spread mulch between them..

J **Compact burning bush** (use 1)

K **Cranberry cotoneaster** (use 1)

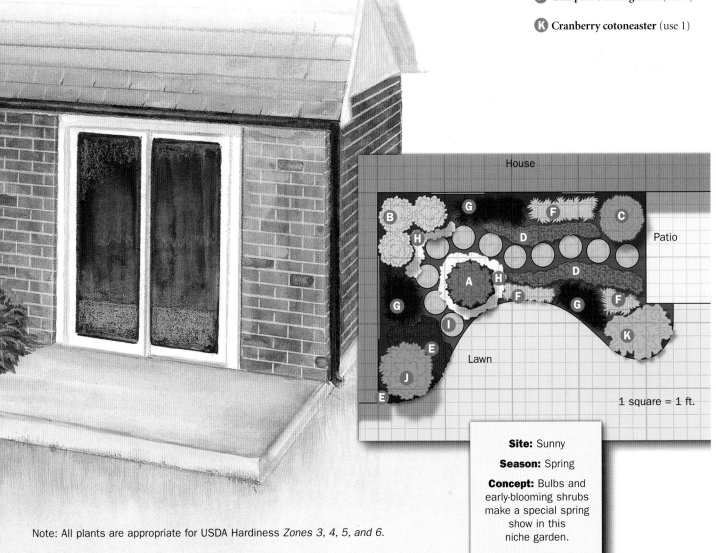

Site: Sunny

Season: Spring

Concept: Bulbs and early-blooming shrubs make a special spring show in this niche garden.

1 square = 1 ft.

Note: All plants are appropriate for USDA Hardiness *Zones 3, 4, 5, and 6.*

A Neighborly Corner

Beautify a Boundary With Easy-care Plants

The corner where your property meets your neighbor's and the sidewalk can be a kind of grassy no-man's-land. This design defines the boundary with a planting that can be enjoyed by both property owners. Good gardens make good neighbors, so we've used well-behaved low-maintenance plants that won't make extra work for the person next door—or for you.

Because of its exposed location, remote from the house and close to the street, this is a less personal planting than those in other more private and frequently used parts of your property. This design is meant, therefore, to be appreciated from a distance. It showcases five handsome shrubs, arranged in blocks, rather like a patchwork quilt, beneath a fine multi-

trunked tree. (An existing fence on the property line, like the one shown here, can help frame the composition.)

Although several of these plants offer attractive flowers, it is their foliage that makes this planting special. As the seasons progress you'll see blues, greens, reds, and yellows, culminating in an eye-popping display of fiery autumn leaves.

Note: All plants are appropriate for USDA Hardiness *Zones 3, 4, 5, and 6.*

Plants and Projects

For the first few years, mulch the planting well to retain moisture and to keep down weeds until the shrubs fill in. This is a very easy planting to maintain if you choose to prune only to maintain the natural shapes of the shrubs, which soften the geometry imposed by the planting plan.

A **Amur maple** *Acer ginnala* (use 1 plant)
A small but fast-growing deciduous tree; pick one that has multiple trunks. Bears pale flowers in spring, green leaves and red fruits in summer, and crimson foliage in autumn.

B **'Gro-Low'** *Rhus aromatica* (use 4)

These tough deciduous shrubs spread to form low mounds beneath the maple. Shiny green leaves turn scarlet in fall.

C **'Anthony Waterer'** *Spiraea × bumalda* (use 3)
Small, fine blue-green leaves set off the rosy pink flowers of this compact deciduous shrub. Blooms in summer.

D **'Blue Star'** *Juniperus squamata* (use 7)
The prickly, rich blue foliage of this low evergreen shrub makes a striking contrast with its neighbors.

E **'Crimson Pygmy'** *Japanese barberry Berberis thunbergii* (use 3)

The small, deep purple leaves of this deciduous shrub are as eye-catching in summer as in fall, when they turn a rich crimson. The low, rounded mounds are set off by the colors of the nearby juniper and sumac.

F **'Goldflame'** *Spiraea × bumalda* (use 4)
The leaves of this small deciduous shrub have a different look in each season: gold in spring, chartreuse in summer, and orange-red in fall. Bears pale pink flowers in summer.

C 'Anthony Waterer' spirea

D 'Blue Star' juniper

Fence

C

D

A

E

B

Sidewalk

F

Lawn

1 square = 1 ft.

Site: Sunny

Season: Summer

Concept: Enhance the property line with a low-care, neighbor-friendly planting of trees and shrubs.

A Amur maple

B 'Gro-Low' sumac

F 'Goldflame' spirea

E 'Crimson Pygmy' Japanese barberry

Streetwise and Stylish

Give Your Curbside Strip a New Look

Homeowners seldom think much about the strip that runs between the sidewalk and street. At best it is a tidy patch of lawn; at worst, a weed-choked eyesore. Yet this is one of the most public parts of your property. Planting this strip attractively can give pleasure to passersby and to visitors who park next to the curb, as well as enhance the streetscape you view from the house. (This property is usually city-owned, so check local ordinances for restrictions before you start a remake.)

In older neighborhoods, mature trees lining the street create more shade than most grass can tolerate. The design shown here replaces thinning turf in a shady site with a lush planting of hostas, ferns, and ground covers. Leaves in a pleasing variety of sizes, shapes, and colors make an inviting display from spring through fall.

It might help to think of this curbside strip as an island bed between two defined boundaries: the street and the sidewalk. The beds are divided by a pedestrian walkway, providing room for visitors to get in and out of their cars. You can expand the beds to fill a longer strip, or plant lawn next to them. This design, or a variation, would also work nicely in a shady location along a patio, property line, or foundation.

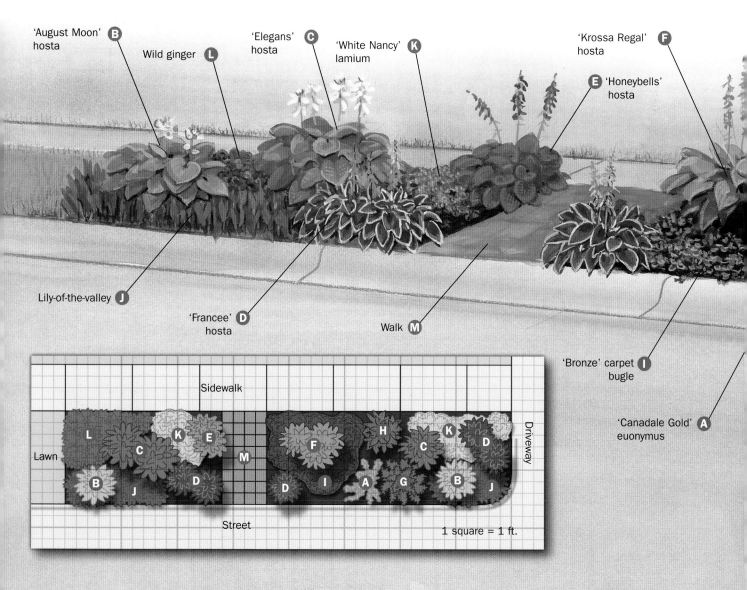

'August Moon' hosta **B**
Wild ginger **L**
'Elegans' hosta **C**
'White Nancy' lamium **K**
'Krossa Regal' hosta **F**
'Honeybells' hosta **E**
Lily-of-the-valley **J**
'Francee' hosta **D**
Walk **M**
'Bronze' carpet bugle **I**
'Canadale Gold' euonymus **A**

Sidewalk
Lawn
Driveway
Street

1 square = 1 ft.

Plants and Projects

This can be a difficult site. Summer drought and shade, winter road salt, pedestrian and car traffic, and errant dogs are usual conditions along the street. Plants have to be tough to perform well here, but they need not look tough. The ones used here make a dramatic impact during the growing season. Then all but the sturdy low-growing euonymus die back in winter, so piles of snow won't hurt them. To help provide adequate moisture, add plenty of organic matter to the soil when you prepare the beds.

A **'Canadale Gold'** *Euonymus fortunei* (use 1 plant)
A broad-leaved evergreen, this shrub forms a low, spreading mound. The small rounded leaves have yellow margins and contrast attractively with the large-leaved hostas.

B **'August Moon'** *Hosta* (use 2)
A perennial (like all hostas), this cultivar forms a broad clump of textured golden yellow leaves. Thin stalks bear white flowers in mid- to late summer.

C **'Elegans'** *Hosta sieboldiana* (use 3)
This hosta's huge blue, textured leaves form imposing mounds at the center of each bed. White flowers in summer.

D **'Francee'** *Hosta* (use 5)
This hosta's dark green heart-shaped leaves are edged with white, and its flowers are lavender.

E **'Honeybells'** *Hosta* (use 2)
Forms a large, broad clump of pale green oblong leaves. The lilac flowers are scented.

F **'Krossa Regal'** *Hosta* (use 3)
Long, powder blue leaves form a large mound, more erect than the other hostas in the planting. Lilac flowers dangle well above the foliage on tall, thin stalks.

G **Japanese painted fern**
Athyrium goeringianum 'Pictum' (use 6)
This elegant perennial is a subtle accent for the planting, with its fronds delicately painted in glowing tones of green, silver, and maroon.

H **Maidenhair fern**
Adiantum pedatum (use 5)
This perennial forms a dainty mass of lacy green fronds on wiry black stems; looks great with the blue hostas.

I **'Bronze' carpet bugle**
Ajuga reptans (use 22)
The dark bronze-green leaves of this fast-spreading perennial ground cover set off the hostas and ferns handsomely. Small bluish purple flowers add color in late spring and early summer.

J **Lily-of-the-valley**
Convallaria majalis (use 32)
A perennial ground cover, it quickly forms a patch of large erect leaves. In spring, tiny white bell-shaped flowers dangle from slender stalks and produce a wonderful sweet scent.

K **'White Nancy'**
Lamium maculatum (use 26)
This perennial ground cover's small silvery leaves edged with green practically shine in the shade. Bears white flowers in early summer.

L **Wild ginger**
Asarum canadense (use 12)
Another perennial ground cover, this produces fuzzy heart-shaped leaves that create a beautiful dull green carpet beneath the blue hosta leaves.

M **Walk**
Use brick, flagstone, or the simple cement pavers shown here. Choose a color to match your house.

> **Site:** Shady
>
> **Season:** Summer
>
> **Concept:** Striking foliage gives a lush look to a shady curbside planting.

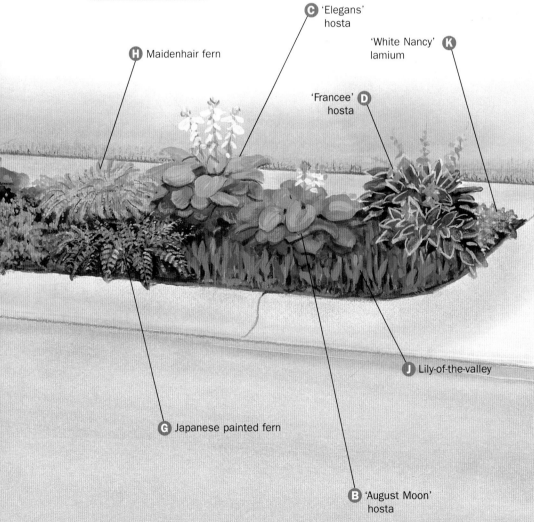

C 'Elegans' hosta

H Maidenhair fern

'White Nancy' lamium **K**

'Francee' **D** hosta

J Lily-of-the-valley

G Japanese painted fern

B 'August Moon' hosta

Note: All plants are appropriate for USDA Hardiness *Zones 3, 4, 5, and 6.*

Landscaping a Low Wall

A Colorful Two-Tier Garden Replaces a Bland Slope

Some things may not love a wall, but plants and gardeners do. For plants, walls offer warmth for an early start in spring and good drainage for roots. Gardeners appreciate the rich visual potential of composing a garden on two levels, as well as the practical advantage of working on two relatively flat surfaces instead of a single sloping one.

This design places two complementary perennial borders above and below a wall bounded at one end by a set of stairs. While each bed is relatively narrow, when viewed from the lower level they combine to form a border almost 10 ft. deep, with plants rising to eye level or more. The planting can be extended farther along the wall with the same or similar plants.

Building the wall that makes this impressive sight possible doesn't require the time or skill it once did. Nor is it necessary to scour the countryside for tons of fieldstone or to hire an expensive contractor. Thanks to precast retaining-wall systems, anyone with a healthy back (or access to energetic teenagers) can install a knee-high do-it-yourself wall in as little as a weekend.

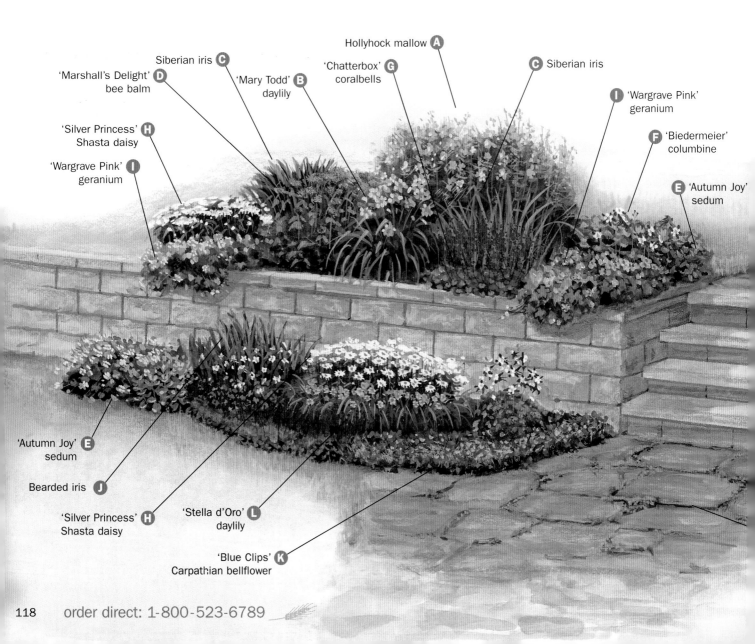

Hollyhock mallow **A**

Siberian iris **C**

'Chatterbox' coralbells **G**

Siberian iris **C**

'Marshall's Delight' bee balm **D**

'Mary Todd' daylily **B**

'Wargrave Pink' geranium **I**

'Silver Princess' Shasta daisy **H**

'Biedermeier' columbine **F**

'Wargrave Pink' geranium **I**

'Autumn Joy' sedum **E**

'Autumn Joy' sedum **E**

Bearded iris **J**

'Silver Princess' Shasta daisy **H**

'Stella d'Oro' daylily **L**

'Blue Clips' Carpathian bellflower **K**

Plants and Projects

composed of durable perennials, this planting offers a summer-long display of flowers in pinks, blues, and whites, with splashes of golden yellow and a hint of violet and purple. Extend the show in spring by planting crocuses in groups of a dozen or more all through the bed. Mulch to control weeds and to conserve moisture; snip off spent blooms to keep things tidy; and cut plants to the ground in late fall or early spring.

Hollyhock mallow *Malva alcea* *'Fastigiata'* (use 3 plants)
In midsummer, this perennial sends up dozens of tall stems, each covered with lovely soft pink flowers. The low mound of bright green foliage looks good the rest of the season.

B **'Mary Todd'** *daylily Hemerocallis* (use 3)
Large, textured yellow flowers of this perennial rise on tall stalks from a handsome clump of grassy foliage, making a striking midsummer centerpiece for the upper bed.

C **Siberian iris** *Iris sibirica* (use 2)
The slender upright leaves of this perennial are attractive all season, and the graceful flowers add brilliant June color. Use any cultivar with blue flowers here.

D **'Marshall's Delight'** *bee balm Monarda* (use 2)
Big, globe-shaped, pink flowers perch atop this perennial's tall leafy stalks in July and August. Spreads to form a loose clump; flowers attract hummingbirds.

E **'Autumn Joy'** *Sedum* (use 4)

This perennial forms a vase-shaped clump of distinctive, fleshy, gray-green leaves. Flat-topped flower clusters appear in August, turning from pale pink to rusty red by October.

F **'Biedermeier'** *columbine Aquilegia* (use 8)
This compact perennial bears lovely blue, pink, or white flowers that dance above mounds of delicate green leaves from late spring into summer.

G **'Chatterbox'** *coralbells Heuchera sanguinea* (use 8)
This low-growing perennial's neat mounds of semievergreen leaves edge the top of the wall and the front of the bed nicely. Tiny red flowers on wiry stems hover above the foliage throughout much of the summer.

H **'Silver Princess'** *Shasta daisy Chrysanthemum × superbum* (use 7)
A low-growing form of an always popular perennial. In July, large white daisies are borne about a foot above a low mat of shiny foliage that looks good all season.

I **'Wargrave Pink'** *Geranium endressii* (use 8)
The bright pink flowers and handsome divided leaves of this peren-

nial create a cheerful, informal effect as they spill over the wall. Blooms heavily in early summer, then off and on until fall.

J **Bearded Iris** (use 3)
The elegant flowers of this perennial last only a week or two, but they are worth every minute. Flat sprays of stiff, swordlike leaves accent the base of the wall. The white-flowered cultivar 'Immortality' (recommended here) blooms in early summer and again in fall.

K **'Blue Clips' Carpathian bellflower** *Campanula carpatica* (use 10)
A perennial offering small spreading mounds of delicate glossy green leaves covered for most of the summer with pretty blue flowers. A perfect edging for the lower path.

L **'Stella d'Oro' daylily** *Hemerocallis* (use 4)
This extraordinary perennial produces a fresh batch of golden yellow flowers each day from mid-June until fall.

M **Retaining wall and steps**
The low, precast retaining wall shown here is easy to install and typical of those available at home and garden centers and local landscaping suppliers.

N **Walk**
The flagstone walk drifts into the lower bed as if inviting strollers to stop and enjoy the view. You can plant thyme in the gaps between the flagstones to further mingle the walk and beds.

Site: Sunny

Season: Summer

Concept: Low retaining wall creates easy-to-maintain beds for a distinctive two-level planting of perennials.

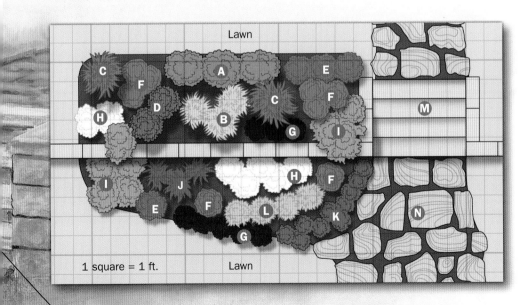

1 square = 1 ft.   Lawn

Note: All plants are appropriate for USDA Hardiness *Zones 3, 4, 5, and 6.*

M Retaining wall and steps

N Walk

Plan #151243

Dimensions: 35' W x 80'6" D
Levels: 1
Square Footage: 1,923
Bedrooms: 3
Bathrooms: 2
Foundation: Crawl space or slab
Materials List Available: No
Price Category: D

Images provided by designer/architect.

This brick home has great styling and offers three bedrooms.

Features:

• Entry: You enter the home though an arched covered entry foyer. On the left, French doors open to bedroom 3. Across the hall is bed room 2, with a large walk-in closet.

• Great Room: This large gathering area, with a 10-ft. boxed ceiling, features a fireplace and access to the grilling porch.

• Kitchen: This kitchen boasts a snack bar and walk-in pantry and is open to the dining room.

• Master Suite: This private area has a 10-ft. boxed ceiling and ample closet storage. The master bath features a corner whirlpool tub with glass blocks, split vanities, and a corner shower.

Copyright by designer/architect.

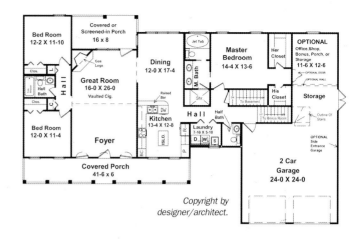

Copyright by
designer/architect.

Plan #351004

Dimensions: 78' W x 49'6" D

Levels: 1

Square Footage: 1,852

Bedrooms: 3

Bathrooms: 2½

Foundation: Crawl space, slab, or basement

Materials List Available: Yes

Price Category: D

Images provided by designer/architect.

Rear Elevation

Bonus Room

Plan #351001

Dimensions: 78'8" W x 51' D

Levels: 1

Square Footage: 1,855

Bedrooms: 3

Bathrooms: 2½

Foundation: Crawl space, slab, or basement

Materials List Available: Yes

Price Category: D

Images provided by designer/architect.

Main Level Floor Plan

Kitchen/Great Room

Bonus Area

Copyright by designer/architect.

Plan #121044

Dimensions: 40' W x 55'8" D
Levels: 2
Square Footage: 1,923
Main Level Sq. Ft.: 1,351
Upper Level Sq. Ft.: 572
Bedrooms: 3
Bathrooms: 3
Foundation: Basement
Materials List Available: Yes
Price Category: D

Images provided by designer/architect.

The layout of this gracious home is designed with the contemporary family in mind.

Features:

• Ceiling Height: 8 ft. unless otherwise noted.

• Foyer: This elegant entry is graced with an open stairway that enhances the sense of spaciousness.

• Kitchen: Located just beyond the entry, this convenient kitchen features a center island that doubles as a snack bar.

• Breakfast Area: A sloped ceiling unites this area with the family room. Here you will find a planning desk for compiling menus and shopping lists.

• Master Bedroom: This bedroom has a distinctively contemporary appeal, with its cathedral ceiling and triple window.

• Computer Loft: Designed to house a computer, this loft overlooks the family room.

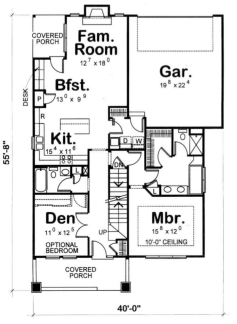

Main Level Floor Plan

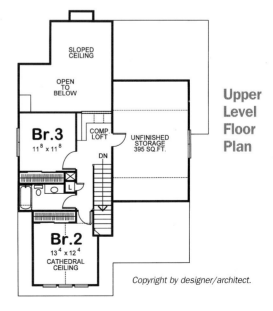

Upper Level Floor Plan

Copyright by designer/architect.

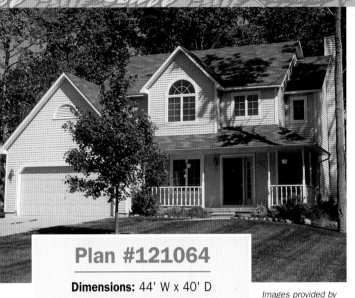

Plan #121064

Dimensions: 44' W x 40' D
Levels: 2
Square Footage: 1,846
Main Level Sq. Ft.: 919
Upper Level Sq. Ft.: 927
Bedrooms: 4
Bathrooms: 2½
Foundation: Basement
Materials List Available: Yes
Price Category: D

Images provided by designer/architect.

Main Level Floor Plan

Upper Level Floor Plan

Copyright by designer/architect.

Plan #321006

Dimensions: 76' W x 45' D
Levels: 1, optional lower
Square Footage: 1,977
Optional Basement Level Sq. Ft.: 1,416
Bedrooms: 4
Bathrooms: 2½
Foundation: Basement
Materials List Available: Yes
Price Category: D

Images provided by designer/architect.

Optional Basement Level Floor Plan

Copyright by designer/architect.

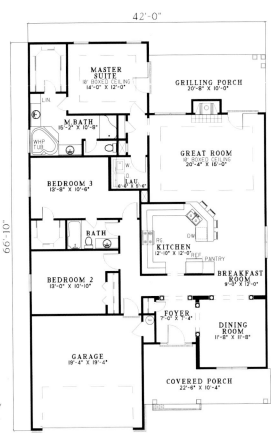

42'-0"

66'-10"

MASTER SUITE
10' BOXED CEILING
14'-0" X 12'-0"

GRILLING PORCH
20'-8" X 10'-0"

LIN.

M.BATH
15'-2" X 10'-8"

WHP TUB

GREAT ROOM
10' BOXED CEILING
20'-4" X 15'-0"

BEDROOM 3
13'-8" X 10'-6"

W.

LAU.
6'-8" X 5'-6"

BATH

KITCHEN
12'-10" X 12'-0"

RG   DW

REF

PANTRY

BEDROOM 2
13'-0" X 10'-10"

BREAKFAST ROOM
9'-0" X 12'-0"

FOYER
7'-0" X 7'-4"

DINING ROOM
11'-8" X 11'-8"

GARAGE
19'-4" X 19'-4"

COVERED PORCH
22'-6" X 10'-4"

Plan #151008

Dimensions: 42' W x 66'10" D

Levels: 1

Square Footage: 1,892

Bedrooms: 3

Bathrooms: 2

Foundation: Crawl space, slab, basement, or daylight basement

Materials List Available: No

Price Category: D

Images provided by designer/architect.

This home, as shown in the photograph, may differ from the actual blueprints. For more detailed information, please check the floor plans carefully.

Copyright by designer/architect.

Great Room/Foyer

Plan #161002

Dimensions: 64'2" W x 44'2" D

Levels: 1

Square Footage: 1,860

Bedrooms: 3

Bathrooms: 2

Foundation: Basement

Materials List Available: Yes

Price Category: D

Images provided by designer/architect.

Rear Elevation

Copyright by designer/architect.

Deck

WALK-IN CLOSET

Master Bedroom
12' x 14'6"
10'10" CEILING

ALCOVE

Great Room
16'6" x 21'2"
11'1" CEILING HT

TV ALCOVE

Breakfast
12'9" x 13'

Porch
11'8" x 11'

Dressing

STAIRS DOWN

Kitchen
12'6" x 10'11"

Laun.
HANGING SPACE

Hall

Bath

Foyer

PANTRY

Bedroom
10' x 12'

Bedroom
11'3" x 11'1"

Porch

Dining Room
10'10" x 12'2"

Garage
19'8" x 23'2"

Plan #391013

Dimensions: 52' W x 41'4" D
Levels: 2
Square Footage: 1,894
Main Level Sq. Ft.: 1,108
Upper Level Sq. Ft.: 786
Bedrooms: 3
Bathrooms: 2½
Foundation: Crawl space, slab, or basement
Materials List Available: Yes
Price Category: D

This home hints at Tudor lineage, with its rising half-timber-effects and peaked roofline. Inside, it's a different, more contemporary story.

Features:

- Living Room. The foyer opens to this room, which basks in the light of a two-story arched window. Even the open dining room enjoys the brightness.

- Family Room: This room warms up with a fireplace, plus a built-in desk, wet bar, and entry to an outdoor deck.

Rear View

- Kitchen: The angular plan of this room, with a convenient pass-through to the dining area, features a picture window with built-in seat for taking time to meditate. Excellent shelving, storage, half-bath, and hall coat closet offer behind-the-scenes support.

- Bedrooms: Bedroom 2 looks over the front yard and shares a bath with bedroom 3, which oversees the backyard.

- Master Bedroom: The second level master bedroom overlooks the living room from a beautiful balcony. Double windows along one wall fill the area with natural light, and a windowed corner illuminates the master bath.

Images provided by designer/architect.

Copyright by designer/architect.

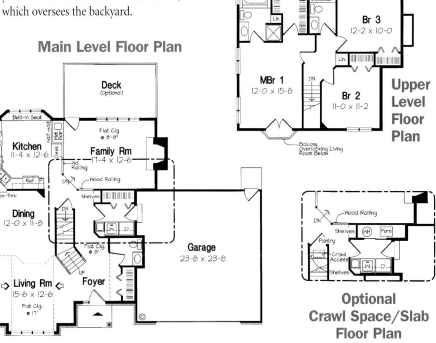

Main Level Floor Plan

Upper Level Floor Plan

Optional Crawl Space/Slab Floor Plan

Main Level Floor Plan

Upper Level Floor Plan

Copyright by designer/architect.

Plan #371038

Images provided by designer/architect.

Dimensions: 52'8" W x 44' D
Levels: 2
Square Footage: 1,896
Main Level Sq. Ft.: 1,253
Upper Level Sq. Ft.: 661
Bedrooms: 4
Bathrooms: 2½
Foundation: Crawl space or slab
Materials List Available: No
Price Category: D

Main Level Floor Plan

Upper Level Floor Plan

Copyright by designer/architect.

Plan #101029

Images provided by designer/architect.

Dimensions: 52' W x 40'4" D
Levels: 2
Square Footage: 1,897
Main Level Sq. Ft.: 995
Upper Level Sq. Ft.: 902
Bedrooms: 4
Bathrooms: 3
Foundation: Basement
Materials List Available: No
Price Category: D

Plan #371039

Dimensions: 60'4" W x 51'4" D
Levels: 1
Square Footage: 1,898
Bedrooms: 3
Bathrooms: 2
Foundation: Slab
Materials List Available: No
Price Category: D

Images provided by designer/architect.

This charming traditional home has everything you need, from the beautifully styled windows to the spacious rooms inside.

Features:

• Living Room: This formal entertaining area, with a 12-ft.-high ceiling and wooden columns, opens into the family room.

• Family Room: A large casual room with a 10-ft.-high ceiling, this room has a cozy fireplace that makes it perfect for entertaining.

• Dining Room: This elegant room has a 10-ft.-high ceiling and wooden columns.

• Kitchen: The breakfast nook opens to this large, fully equipped kitchen, which has a raised bar that brings the nook and the family room together.

• Master Suite: This secluded suite boasts a luxurious bathroom with his and her vanities and two walk in closets.

• Bedrooms: The two secondary bedrooms with sloped ceilings and walk-in closets share a convenient bathroom with a separate dressing room.

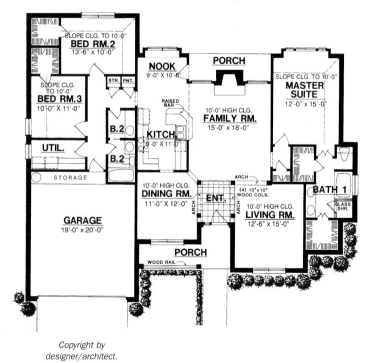

Copyright by designer/architect.

Plan #371075

Dimensions: 49'8" W x 54'6" D

Levels: 1

Square Footage: 1,904

Bedrooms: 4

Bathrooms: 2

Foundation: Crawl space or slab

Materials List Available: No

Price Category: E

Images provided by designer/architect.

This beautiful traditional brick home will make you feel right at home.

Features:

- Living Room: With high ceilings spelling luxury, this large entertaining area also has a media center, fireplace, and large window overlooking the back porch.

- Kitchen: This large gourmet kitchen has a raised bar that brings the dining area and living room together.

- Master Suite: With a stepped-up ceiling, this large, relaxing area boasts a luxurious master bathroom with his and her vanities, a marble tub, and two walk-in closets.

- Bedrooms: The additional three bedrooms, with walk-in closets, share a convenient hall bathroom.

Copyright by designer/architect.

Plan #391003

Dimensions: 47' W x 39' D
Levels: 2
Square Footage: 1,907
Main Street Sq. Ft.: 1,269
Upper Street Sq. Ft.: 638
Bedrooms: 3
Bathrooms: 2½
Foundation: Crawl space, slab, or basement
Materials List Available: Yes
Price Category: D

Images provided by designer/architect.

A family-loving wraparound porch and the quaint clapboard exterior open to an interior that boasts current styling.

Features:

- Foyer: This light-filled two-story room evokes a special aura, with a high-perching ledge for growing plants or showcasing treasures.

- Living Room: The woodstove basks in light from the soaring sky-lit ceiling. Sliding doors go out to the deck or backyard.

- Kitchen: This room features a spacious back-room laundry area and a curved counter that also serves the dining room.

- Dining Room: A beautiful bay window illuminates this room.

- Master Suite: This main-floor suite enjoys sliders to the deck, plus generous windows even in the private bath.

- Bedrooms: Two secondary bedrooms embrace their own unique storybook character with gabled reading nooks, sloped roof detailing, and walk-in closets. A full bath is situated smartly between them.

Upper Level Floor Plan

Br 2 10-4 x 14
Br 3 11 x 14
skylight
open to below
Balcony
DN
plant ledge
slope

Main Level Floor Plan

Optional Deck
Living Rm 13 x 19-6
Ldry
MBr 1 13-6 x 14
wood stove
Kitchen 11 x 12
DN
Dining Rm 12-10 x 13-6
Foyer
pan.
W D

Slab/Crawl Space Option

Copyright by designer/architect.

Rear View

Plan #371014

Dimensions: 46' W x 70'10" D
Levels: 1
Square Footage: 1,908
Bedrooms: 3
Bathrooms: 2
Foundation: Slab
Materials List Available: No
Price Category: D

This elegant French-style stucco home will show off your good taste.

Features:

- Living Room: This large area has a 12-ft.-high ceiling with a media center and fireplace, which makes it great for entertaining.

- Dining Room: Elegant columns separate this formal room from the living room.

- Kitchen: This kitchen has a raised bar and a breakfast nook with a built-in hutch and butler's pantry.

- Master Suite: You'll find a luxurious bath room with a marble tub, a glass shower, a his-and-her vanity, and large walk in closets in this suite.

- Bedrooms: The two secondary bedrooms share a private bathroom.

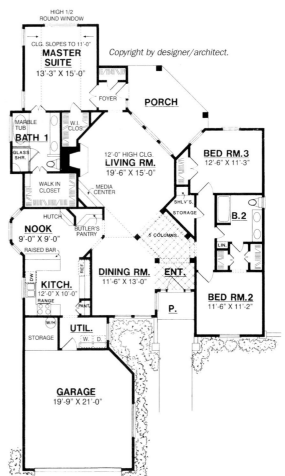

Plan #391022

Dimensions: 39' W x 48' D
Levels: 2
Square Footage: 1,908
Main Level Sq. Ft.: 1,316
Upper Level Sq. Ft.: 592
Bedrooms: 3
Bathrooms: 2
Foundation: Crawl space, slab, or basement
Materials List Available: Yes
Price Category: D

This home is made for today's environment-minded homeowners. Sun-loving walls of windows and effortless sliding doors to the outdoor deck seem to commune with nature while interior spaces seem to flow with each other.

Features:

- Kitchen: The dining room and this kitchen, a well-matched pair, open generously to the living room, with its sloped ceiling and far-reaching fireplace.

- Stairs: An abbreviated staircase tucks in two secondary bedrooms and a conveniently located laundry room. Ascend a second short set of steps for the master suite, which rivals most others.

- Master Suite: An entirely private level is devoted to this master retreat. A sloped ceiling, restful balcony, plus a spa-style step-up bathtub in the master bath showcase beauty and innovation.

- Storage: Excellent closeting and attic access are among many hardworking components of the home.

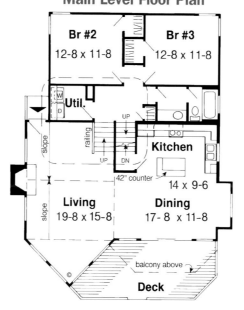

Rear View

Upper Level Floor Plan

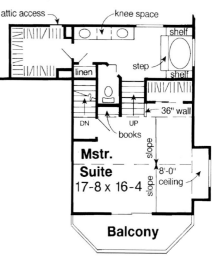

attic access — knee space

shelf

linen

step

shelf

36" wall

DN   UP

books

Mstr. Suite
17-8 x 16-4

slope

slope

8'-0" ceiling

slope

Balcony

Main Level Floor Plan

Br #2
12-8 x 11-8

Br #3
12-8 x 11-8

Util.

slope

UP

railing

UP   DN

42" counter

Kitchen
14 x 9-6

Living
19-8 x 15-8

slope

Dining
17-8 x 11-8

balcony above

Deck

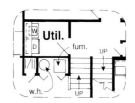

Util.

furn.

UP

w.h.   UP

Pier/Crawl Space Option

Plan #181242

Dimensions: 48' W x 35'4" D
Levels: 2
Square Footage: 1,826
Main Level Sq. Ft.: 918
Upper Level Sq. Ft.: 908
Bedrooms: 3
Bathrooms: 2
Foundation: Basement
Materials List Available: Yes
Price Category: D

Images provided by designer/architect.

This charming home has room for everyone.

Features:

• Foyer: This closed entry space will work as an "air-lock" to help keep heating and cooling costs down.

• Kitchen: L-shaped, with an eat-in design, this kitchen has a lunch counter for added seating space.

• Family Room: This relaxing area has a cozy fireplace and a large window looking onto the front yard.

• Master Bedroom: A his-and-her walk-in closet graces this large bedroom.

• Bedrooms: The two secondary bedrooms have large closets, and each has a unique nook.

Main Level Floor Plan

Copyright by designer/architect.

Upper Level Floor Plan

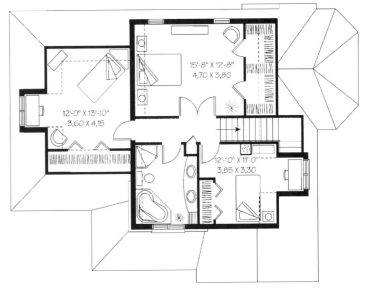

Plan #151244

Dimensions: 35' W x 80'6" D
Levels: 1
Square Footage: 1,923
Bedrooms: 3
Bathrooms: 2
Foundation: Crawl space or slab
Materials List Available: No
Price Category: D

Images provided by designer/architect.

This brick home, with stone accents on the front elevation, has great styling and offers three bedrooms.

Features:

- Entry: You enter the home though an arched covered entry foyer. On the left, French doors open to bedroom 3. Across the hall is bedroom 2, with a large walk-in closet.

- Great Room: This large gathering area, with a 10-ft. boxed ceiling, features a fireplace and access to the grilling porch.

- Kitchen: This kitchen boasts a snack bar and walk-in pantry and is open to the dining room.

- Master Suite: This private area has a 10-ft. boxed ceiling and ample closet storage. The master bath features a corner whirlpool tub with glass blocks, split vanities, and a corner shower.

Copyright by designer/architect.

Plan #401011

Dimensions: 56'8" W x 48'4" D
Levels: 2
Square Footage: 2,097
Main Level Sq. Ft.: 1,445
Upper Level Sq. Ft.: 652
Bedrooms: 4
Bathrooms: 2½
Foundation: Basement
Materials List Available: Yes
Price Category: D

Images provided by designer/architect.

A portico entry, graceful arches, and brick detailing provide appeal and a low-maintenance exterior for this design.

Features:

- Entry: A half-circle transom over this entry lights the two-story foyer, and a plant shelf lines the hallway to the sunken family room.

- Living Room: This space holds a vaulted ceiling, masonry fireplace, and French door access to the railed patio.

- Kitchen: This nearby kitchen has a center food-preparation island, a built-in desk over-looking the family room, and extensive pantries in the breakfast area.

- Formal Dining Room: This room has a tray ceiling and access to the foyer and the central hall.

- Master Suite: Located on the first level for privacy and convenience, this suite features a walk-in closet and lavish bathroom with twin vanities, a whirlpool tub, and separate shower.

- Bedrooms: The second floor holds three family bedrooms, two with built-in desks.

Rear Elevation

Right Side Elevation

Left Side Elevation

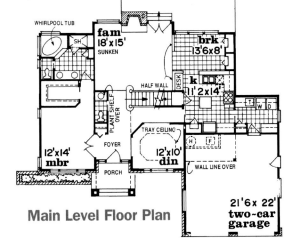

Main Level Floor Plan

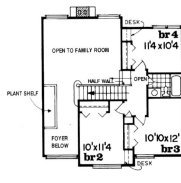

Upper Level Floor Plan

Copyright by designer/architect.

Plan #401037

Dimensions: 53' W x 44' D
Levels: 2
Square Footage: 1,924
Main Level Sq. Ft.: 1,007
Upper Level Sq. Ft.: 917
Bedrooms: 3
Bathrooms: 2½
Foundation: Basement
Materials List Available: Yes
Price Category: D

This charming country exterior conceals an elegant interior, starting with formal living and dining rooms, each with a bay window. Decorative columns help define an elegant dining room.

Features:

- **Kitchen:** This gourmet kitchen features a work island and a breakfast area with its own bay window.

- **Family Room:** A fireplace warms this room, which opens to the rear porch through French doors.

- **Master Suite:** Located on the second floor, this area boasts a vaulted ceiling, a walk-in closet, and a tiled bath.

- **Bedrooms:** Upstairs, two family bedrooms share a full bath and a gallery hall with a balcony overlook to the foyer.

**Main Level
Floor Plan**

Left Side Elevation

Right Side Elevation

**Upper Level
Floor Plan**

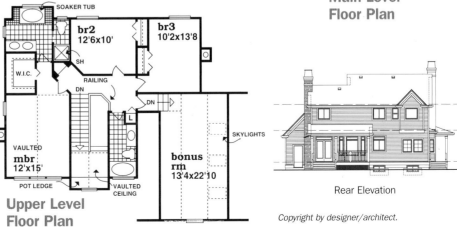

Rear Elevation

WHIRLPOOL TUB

br3
10'x10'2

br4
11'x9'10

SH

RAILING

**Upper Level
Floor Plan**

13'8x11'
br2

OPEN TO
BELOW

12'x14'6
mbr

47' (14.3m)

brk

din
10'x 12'

k
11'8x11'8

14'x15'6
fam

42' (12.8m)

ldr

W
D

RAILING

12'x15'
liv

LINE OF 2nd
FLOOR

**Main Level
Floor Plan**

Copyright by designer/architect.

20'6 x 23'
**two~car
garage**

PORCH

RAILING

Plan #401002

*Images provided by
designer/architect.*

Dimensions: 47' W x 42' D
Levels: 2
Square Footage: 1,938
Main Level Sq. Ft.: 936
Upper Level Sq. Ft.: 1002
Bedrooms: 4
Bathrooms: 2½
Foundation: Basement
Materials List Available: Yes
Price Category: D

**Main Level
Floor Plan**

13'-10" x 10'-4"
4.15 x 3.10

11'-0" x 11'-0"
3.30 x 3.30

35'-8"
10.7 m

11'-8" x 21'-0"
3.50 x 6.30

14'-8" x 21'-0"
4.40 x 6.30

32'-4"
9.7 m

11'-0" x 9'-10"
3.30 x 2.95

12'-0" x 15'-8"
3.60 x 4.70

11'-0" x 9'-10"
3.30 x 2.95

11'-0" x 11'-8"
3.30 x 3.50

**Upper Level
Floor Plan**

Plan #181230

*Images provided by
designer/architect.*

Dimensions: 32'4" W x 35'8" D
Levels: 2
Square Footage: 1,943
Main Level Sq. Ft.: 836
Upper Level Sq. Ft.: 1,107
Bedrooms: 3
Bathrooms: 2½
Foundation: Basement
Materials List Available: Yes
Price Category: D

Copyright by designer/architect.

Images provided by designer/architect.

Plan #371040

Dimensions: 58' W x 64'6" D

Levels: 1

Square Footage: 1,913

Bedrooms: 3

Bathrooms: 2

Foundation: Slab

Materials List Available: No

Price Category: D

Images provided by designer/architect.

Plan #101028

Dimensions: 57'8" W x 57'6" D

Levels: 1

Square Footage: 1,963

Bedrooms: 3

Bathrooms: 2

Foundation: Basement

Materials List Available: No

Price Category: D

Bonus Area Floor Plan

Storage
17-4x5-8

Garage
20-4x21-4

Porch
17-4x10-0

Master
Bedroom
17-4x13-6

*Copyright by
designer/architect.*

Laundry
7-4x6-3

1/2 Bath

Pantry

Greatroom
17-4x17-4

Bath

M.Bath

Kitchen/
Breakfast
13-3x20-5

Dining
11-3x13-4

Foyer

Bedroom
11-3x10-1

Bedroom
11-4x11-4

Porch
31-0x8-0

1/2
Bath

Greatroom

Kitchen

**Basement
Stair Location**

Plan #311011

Dimensions: 56'4" W x 67'4" D

Levels: 1

Square Footage: 1,955

Bedrooms: 3

Bathrooms: 2½

Foundation: Crawl space, slab, or basement

Materials List Available: Yes

Price Category: D

*Images provided by
designer/architect.*

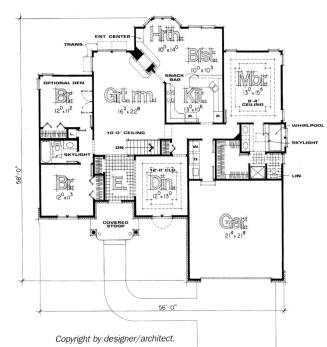

Plan #121001

Dimensions: 56' W x 58' D

Levels: 1

Square Footage: 1,911

Bedrooms: 3

Bathrooms: 2

Foundation: Basement

Materials List Available: Yes

Price Category: D

*Images provided by
designer/architect.*

Copyright by designer/architect.

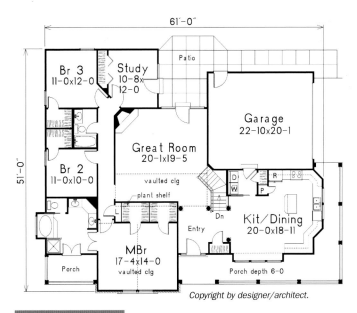

Images provided by designer/architect.

Copyright by designer/architect.

Plan #321030

Dimensions: 61' W x 51' D
Levels: 1
Square Footage: 2,029
Bedrooms: 4
Bathrooms: 2
Foundation: Crawl space, slab, basement, or walkout
Materials List Available: Yes
Price Category: D

SMARTtip

Measuring Angles

A sure-fire way to accurately measure the wall-frame acute angle is to cut a piece of scrap lumber to emulate the angle, and then measure it.

Upper Level Floor Plan

Main Level Floor Plan

Copyright by designer/architect.

Plan #161020

Dimensions: 60' W" x 50'4" D
Levels: 2
Square Footage: 2,082; 2,349 with bonus space
Main Level Sq. Ft.: 1,524
Upper Level Sq. Ft.: 558
Bedrooms: 3
Bathrooms: 2½
Foundation: Basement
Materials List Available: Yes
Price Category: D

Images provided by designer/architect.

Plan #391007

Dimensions: 74' W x 41'6" D
Levels: 2
Square Footage: 2,083
Main Level Sq. Ft.: 1,113
Upper Level Sq. Ft.: 970
Bedrooms: 3
Bathrooms: 2½
Foundation: Crawl space, slab, or basement
Materials List Available: Yes
Price Category: D

Images provided by designer/architect.

With a wide-wrapping porch and a pretty Palladian window peeking from a sky-high dormer, this charming home is cheerfully reminiscent of the good old days.

Features:

• Dining and Living Rooms: Over the threshold, this dining room engages one side of the staircase and the living room with fireplace occupies the other to maintain balance.

• Kitchen: One section of this functional kitchen looks out at the deck, feeds into the breakfast area, and flows into the great-sized family room while the other leads to the laundry area, half bath, mudroom, and garage.

• Master Suite: The second level delivers the master suite, with its wide walk-in closet and a full bath with separate shower and tub areas, double sinks, and a bright window.

• Bedrooms: Each of the two equally spacious secondary bedrooms with wall-length closets and large windows shares a full-size bath uniquely outfitted with double sinks so that no one has to wait to primp.

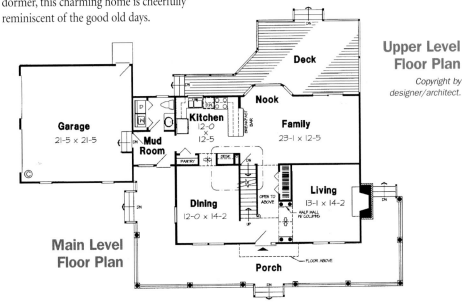

Main Level Floor Plan

Upper Level Floor Plan

Copyright by designer/architect.

Crawl Space/Slab Option

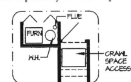

Rear View

Rear View

Loft Area

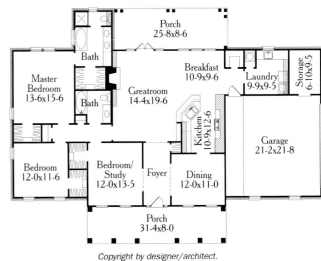

Porch
25-8x8-6

Bath

Master
Bedroom
13-6x15-6

Bath

Greatroom
14-4x19-6

Breakfast
10-9x9-6

Laundry
9-9x9-5

Storage
6-10x9-5

Kitchen
10-9x12-6

Garage
21-2x21-8

Bedroom
12-0x11-6

Bedroom/
Study
12-0x13-5

Foyer

Dining
12-0x11-0

Porch
31-4x8-0

Images provided by designer/architect.

Copyright by designer/architect.

Plan #311018

Dimensions: 70'6" W x 51' D
Levels: 1
Square Footage: 1,867
Bedrooms: 3
Bathrooms: 2
Foundation: Crawl space, slab, or basement
Materials List Available: Yes
Price Category: C

Basement Stair Location

Laundry
9-9x5-6

Storage

Plan #121015

Dimensions: 52' W x 47'4" D
Levels: 2
Square Footage: 1,999
Main Level Sq. Ft.: 1,421
Upper Level Sq. Ft.: 578
Bedrooms: 4
Bathrooms: 2½
Foundation: Basement
Materials List Available: Yes
Price Category: D

Images provided by designer/architect.

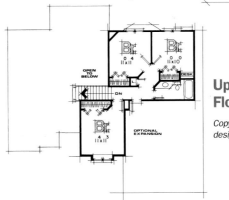

Main Level Floor Plan

TRANSOMS

LIN.

Grt. rm.
15x19
12'-10" CEILING

Bfst.
14x13

SNACK BAR

Kit.
10x11

DESK

LAUNDRY

UP

DN

Mbr
13x16
11'-4" CEILING

Dn.
12x12

HUTCH

Gar.
20x23

COVERED PORCH

52'-0"

47'-4"

Upper Level Floor Plan

Br
11x12

Br
11x10

DESK

OPEN TO BELOW

DN

Br
11x11

OPTIONAL EXPANSION

Copyright by designer/architect.

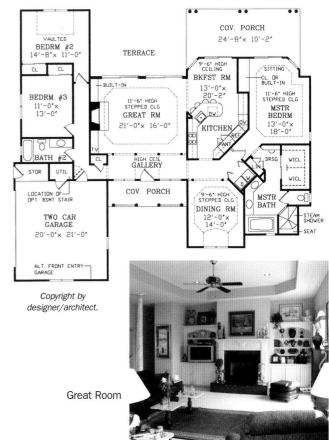

Images provided by designer/architect.

Copyright by designer/architect.

Plan #131009

Dimensions: 64'10" W x 57'8" D
Levels: 1
Square Footage: 2,018
Bedrooms: 3
Bathrooms: 2
Foundation: Crawl space, slab, or basement
Materials List Available: Yes
Price Category: D

Great Room

Plan #161008

Dimensions: 64'2" W x 46'6" D
Levels: 1
Square Footage: 1,860
Bedrooms: 3
Bathrooms: 2
Foundation: Slab
Materials List Available: No
Price Category: D

Images provided by designer/architect.

Copyright by designer/architect.

SMARTtip

Espaliered Fruit Trees

Try a technique used by the royal gardeners at Versailles—espalier. They trained the fruit trees to grow flat against the walls, creating patterns. It's not difficult, especially if you go to a reputable nursery and purchase an apple or pear tree that has already been espaliered. Plant it against a flat surface that's in a sunny spot.

Clutter-Cutting Tips for Your Home

One of the great things about moving into a new home is all that new, uncluttered closet space you gain. But if you are like most homeowners, storage of all types will quickly become scarce, especially in a smaller cottage home. Here are some tips for expanding and organizing storage space.

Home offices require a mix of storage options: open shelving, drawers, and file cabinets.

Shelving Types

Shelving is an easy and economical way to add extra storage space in almost any part of your home—along walls, inside closets, and even in the basement or garage. Building shelves doesn't usually require a lot of skill or specialized tools, so this is one project just about any do-it-yourselfer can handle. And unless you decide to use hardwood—which looks great but costs a bundle—it won't cost a lot to install them either.

Solid wood shelving is the way to go when you want to show off the wood or your work.

Plywood and particleboard offer a couple of advantages when it comes to shelving, though. They cost less than solid wood, and can be bought faced with decorative surfaces. They also come in sheets, which makes them ideal for a really wide shelf. Inexpensive, manufactured storage units ready for assembly often are made from melamine-coated particleboard.

Wood trim will help match your new shelves to the rest of the room or add some interesting detail. Trim is also a handy way to hide seams, gaps, exposed edges of plywood, and other blemishes. You can get trim in either hardwood or softwood. If you plan on finishing a project with stain or sealer, make sure the trim matches the wood you used for the rest of the project.

Bracket Options

There are two basic types of ready-to-hang shelving supports: stationary shelf brackets and shelving standards. Stationary brackets come in many sizes and styles, and range from utilitarian to decorative. Shelving standards are slotted metal strips that support various types of shelf brackets.

Mounting Brackets

For maximum strength, anchor shelf supports to wall studs. If your shelf will carry a light load, you can anchor its supports between studs with mollies or toggle bolts. Attaching supports directly to the studs is always better, though, because sooner or later something heavy will wind up on the shelf. Use masonry anchors to attach shelf supports to brick or concrete. You can also attach shelf supports to a ledger attached to wall studs with 3-inch drywall screws.

Ready-made shelving, above, offers a quick alternative to building your own shelves.

Mud rooms and areas near the entrance the family uses most should have storage for coats, hats, and boots.

Shelf Standards. Metal shelf standards can be mounted directly to walls or, for a more decorative look, you can insert the standards in grooves routed into the wood itself or into hardwood strips.

Cut the standards to fit with a hacksaw, and attach them to wall studs with 3-inch drywall screws. Use a carpenter's level to make sure that both standards are plumb and that the corresponding mounting slots are level. Mount standards 6 inches from the ends of shelving to prevent sagging. For long wall shelves, install standards every 48 inches.

Many kitchen and closet storage systems use wire grids that attach to walls with molded plastic brackets. If you anticipate light loads, you can mount these brackets to drywall using the screws and expansion anchors usually included with such systems. But for heavier loads, use drywall screws to fasten the brackets directly to the wall studs.

Customized Storage

Built-in storage units are an excellent way to make the most of existing storage space in your home. Ready-made or custom-made built-in shelving units, entertainment centers, kitchen cabinets, medicine cabinets, window seats, and under-bed drawers are not only inexpensive and easy to assemble, they allow you to add a unique, personalized touch to your living spaces.

Built-in Shelving

A built-in shelving unit can create valuable storage capacity from an overlooked wall space, such as the area between windows or between a door and its adjacent corner. To construct the shelving, you'll need 1x10 or 1x12 lumber for side panels, top and base panels, and shelves; four 2x2 strips for spreaders; trim molding to conceal gaps along the top and bottom of the unit; 12d

common nails and 6d finishing nails. If the unit will be bearing heavy loads, use hardwood boards, and make sure that the shelves span no more than 36 inches. To make installation easier, cut the side pieces an inch shorter than the ceiling height. (This way, you'll be able to tilt the unit into position without scraping the ceiling.) Paint or stain the wood pieces before assembling the unit. Hang the shelves from pegs or end clips inserted into holes drilled in the side pieces.

Adding Closet Space

What homeowner, even a new homeowner, hasn't complained about having too little closet space? Fortunately, there are almost always ways to find a bit more closet space or to make the closet space you have more efficient. Often, it isn't the space that is lacking but how the space is organized that is the problem. The trick is to find ways to help you organize the space.

Ventilated closet systems help keep your belongings neat and within easy reach.

Organizing Systems. The easiest and most obvious solution is one of the many commercial closet organizing systems now on the market. There are a number of configurations available, and you can customize most systems to meet your needs. Constructing your own version of a commercial closet organizer is another option. With a combination of shelves and plywood partitions, you can divide a closet into storage zones, with a single clothes pole on one side for full-length garments; double clothes poles on the other side for half-length garments like jackets, skirts, or slacks; a column of narrow shelves between the two for folded items or shoes; and one or more closet-wide shelves on top.

Before designing a closet system, above, inventory all of the items you want to store in the closet.

Metal shelf standards can provide a quick solution for creating shelving in areas where it is needed.

Cedar Closets

Both solid cedar boards and composite cedar panels have only moderate resistance to insects, and are used more for their pleasant aroma and appearance. The sheets of pressed red and tan particles are no less aromatic than solid wood, but the panels are 40 to 50 percent less expensive, and are easier to install. Solid boards require more carpentry work, and are likely to produce a fair amount of waste unless you piece the courses and create more joints. To gain the maximum effect, every inside surface should be covered, including the ceiling and the back of the door. The simplest option is to use ¼-inch-thick panels, which are easy to cut into big sections that cover walls in one or two pieces. Try to keep cedar seams in boards or panels from falling over drywall seams. No stain, sealer, or clear finish is needed; just leave the wood raw. The cedar aroma will fade over the years as natural oils crystallize on the surface. But you can easily regenerate the

For garages and basements, you'll find a combination of shelving and hanging hooks keeps tools and equipment organized, left.

Storage for basements, garages, and workshops, opposite below, should include a cabinet that locks for storage of dangerous chemicals.

Specialized storage accessories, such as the sports storage system shown at right, not only keeps items organized but they also keep them in ready-to-play condition.

scent from the panels by scuffing the surface with fine sandpaper.

Ideas for Basements, Garages, and Workshops

Workshops and other utility areas such as garages, attics, and basements can benefit from storage upgrades as much as any other room in the home—perhaps even more so, as utility areas are prone to clutter. Convenience, flexibility, and safety are the things to keep in mind when reorganizing your work space. Try to provide storage space for tools and hardware as near as possible to where they'll be used. In addition to a sturdy workbench, utility shelving

is a mainstay in any workshop. You can buy ready-to-assemble units or make your own using ¾-inch particleboard or plywood shelves and ¾x1½-inch (1x2) hardwood stock for cleats (nailed to the wall), ribs (nailed to the front underside of the shelves), and vertical shelf supports.

DIY Utility Storage. Don't forget about pegboard. To make a pegboard tool rack, attach washers to the back of the pegboard with hot glue, spacing the washers to coincide with wall studs. Position the pegboard so that the rear washers are located over studs. Drive drywall screws through finish washers and the pegboard into studs. (Use masonry anchors for concrete walls.)

Finally, try to take advantage of any oth-

erwise wasted space. The area in your garage above your parked car is the ideal spot for a U-shaped lumber storage rack, made of 1x4 stock and connecting plates. The space in front of the car could be used for a storage cabinet or even a workbench.

Instant Storage. To utilize the overhead space in your garage, build deep storage platforms supported by ledgers screwed to wall studs and threaded rods hooked to ceiling joists or rafters. You can also hang tools from the walls by mounting pegboard. You can buy sets with a variety of hooks and brackets for tools. For small items, such as jars of nails, make shallow shelves by nailing 1x4 boards between the exposed studs.

Suit storage to your needs. The narrow pullout pantry above is located between the refrigerator and a food-preparation area. Notice how you can access the shelves from both sides of the pantry when it is extended.

Kitchen Storage

The type of storage in a kitchen is almost as important as the amount. Some people like at least a few open shelves for displaying attractive china or glassware; others want absolutely everything tucked away behind doors.

What are your storage needs? The answer depends partly on your food shopping habits and partly on how many pots, pans, and other pieces of kitchen equipment you have or would like to have. A family that goes food shopping several times a week and prepares mostly fresh foods needs more refrigerator space, less freezer capacity, and fewer cabinets than a family that prefers packaged or prepared foods and makes only infrequent forays to the local supermarket.

Planning

To help clarify your needs, mentally walk yourself through a typical meal and list the utensils used to prepare food, where you got them, and your progress throughout the work area. And don't limit yourself to full-scale meals. Much kitchen work is devoted to preparing snacks, reheating leftovers, and making lunches for the kids to take to school.

Food Preparation. During food preparation, the sink and stove come into use. Some families rely heavily on the microwave for reheating. Using water means repeated trips to the sink, so that area might be the best place to keep a steamer, salad spinner, and coffee and tea canisters, as well as glassware and cups. Near the stove you may want storage for odd-shaped items such as a fish poacher or wok. You can hang frequently used pans and utensils from a convenient rack; stow other items in cabinets so that they do not collect grease.

During the Meal. When the food is ready, you must take it to the table. If the eating space is nearby, a work counter might turn into a serving counter. If the dining space is in another room, a pass-through facilitates serving.

Storage accessories, such as the pullout pot holder above, come as options from some cabinet manufacturers, or you can install them later yourself. Notice how the side rails hold the pot lids in place. The cabinet below features space for small baskets.

After the Meal. When the meal ends, dishes must go from the table to the sink or dishwasher, and leftovers to storage containers and the refrigerator. Now the stove and counters need to be wiped down and the sink scoured. When the dishwasher finishes its cycle, everything must be put away.

Open versus Closed Storage.

Shelves, pegboards, pot racks, cup hooks, magnetic knife racks, and the like put your utensils on view, which is a good way to personalize your kitchen.

But open storage has drawbacks. Items left out in the open can look messy unless they are kept neatly arranged. Another option is to install glass doors on wall cabinets. This handily solves the dust problem but often costs more than solid doors.

Plan #151205

Dimensions: 65' W x 56' D
Levels: 1
Square Footage: 1,969
Bedrooms: 3
Bathrooms: 2
Foundation: Crawl space or slab
Materials List Available: No
Price Category: C

Images provided by designer/architect.

This attractive home is sure to charm the neighborhood.

Features:

- Entry Porch: This covered porch welcomes you home and has decorative columns.

- Great Room: Gather your family around this room's fireplace on cold winter nights.

- Kitchen: The family chef will love preparing meals in this kitchen almost as much as serving them in the dining room defined by round columns. The fully equipped kitchen has a breakfast bar and is open to the breakfast room.

- Master Suite: This area features French doors that lead to the rear grilling porch and has a beautiful private bathroom.

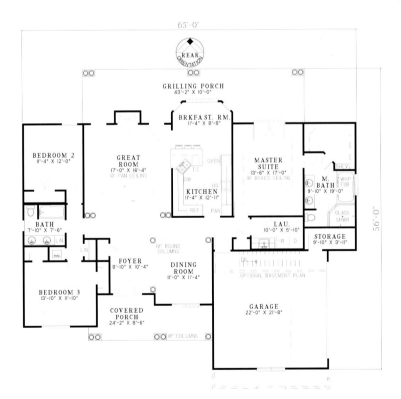

Copyright by designer/architect.

Plan #391046

Dimensions: 67'6" W x 39'6" D
Levels: 2
Square Footage: 1,978
Main Level Sq. Ft.: 1,034
Upper Level Sq. Ft.: 944
Bedrooms: 4
Bathrooms: 2½
Foundation: Crawl space, slab, or basement
Materials List Available: Yes
Price Category: D

This could be your coastal cottage or the pretty place you come home to every day.

Features:

- Porch: This wraparound porch leads inside to an airy front entry with coat closet.

- Staircase: This central staircase divides the layout, with a versatile den/guest room and powder room on one side and a stylish dining room on the other.

- Kitchen: Surrounded by counters and cabinetry, this kitchen features a centralized lunch island that is made for two but gathers more.

- Living Room: The fireplace is a big draw, and there's more than one way to reach the family's favorite space.

- Bedrooms: A bi-level staircase reaches the second-level sitting area and all three bed rooms. Two secondary bedrooms enjoy unique character as well as wall-length closets and excellent windowing.

- Master Suite: This area is a masterpiece, with its cathedral ceilings, L-shaped walk-in closet, corner tub, separate shower and toilet, and double sinks.

Images provided by designer/architect.

Front View

Rear View

Main Level Floor Plan

Upper Level Floor Plan

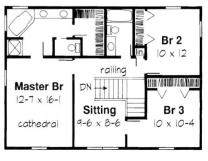

Copyright by designer/architect.

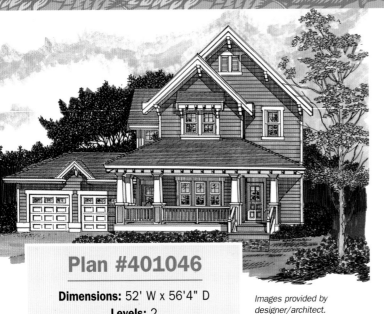

Main Level Floor Plan

fam
12'x14'4

PORCH

brk
9'x9'
BREAKFAST BAR

Furn. & HWT location
for crawlspace version

FREEZER

two car
garage
23'6x21'

D W T

k
13'x10'

din
14' & 13'x10'

liv
17'6x15'

UP

DN

PORCH

br2
10'4x12'

br3
10'4x12'

W.I.C.

DN

OPEN
TO
BELOW

mbr
12'x15'4

Upper Level Floor Plan

Copyright by designer/architect.

Plan #401046

Dimensions: 52' W x 56'4" D

Levels: 2

Square Footage: 1,990

Main Level Sq. Ft.: 1,074

Upper Level Sq. Ft.: 916

Bedrooms: 3

Bathrooms: 2½

Foundation: Basement

Materials List Available: Yes

Price Category: D

*Images provided by
designer/architect.*

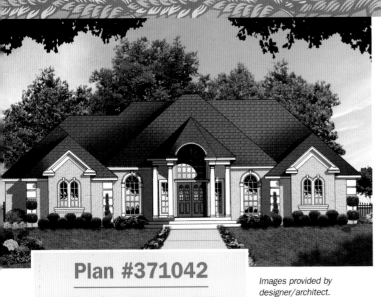

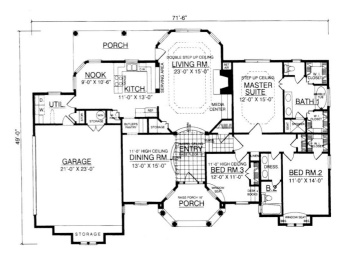

Copyright by designer/architect.

71'-6"

PORCH

NOOK
9'-0" X 10'-6"

KITCH.
11'-0" X 13'-0"

DOUBLE STEP UP CEILING
LIVING RM.
23'-0" X 15'-0"

SERVING AREA

STEP UP CEILING
MASTER
SUITE
12'-0" X 15'-0"

W. I.
CLOSET

BATH

UTIL.

D.

W.

BUTLER'S
PANTRY

STORAGE

REF

STORAGE

MEDIA
CENTER

SEAT

SHOWER

W. I.
CLOSET

49'-0"

GARAGE
21'-0" X 23'-0"

DINING RM.
13'-0" X 15'-0"

11'-0" HIGH CEILING

ENTRY

11'-0" HIGH CEILING
BED RM.3
12'-0" X 11'-0"

DRESS

B.2

BED RM.2
11'-0" X 14'-0"

WINDOW
SEAT

RAISE PORCH 18"

PORCH

WINDOW SEAT

STORAGE

Plan #371042

Dimensions: 71'6" W x 49' D

Levels: 1

Square Footage: 1,999

Bedrooms: 3

Bathrooms: 2

Foundation: Slab

Materials List Available: No

Price Category: D

*Images provided by
designer/architect.*

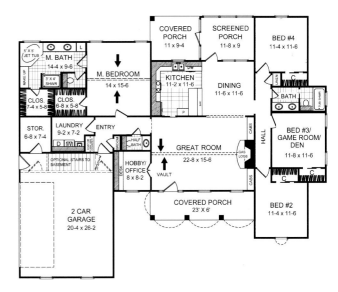

Plan #351044

Dimensions: 68' W x 55'8" D

Levels: 1

Square Footage: 2,000

Bedrooms: 4

Bathrooms: 2½

Foundation: Crawl space, slab, or basement

Materials List Available: Yes

Price Category: E

Images provided by designer/architect.

Copyright by designer/architect.

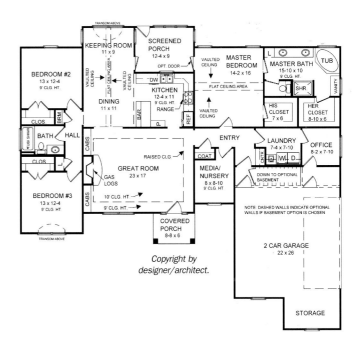

Plan #351045

Dimensions: 66' W x 60' D

Levels: 1

Square Footage: 2,000

Bedrooms: 3

Bathrooms: 2

Foundation: Crawl space, slab, or basement

Materials List Available: Yes

Price Category: E

Images provided by designer/architect.

Copyright by designer/architect.

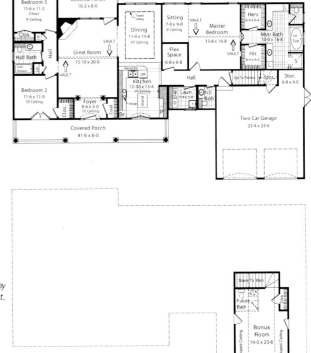

Main Level Floor Plan

Upper Level Floor Plan

Plan #351049

Dimensions: 78' W x 49'6" D

Levels: 1

Square Footage: 2,004

Bedrooms: 3

Bathrooms: 2½

Foundation: Crawl space or slab

Materials List Available: Yes

Price Category: E

Images provided by designer/architect.

Copyright by designer/architect.

Main Level Floor Plan

Upper Level Floor Plan

Copyright by designer/architect.

Plan #391033

Dimensions: 48' W x 48' D

Levels: 2

Square Footage: 2,007

Main Level Sq. Ft.: 1,345

Upper Level Sq. Ft.: 662

Bedrooms: 3

Bathrooms: 2½

Foundation: Crawl space, slab, or basement

Materials List Available: Yes

Price Category: D

Images provided by designer/architect.

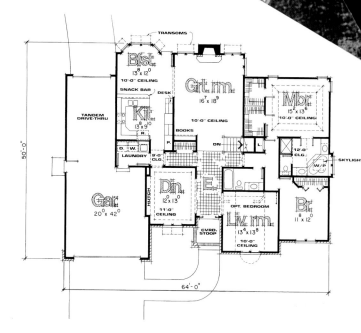

Plan #121050

Dimensions: 64' W x 50' D

Levels: 1

Square Footage: 1,996

Bedrooms: 2

Bathrooms: 2

Foundation: Basement

Materials List Available: Yes

Price Category: D

Images provided by designer/architect.

Copyright by designer/architect.

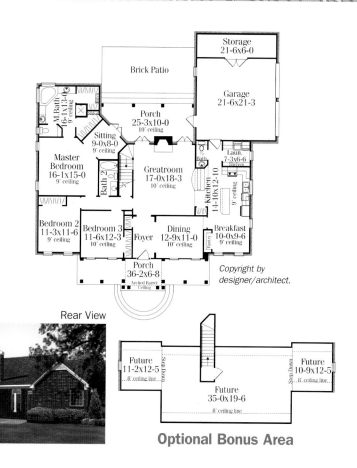

Plan #311001

Dimensions: 65'11" W x 67'9" D

Levels: 1

Square Footage: 2,085

Bedrooms: 3

Bathrooms: 2½

Foundation: Crawl space, slab, or basement

Materials List Available: No

Price Category: D

Images provided by designer/architect.

Copyright by designer/architect.

Rear View

Optional Bonus Area

Plan #371043

Dimensions: 40' W x 56'6" D

Levels: 2

Square Footage: 2,013

Main Level Sq. Ft.: 1,323

Upper Level Sq. Ft.: 690

Bedrooms: 4

Bathrooms: 2½

Foundation: Slab

Materials List Available: No

Price Category: E

Images provided by designer/architect.

This charming country home will make you feel right at home. Exquisite country trim gives it character, and the front dormers give it charm.

Features:

• **Living Room:** This large entertaining area, with its 10-ft.-high ceiling and corner fireplace, is open to the kitchen and breakfast nook.

• **Dining Room:** This formal room has a 10-ft.-high ceiling, bay window, and easy access to the kitchen.

• **Kitchen:** The pantry, raised bar, and cozy breakfast nook are three reasons why this large kitchen is a winner.

• **Master Suite:** This private area has a cozy sitting area and a luxurious bathroom with two large walk-in closets.

• **Bedrooms:** Upstairs you'll find three large bedrooms, which share a convenient hall bathroom.

Main Level Floor Plan

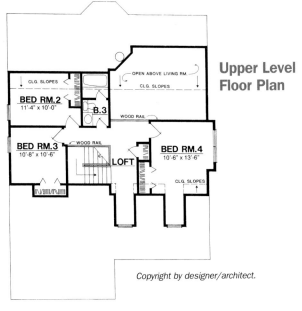

Upper Level Floor Plan

Copyright by designer/architect.

Plan #391001

Dimensions: 32' W x 40' D
Levels: 2
Square Footage: 2,015
Main Level Sq. Ft.: 1,280
Upper Level Sq. Ft.: 735
Bedrooms: 3
Bathrooms: 2½
Foundation: Crawl space
Materials List Available: Yes
Price Category: D

Images provided by designer/architect.

- **Kitchen:** This L-shaped kitchen features an expansive cooktop/lunch counter.

- **Utility Areas:** A utility room handles the laundry and storage, and a half bath with linen closet takes care of other necessities.

- **Master Suite:** This main-floor master suite is just that—sweet! The spa-style bath features a corner tub nestled against a greenhouse window. Plus, there are double sinks and a separate shower.

- **Upstairs:** The sun-washed loft overlooks the activity below while embracing two dreamy bedrooms and a sizable bath with double sinks.

Follow your dream to this home surrounded with decking. The A-frame front showcases bold windowing (on two levels), and natural lighting fills the house.

Features:

- **Dining Room:** This dining room and the family room are completely open to each other, perfect for hanging out in the warmth of the hearth.

Main Level Floor Plan

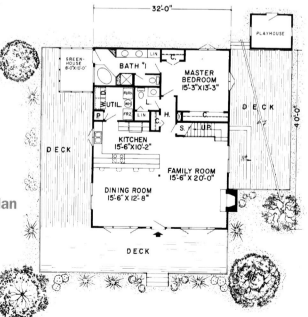

Upper Level Floor Plan

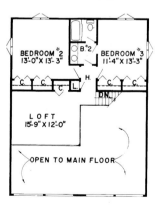

Copyright by designer/architect.

Plan #161082

Dimensions: 52' W x 36'4" D

Levels: 2

Square Footage: 2,049

Main Level Sq. Ft.: 902

Upper Level Sq. Ft.: 1,147

Bedrooms: 4

Bathrooms: 2½

Foundation: Basement

Materials List Available: Yes

Price Category: D

This charming two-story home has everything your family needs.

Features:

- Parlor/Library: Located just off the entry, this area welcomes guests into your home.

- Great Room: With its fireplace and view onto the backyard, this enormous room is perfect for entertaining.

- Kitchen: This U-shaped kitchen has counter seating and is open to the great room and the dining room.

- Master Suite: Walk up to the second floor, and you'll find this large area, which has a spacious walk-in closet and a luxurious private bath.

- Bedrooms: Three additional bedrooms, two with walk-in closets, share a full bathroom.

Images provided by designer/architect.

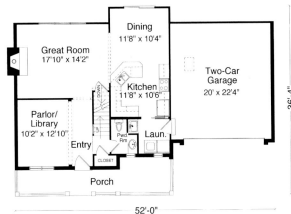

Copyright by designer/architect.

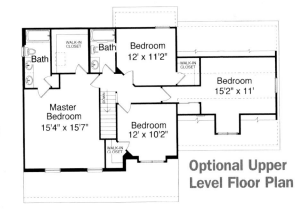

Optional Upper Level Floor Plan

Rear Elevation

Left Side Elevation

Right Side Elevation

Plan #401001

Dimensions: 56' W x 43'4" D
Levels: 2
Square Footage: 2,071
Main Level Sq. Ft.: 1,204
Upper Level Sq. Ft.: 867
Bedrooms: 3
Bathrooms: 2½
Foundation: Basement
Materials List Available: Yes
Price Category: D

Images provided by designer/architect.

This transitional design carries the best of both worlds—popular details of both traditional and contemporary architecture. The high rooflines allow for dramatic full-height windows and vaulted ceilings in the formal areas.

Features:

- Open Plan: The open casual areas include the hearth-warmed family room, bayed breakfast nook, and island kitchen.

- Den: Located just off the foyer, this room is a well-appreciated haven for quiet time. Note the half-bath just beyond the den.

- Master Suite: This area has two walk-in closets and a full bath with a separate shower and tub.

- Bedrooms: Three bedrooms occupy the second floor and include two family bedrooms—one with a vaulted ceiling.

- Utility Areas: A laundry alcove leads to the two-car garage with extra storage space.

Main Level Floor Plan

Rear Elevation

Left Side Elevation

Upper Level Floor Plan

Right Side Elevation

Copyright by designer/architect.

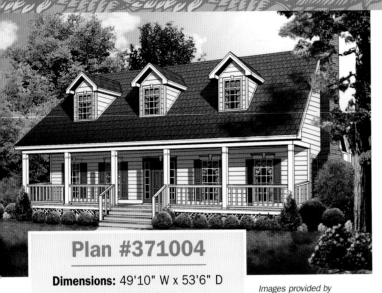

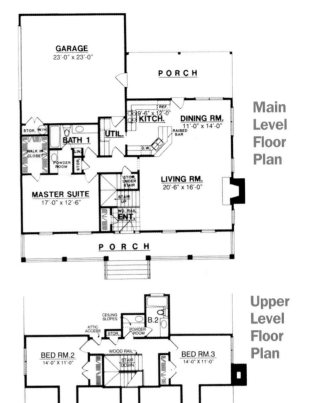

Main Level Floor Plan

GARAGE
23'-0" x 23'-0"

PORCH

KITCH.
9'-6" x 13'-0"

DINING RM.
11'-0" x 14'-0"
raised bar

STOR. W/H

BATH 1

UTIL.

POWDER ROOM

STOR.

LIVING RM.
20'-6" x 16'-0"

MASTER SUITE
17'-0" x 12'-6"

STOR. UNDER STAIR

STAIR UP

WD. RAIL

ENT.

PORCH

Images provided by designer/architect.

Plan #371004

Dimensions: 49'10" W x 53'6" D
Levels: 2
Square Footage: 1,815
Main Level Sq. Ft.: 1,245
Upper Level Sq. Ft.: 570
Bedrooms: 3
Bathrooms: 2
Foundation: Slab
(crawl space option for fee)
Materials List Available: No
Price Category: D

Upper Level Floor Plan

CEILING SLOPES

ATTIC ACCESS

B.2

POWDER ROOM

STOR.

BED RM.2
14'-0" x 11'-0"

WOOD RAIL

STAIR DOWN

BED RM.3
14'-0" x 11'-0"

Copyright by designer/architect.

Main Level Floor Plan

51'-4"

PORCH
14'-0" X 12'-0"

NOOK
13'-0" X 9'-6"

MASTER SUITE
17'-0" x 12'-0"

DINING RM.
13'-6" X 10'-0"

KITCH.
14'-0" X 11'-0"

BATH 1

2 STORY CEILING
LIVING RM.
17'-6" X 16'-0"

UTIL.

STORAGE

ENT.

PORCH
WOOD POSTS AND RAIL

GARAGE
25'-0" X 21'-0"

56'-6"

Plan #371079

Dimensions: 51'4" W x 56'6" D
Levels: 2
Square Footage: 2,089
Main Level Sq. Ft.: 1,441
Upper Level Sq. Ft.: 648
Bedrooms: 3
Bathrooms: 2½
Foundation: Slab
Materials List Available: No
Price Category: D

Images provided by designer/architect.

Upper Level Floor Plan

BED RM.3
11'-0" X 11'-6"

ATTIC AREA

ATTIC AREA

LOFT

B.3

BED RM.2
10'-0" X 12'-6"

OPEN ABOVE LIVING ROOM

STUDY AREA

PLANT SHELF

BONUS RM.
11'-6" X 22'-0"

ATTIC SPACE

Copyright by designer/architect.

Copyright by designer/architect.

SCREENED PORCH 15'4" x 13'10"

DECK 11'0" x 7'6"

14' CEILING

SITTING

BEDROOM 3 13'0" x 11'0"

8' HIGH OPENING

BRKFST 11'0" x 10'10

MASTER SUITE 21'4" x 15'0"

FAMILY ROOM 16'0" x 24'1"

KITCHEN 13'8" x 9'6"

PANTRY

13'-10" CEILING

10' CEILING

OPTIONAL STAIRS TO BASEMENT

LINEN

BEDROOM 2 13'0" x 11'0"

13'-4" CEILING

DINING 11'0" x 12'0"

TRAY CEILING

9' CEILING

LIVING 11'0" x 12'0"

PORCH 15'4" x 5'4"

3 CAR GARAGE 21'4" x 29'10"

57'-2"

2 CAR GARAGE OPTION

◄63'-0►

Images provided by designer/architect.

Plan #101005

Dimensions: 63' W x 57'2" D

Levels: 1

Square Footage: 1,992

Bedrooms: 3

Bathrooms: 2½

Foundation: Crawl space, slab, or basement

Materials List Available: Yes

Price Category: D

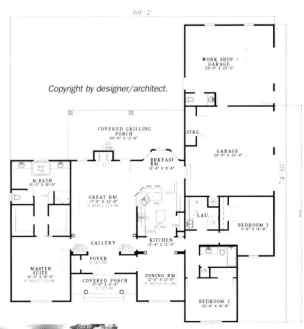

Rear View

Plan #151050

Dimensions: 69'2" W x 74'10" D

Levels: 1

Square Footage: 2,096

Bedrooms: 3

Bathrooms: 2½

Foundation: Crawl space, slab, or basement

Materials List Available: No

Price Category: D

Images provided by designer/architect.

69'-2"

WORK SHOP / GARAGE 23'-0" X 20'-0"

Copyright by designer/architect.

COVERED GRILLING PORCH 30'-6" X 12'-6"

STRG.

GARAGE 23'-0" X 22'-4"

74'-10"

M. BATH 15'-2" x 18'-0"

BRKFAST RM. 12'-4" X 9'-6"

GREAT RM. 17'-0" X 22'-8" 9' BOXED CEILING

KITCHEN 12'-4" X 12'-0"

LAU.

BEDROOM 3 11'-8" X 14'-4"

GALLERY

FOYER 9' CEILING

MASTER SUITE 15'-2" X 16'-0" 9' BOXED CEILING

COVERED PORCH 17'-0" X 5'-0" 9' CEILING

DINING RM. 12'-4" X 12'-0" 9' BOXED CEILING

BEDROOM 2 13'-4" X 10'-4"

Optional Front View

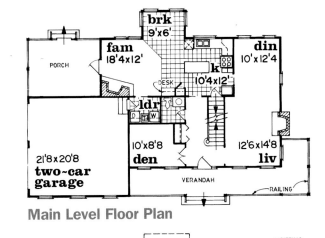

Main Level Floor Plan

Upper Level Floor Plan

Copyright by designer/architect.

Plan #401010

Dimensions: 62'6" W x 40' D

Levels: 2

Square Footage: 2,094

Main Level Sq. Ft.: 1,098

Upper Level Sq. Ft.: 996

Bedrooms: 4

Bathrooms: 2½

Foundation: Basement

Materials List Available: Yes

Price Category: D

Images provided by designer/architect.

Rear Elevation

Plan #371044

Dimensions: 57'4" W x 63'8" D

Levels: 1

Square Footage: 2,094

Bedrooms: 4

Bathrooms: 2 1/2

Foundation: Slab

Materials List Available: No

Price Category: D

Images provided by designer/architect.

Copyright by designer/architect.

Plan #151245

Dimensions: 35' W x 80'6" D
Levels: 1
Square Footage: 1,923
Bedrooms: 3
Bathrooms: 2
Foundation: Crawl space or slab
Materials List Available: No
Price Category: D

Images provided by designer/architect.

This brick home, with a stone-and-wood-sided front elevation, has great styling and offers three bedrooms.

Features:

- **Entry:** You enter the home though an arched covered entry foyer. On the left, French doors open to bedroom 3. Across the hall is bedroom 2, with a large walk-in closet.

- **Great Room:** This large gathering area, with a 10-ft. boxed ceiling, features a fireplace and access to the grilling porch.

- **Kitchen:** This kitchen boasts a snack bar and walk-in pantry and is open to the dining room.

- **Master Suite:** This private area has a 10-ft. boxed ceiling and ample closet storage. The master bath features a corner whirlpool tub with glass blocks, split vanities, and a corner shower.

Copyright by designer/architect.

Flooring Options

Selecting a flooring material is one of the most important decisions you will make when decorating a room. The right material can enhance the color scheme and the overall look of the room, and flooring provides a unique tactile component to the design.

If you are are acting as your own designer, one of the first things you should do is learn about the various types of flooring—from wood to stone to vinyl—on today's market. The choices are myriad and innovations in technology have widened the range of finishes.

Choices in Wood

In bygone eras, a wood floor was simply one that was created by laying wide wood planks side by side. Later, as the milling of lumber improved, homeowners were able to choose narrower planks that look more refined than rustic. Parquet floors were created by woodcrafters with a flair for the dramatic and an appreciation of the artistic richness of wood grains set in nonlinear patterns.

Today's manufacturers have made it possible to have it all. The wood floor, factory- or custom-stained to suit a particular style or mood in a room, is still a traditional favorite. It's readily available in strips of 1 to 2¼ inches wide, or in country-style planks of 3 to 8 inches wide. The formal, sophisticated look of a parquet floor is unparalleled for richness of visual texture.

Types of Wood Flooring
Wood varieties available as a surface material are vast, and cost varies widely, depending on the type and grade of wood and on the choice of design.

Softwoods, like pine and fir, are often used to make simple tongue-and-groove floorboards. These floors are less expen-

sive than hardwoods but also less durable. The hardwoods—maple, birch, oak, ash—are far less likely to mar with normal use. A hardwood floor is not indestructible; however, it will stand up to demanding use.

Both hardwoods and softwoods are graded according to their color, grain, and imperfections. The top of the line is known as clear, followed by select, No. 1 common, and No. 2 common. In addition to budget considerations, the decision whether to pay top dollar for clear wood or to economize with a lesser grade depends on use factors and on the design objectives. For example, if you plan to install a wood floor in a small room and then cover most of it with an area rug, the No. 2 common grade may be a good

choice; lesser grades are also fine for informal rooms where a few defects just enhance a lived-in look. If your design calls for larger areas of rich wood grain that will be exposed, with scatter rugs used for color accents, a clear or select grade will make an attractive choice.

Finishing Options
Color stains—reds, blues, and greens—may work in settings where a casual or rustic feeling is desired. This, however, is a departure from the traditional use of

Wood flooring, below, fits well in both formal and informal spaces.

Laminate flooring, opposite, can mimic the look of real wood or natural stone.

Laminate Flooring

Laminate flooring is the great pretender among flooring materials. When your creative side tells you to install wood but your practical side knows it just won't hold up in the traffic-heavy location for which you're considering it, a wood floor look-alike might be just the thing. Faux wood and faux stone laminate floors provide you with the look you want, tempered with physical wear and care properties that you and your family can live with. Laminate is particularly suited to rooms where floors are likely to see heavy duty—kitchens, family rooms, hallways, and children's bedrooms and playrooms—anywhere stain and scratch resistance and easy cleanup count. Prolonged exposure to moisture will damage some laminate products, but many can now be used in wet areas. Manufacturers of laminate offer warranties against staining, scratching, cracking, and peeling for up to 25 years.

Laminate is made from paper impregnated with melamine, an organic resin, and bonded to a core of particleboard, fiberboard, or other wood by-products. It can be laid over virtually any subflooring surface, including wood and concrete. It can also be applied on top of an existing wood, ceramic, or vinyl tile, as well as vinyl or other sheet flooring. You can even install it over certain types of carpeting, but check the manufacturer's guidelines before doing so.

Installation and Care

The installation of laminate flooring is a reasonably quick and relatively easy do-it-yourself project. It requires sheets of a special foam underlayment followed by the careful placement, cutting, and gluing of the laminate.

Laminate is available in sheets that are ideal when your design calls for a uniform look, such as monotone stone, or a linear design that mimics strip or plank wood flooring. Laminate planks, squares, and blocks offer added design flexibility: with them, you can design your own tile patterns, lay strips of wood-look planks with alternating "stain" finishes, or border your floor with a contrasting color.

wood. Wood is not typically used to deliver color impact; instead it blends with and subtly enhances its surroundings. Natural wood stains range from light ash tones to deep, coffee-like colors. Generally, lighter stains make a room feel less formal, and darker, richer stains suggest a stately atmosphere. As with lighter colors, lighter stains create a feeling of openness; darker stains foster a more intimate feeling and can reduce the visual vastness of a large space.

Installation

If the design plan calls for the laying of unfinished wood strips, factor the cost of hiring a skilled professional into your budget. Many manufacturers offer products with installation kits that make wood flooring a do-it-yourself option for those whose skills are good but don't necessarily approach a professional carpenter's level. Some make strips or planks already finished and sealed. Most parquet tiles come finished and sealed as well.

Vinyl Sheet & Tile Flooring

Like laminate, resilient flooring is also available in design-friendly sheet or tile form. Resilient floors can be made from a variety of materials, including linoleum, asphalt, cork, or rubber. However, the most commonly used material in manufacturing today's resilient floors for homes is vinyl.

Price, durability, and easy maintenance make resilient flooring an attractive and popular choice. Do-it-yourself installation, an option even for those who are not particularly skilled, can mean further savings.

Sheet versus Tiles
Resilient flooring comes in an enormous array of colors and patterns, plus many of the flooring styles have a textured surface. With the tiles, you can combine color and pattern in limitless ways. Even the sheet form of resilient flooring can be customized with inlay strips.

Cushioned sheet vinyl offers the most resilience. It provides excellent stain resistance; it's comfortable and quiet underfoot and easy to maintain, with no-wax and never-wax finishes often available. These features make the floor especially attractive for areas with lots of kid traffic. Beware though: only the more expensive grades show an acceptable degree of resistance to nicking and denting. In rooms where furniture is often moved around, this could be a problem. Although the range of colors, patterns, and surface textures is wide, sheet floor-

Vinyl sheet flooring, left, is a good choice for high-traffic areas, such as kitchens, family rooms, and playrooms. Most products have a no-wax finish that is easy to maintain.

Vinyl flooring, above, comes in a variety of styles and colors. Tiles and sheet flooring can look like ceramic tiles and natural stone.

Ceramic tile, opposite, offers a number of possibilities—from simple patterns to more elaborate designs that feature borders and inlays.

ing is not as flexible as vinyl tile when it comes to customizing your look.

Regular sheet vinyl is less expensive than the cushioned types, but it carries the same disadvantages and is slightly less resilient. Except for the availability of no-wax finishes, a vinyl tile floor is as stain resistant and as easy to maintain as the sheet-vinyl products. Increased design possibilities are the trade-off.

Here, as with other flooring materials, one possible way out of the choice maze is to take the unconventional step of mixing flooring materials. For example, use a durable cushioned sheet vinyl in more trafficked areas, but frame it with a pretty vinyl tile or laminate border.

Ceramic Choices

Ceramic tile—actually fired clay—is an excellent choice for areas subject to a lot of traffic and in rooms where resistance to moisture and stains is needed. These features, combined with easy cleanup, have made ceramic tile a centuries-old tradition for flooring, walls, and ceilings in bathrooms and kitchens. Color, texture, and pattern choices available today make ceramic tile the most versatile flooring option in terms of design possibilities.

Tile Options

Some handcrafted ceramic tiles are very costly, but manufacturers have created a market full of design and style options.

Tiles come in a variety of sizes, beginning with 1-inch-square mosaic tiles up to large 16 x 16-inch squares. Other shapes, such as triangles, diamonds, and rectangles, are also available. Tile textures range from shiny to matte-finished and from glass-smooth to ripple-surfaced. Tiles are available either glazed or unglazed. Glazed tiles have a hard, often colored, surface that is applied during the firing process; the resulting finish can range from glossy to matte. Unglazed tiles, such as terra-cotta or quarry tiles, have a matte finish, are porous, and need to be sealed to prevent staining.

Consider using accent borders to create unique designs, such as a faux area rug, that visually separate sections of a room or separate one room from another. When added in a random pattern, embossed accent tiles add interest, variety, and elegance to an expanse of single-colored tiles.

Alas, no surfacing material is perfect. Ceramic tile offers long-lasting beauty, design versatility, and simplicity of maintenance, but it also has some hard-to-live-with features. Tile is cold underfoot, noisy when someone walks across it in hard-soled shoes, and not at all resilient—always expect the worst when something breakable falls on a tile floor. If you have infants and toddlers around, it may be best to wait a few years for your tiled floor.

Natural Stone

Like ceramic tile, stone and marble are classified as "non-resilients." Like tile, these materials offer richness of color, durability, moisture and stain resistance, and ease of maintenance. They also share with tile the drawbacks of being cold to the touch, noisy to walk on, and unforgivingly hard.

Stone and marble floors are clearly, unmistakably natural. As remarkably good as some faux surfaces look, no product manufactured today actually matches the rustic irregularity and random color variation of natural stone.

Picking a Flooring Material

Now that you've got the facts about each floor surface option, picking the right one for your design will be much less confusing. The following steps can make it downright simple.

Step 1: Make a "Use/Abuse" Analysis. Begin by asking yourself the most important question: How will this room used? Your answer should tell you just what kind of traffic the future floor surface will endure. With a relatively expensive investment like a floor, it's best not to guess. Instead, use this system to arrive at an accurate use/abuse analysis.

On a piece of paper, make columns headed "Who" and "Activities," and then list who in the family will use the room and what activities will occur there. Will the kids play with toys on the floor? Will they do arts and crafts projects with paint, glue, and glitter? Will the family gather on Saturday afternoons and snack while watching a football game on television? Is it a formal living room where you will entertain your friends and business clients? Is it a busy kitchen? Does the hallway extend from your front entrance or from a busier back door where the kids will drop off their hockey skates?

The answers to these questions will help you to determine how durable and resilient a flooring surface needs to be, whether warmth and softness are requirements, and how much maintenance will be necessary to keep the surface clean.

Step 2: Determine Your Design Objectives. Your choices are limited by the other elements in the room. Your color choices can enhance the color palette you are planning. Because you will be starting from scratch—including walls, furniture, and accessories—you have more flexibility, although your job is a bit more complex and involves more decisions.

Once you've determined your design objectives, compare your use/abuse analysis

High-traffic areas, below left, require flooring that can stand up to abuse.

Laminate flooring, below right, is a good choice for a variety of rooms.

to the types of flooring that meet both your style and use needs. From the list of options that are left, you can narrow down your choices even more.

Step 3: Draw and Use a Floor Plan.

After you have completed the use/abuse analysis and the list of design objectives, draw up a floor plan—a separate one for experimenting with your flooring ideas. Follow these guidelines: measure the length and width of the room, and plot it on graph paper, using a scale of 1 inch to 1 foot. If your room is larger than 8 x 10 feet, you can tape two pieces of 8½- x 11-inch graph paper together. Measure and mark the locations of entryways and any permanent features in the room, such as cabinets, fixtures, or appliances.

Make several photocopies of your floor plan. Reserve one copy as a template. Use the other copies for previewing pattern ideas for flooring that comes in tiles (ceramic, vinyl, or carpeting tiles). Buy

multicolored pencils, and fill in your grid. You'll be able to determine not only how the pattern will look but also how many tiles of various colors you'll need to buy to complete the project. Don't forget to include such items as borders and inlays.

Step 4: Convert Your Overall Budget to Cost per Square Foot.

After you've completed the use/abuse analysis, determined your design objectives, and created a floor plan, the next step is determining cost.

Most flooring is priced in terms of square feet. To determine how many square feet are in your room, round the measurements up to the next foot. Then simply multiply the length by the width. For example, for a room measuring 10 feet 4 inches x 12 feet 6 inches, round the figures to 11 x 13 feet. Multiply 11 x 13 feet (that's 143 square feet). You will end up with extra flooring, but it is better to have more than less.

Some flooring—like carpeting—is priced in terms of square yards. To determine the number of square yards in your room, divide the number of square feet by nine. In our example, there are just under 16 square yards in 143 square feet.

Let's say you have a budget of $850 to purchase tile for your 10-foot-4-inch x 12-foot-6-inch room. For the sake of the illustration, let's assume your subflooring is adequate, you have the tools, and the cost of adhesive and grout for your room is about $75. That leaves you with $775. To determine how much you can spend per tile, divide the remainder by the number of square feet in the room. In our example, $775 divided by 143 square feet equals about $5.40 per square foot of tile.

Light colors, below left, make a room feel more open than darker colors.

Consider the rest of the room, below, when selecting flooring.

Plan #401038

Dimensions: 47' W x 48' D
Levels: 2
Square Footage: 2,142
Main Level Sq. Ft.: 1,092
Upper Level Sq. Ft.: 1,050
Bedrooms: 4
Bathrooms: 2½
Foundation: Basement
Materials List Available: Yes
Price Category: D

Images provided by designer/architect.

There is much to recommend this charming home. It begins with a quaint front porch opening to a raised foyer.

Features:

- **Living/Dining Room:** On the left side of the plan are this dining room with buffet space and living room with a tray ceiling and fireplace.

- **Kitchen:** This practical kitchen opens to the breakfast nook, which has double doors to the rear porch.

- **Family Room:** Open to the kitchen and breakfast nook to form one great gathering space, this room is warmed by a fireplace.

- **Utility Areas:** Access the two-car garage is through the laundry room and mudroom, near the half-bath at the entry.

- **Master Suite:** This area boasts a vaulted ceiling, a large walk-in closet, and a lavish full bathroom with twin vanities and a whirlpool spa.

- **Bedrooms:** Three additional bedrooms share a skylighted bathroom that includes a soaking tub.

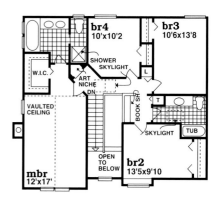

Upper Level Floor Plan

Main Level Floor Plan

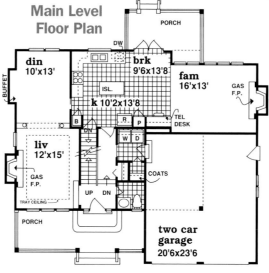

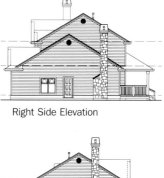

Right Side Elevation

Left Side Elevation

Rear Elevation

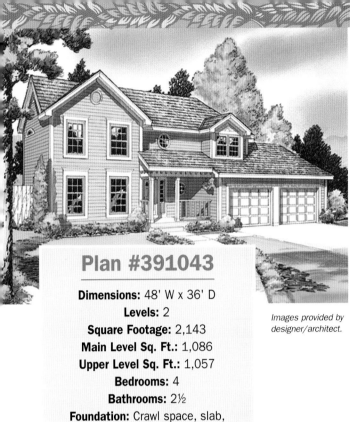

Main Level Floor Plan

48'-0"

36'-0"

Optional Deck

decor. ceiling

Dining Rm 11-6 x 13-4

Kitchen 10 x 11-8

Brkfst 8 x 11-8

9'-0" ceiling ht.

Hearth Rm 14 x 13-4

slope

Living Rm 14 x 15-4

D W

DN

pan

Foy UP

Garage 21-8 x 21-4

Images provided by designer/architect.

Br 2 10 x 10-6

Br 3 10-6 x 11

DN

MBr 1 14x 15-4 decor. ceiling

Br 4 10-10 x 11

open to below

Upper Level Floor Plan

Copyright by designer/architect.

Plan #391043

Dimensions: 48' W x 36' D

Levels: 2

Square Footage: 2,143

Main Level Sq. Ft.: 1,086

Upper Level Sq. Ft.: 1,057

Bedrooms: 4

Bathrooms: 2½

Foundation: Crawl space, slab, or basement

Materials List Available: Yes

Price Category: D

Plan #151206

Dimensions: 62'6" W x 62'4" D

Levels: 1

Square Footage: 2,151

Bedrooms: 3

Bathrooms: 2

Foundation: Crawl space or slab

Materials List Available: No

Price Category: D

Images provided by designer/architect.

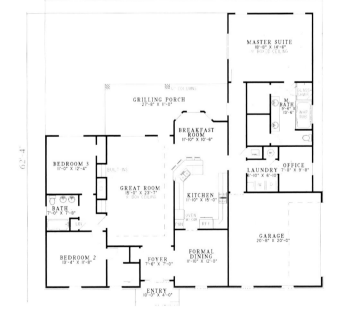

62'-6"

62'-4"

MASTER SUITE 18'-8" X 14'-6" W/ BOXED CEILING

GRILLING PORCH 27'-8" X 11'-6"

BREAKFAST ROOM 11'-10" X 10'-6"

M. BATH 9'-6" X 13'-6"

WHP TUB

BEDROOM 3 11'-0" X 12'-4"

BUILT-INS

GREAT ROOM 15'-0" X 23'-7" W/ BOX CEILING

KITCHEN 11'-0" X 15'-0"

OVEN

REF

LAUNDRY 6'-10" X 6'-10"

OFFICE 7'-8" X 9'-8"

BATH 7'-0" X 7'-8"

GARAGE 20'-8" X 20'-0"

BEDROOM 2 13'-4" X 11'-8"

FOYER 7'-6" X 7'-0"

FORMAL DINING 11'-10" X 12'-0"

ENTRY 10'-0" X 4'-0"

Copyright by designer/architect.

Plan #391012

Dimensions: 54' W x 46' D
Levels: 2
Square Footage: 2,157
Main Level Sq. Ft.: 1,590
Upper Level Sq. Ft.: 567
Bedrooms: 3
Bathrooms: 2½
Foundation: Crawl space, slab, or basement
Materials List Available: Yes
Price Category: D

This home, as shown in the photograph, may differ from the actual blueprints. For more detailed information, please check the floor plans carefully.

Images provided by designer/architect.

Creativity comes home to roost in this two-story ultra-comfortable abode, with its covered porch and welcoming entrance.

Features:

- Dining Room: Located on the opposite side of the kitchen, this room opens into formal living space that makes room for large-scale entertaining.

- Family and Breakfast Rooms: These rooms share a double-sided fireplace. An exterior deck draws folks outdoors. Laundry facilities and a powder room are tucked away neatly.

- Master Suite: This main-floor master suite features a tray ceiling, deep walk-in closet, and private bath with double sinks.

- Bedrooms: Upstairs along the open mezzanine, two secondary bedrooms nestle near a shared bath, and a loft-style media room with window overlooks the front of the house.

Rear View

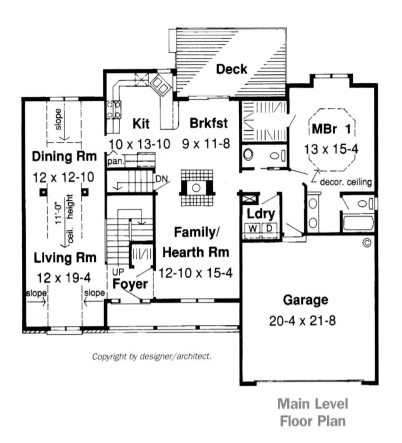

Dining Rm
12 x 12-10

Living Rm
12 x 19-4

Kit
10 x 13-10

Brkfst
9 x 11-8

Deck

MBr 1
13 x 15-4

decor. ceiling

Family/
Hearth Rm
12-10 x 15-4

Foyer

Ldry

Garage
20-4 x 21-8

Copyright by designer/architect.

**Main Level
Floor Plan**

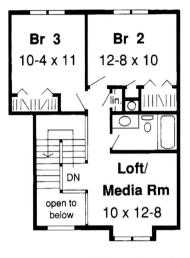

Br 3
10-4 x 11

Br 2
12-8 x 10

Loft/
Media Rm
10 x 12-8

open to
below

**Upper Level
Floor Plan**

Family Hearth Room/Kitchen

Living Room

Plan #371081

Dimensions: 54'6" W x 41'10" D

Levels: 2

Square Footage: 2,143

Main Level Sq. Ft.: 1,535

Upper Level Sq. Ft.: 608

Bedrooms: 4

Bathrooms: 3

Foundation: Slab or basement

Materials List Available: No

Price Category: D

The cozy wraparound front porch of this beautiful country home invites you to stay awhile.

Features:

- **Family Room:** This large gathering area features a wonderful fireplace and is open to the dining room.

- **Kitchen:** The island cabinet in this fully functional kitchen brings an open feel to this room and the adjoining dining room.

- **Master Suite:** Mom and Dad can relax downstairs in this spacious master suite, with their luxurious master bathroom, which has double walk-in closets and a marble tub.

- **Bedrooms:** The kids will enjoy these two large secondary bedrooms and the study area with bookcases upstairs.

Rear Elevation

Upper Level Floor Plan

Main Level Floor Plan

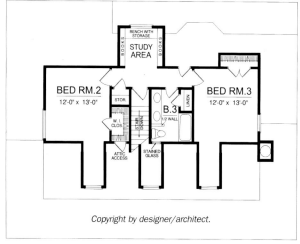

Copyright by designer/architect.

Plan #401028

Dimensions: 25'6" W x 54'9" D
Levels: 2
Square Footage: 2,219
Main Level Sq. Ft.: 1,136
Upper Level Sq. Ft.: 1,083
Bedrooms: 4
Bathrooms: 2½
Foundation: Basement
Materials List Available: Yes
Price Category: E

This inviting narrow-lot design borrows classic details from a bygone era—a covered veranda in the front, a gabled roof, and fish-scale detailing. Ideal for city lots, this design features four bedrooms

Features:

- Living Room: Located on the first floor with a gas fireplace, this formal room opens to a dining room.

- Kitchen: Toward the rear of the home, this kitchen overlooks a breakfast nook

- Family Room: A second gas fireplace warms this cozy area.

- Master Suite: This area has a walk-in closet and a private bath that includes a separate tub and shower and double vanities.

- Bedroom: A box window graces one of the family bedrooms.

Images provided by designer/architect.

Optional Main Level Floor Plan

Main Level Floor Plan

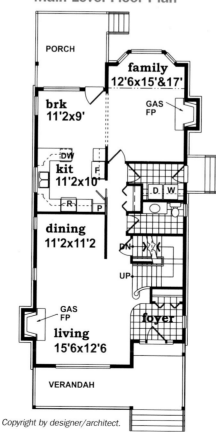

Copyright by designer/architect.

Upper Level Floor Plan

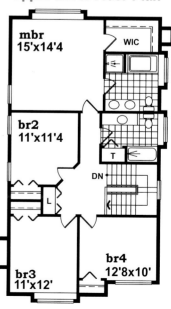

Plan #161016

Dimensions: 59'4" W x 58'8" D
Levels: 2
Square Footage: 2,101
Main Level Sq. Ft.: 1,626
Upper Level Sq. Ft.: 475
Bedrooms: 3
Bathrooms: 2½
Foundation: Basement, optional crawl space available for extra fee
Materials List Available: Yes
Price Category: D

Images provided by designer/architect.

Upper Level Floor Plan

Main Level Floor Plan

Copyright by designer/architect.

Plan #151004

Dimensions: 64'8" W x 62'1" D
Levels: 1
Square Footage: 2,107
Bedrooms: 4
Bathrooms: 2½
Foundation: Crawl space, slab, or basement
Materials List Available: No
Price Category: D

Images provided by designer/architect.

Copyright by designer/architect.

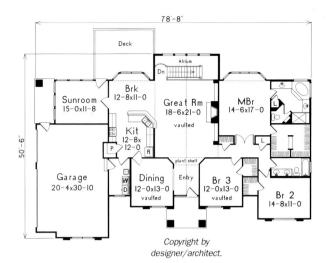

Copyright by
designer/architect.

Plan #321037

Dimensions: 78'8" W x 50'6" D

Levels: 1

Square Footage: 2,397

Bedrooms: 3

Bathrooms: 2

Foundation: Basement or walkout

Materials List Available: Yes

Price Category: E

*Images provided by
designer/architect.*

**Optional
Basement Level
Floor Plan**

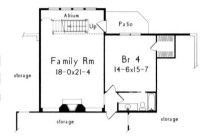

Plan #151034

Dimensions: 58'6" W x 64'6" D

Levels: 1

Square Footage: 2,133

Bedrooms: 3

Bathrooms: 2

Foundation: Crawl space, slab,
or basement

Materials List Available: No

Price Category: D

*Images provided by
designer/architect.*

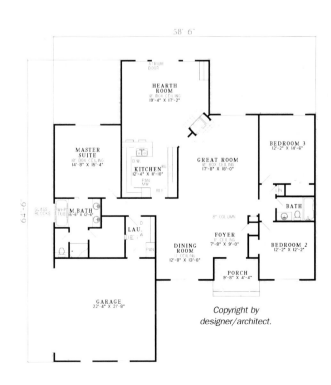

Copyright by
designer/architect.

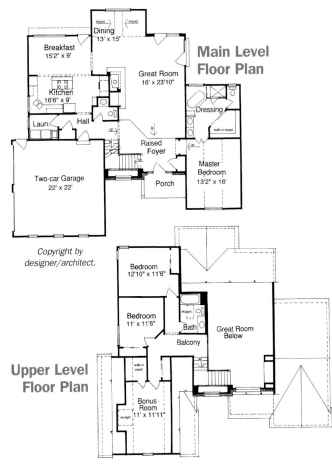

Main Level Floor Plan

Dining 13' x 15'

Breakfast 15'2" x 9'

Great Room 16' x 23'10"

Kitchen 16'6" x 9'

Dressing

Laun.

Hall

walk-in closet

up

Two-car Garage 22' x 22'

Raised Foyer

up

Master Bedroom 13'2" x 16'

Porch

Copyright by designer/architect.

Images provided by designer/architect.

Plan #161034

Dimensions: 56' W x 53' D

Levels: 2

Square Footage: 2,156

Main Level Sq. Ft.: 1,605

Upper Level Sq. Ft.: 551

Bedrooms: 3

Bathrooms: 2½

Foundation: Basement

Materials List Available: No

Price Category: D

Bedroom 12'10" x 11'6"

Bedroom 11' x 11'6"

Bath

skylight

Balcony

Great Room Below

walk-in closet

Bonus Room 11' x 11'11"

skylight

Upper Level Floor Plan

Plan #211006

Dimensions: 61' W x 77' D

Levels: 1

Square Footage: 2,177

Bedrooms: 3

Bathrooms: 2

Foundation: Crawl space or slab

Materials List Available: Yes

Price Category: D

Images provided by designer/architect.

SMARTtip

DECK Furniture Style

Mix-and-match tabletops, frames, and legs are stylish. Combine materials such as glass, metal, wood, and mosaic tiles.

shv

mbr 18 x 12

shr

sitting 11 x 10

shv

lin

porch 29 x 6

eating 11 x 10

br 3 12 x 12

living 21 x 17

bar

kit 13 x 12

bar

desk shv

shv

lin

sto 10x7

ov

dw

frz

d w

foy

r/a

utii

sto

dining 15 x 12

por 11x5

br 2 15 x 12

garage 22 x 22

Copyright by designer/architect.

**Main Level
Floor Plan**

Plan #181151

Dimensions: 50' W x 46' D

Levels: 2

Square Footage: 2,283

Main Level Sq. Ft.: 1,274

Second Level Sq. Ft.: 1,009

Bedrooms: 3

Bathrooms: 2½

Foundation: Basement

Materials List Available: Yes

Price Category: E

*Images provided by
designer/architect.*

**Upper Level
Floor Plan**

*Copyright by
designer/architect.*

**Upper Level
Floor Plan**

Plan #181239

Dimensions: 37' W x 38' D

Levels: 2

Square Footage: 2,181

Main Level Sq. Ft.: 1,307

Upper Level Sq. Ft.: 874

Bedrooms: 4

Bathrooms: 2½

Foundation: Basement

Materials List Available: Yes

Price Category: D

*Images provided by
designer/architect.*

**Main Level
Floor Plan**

*Copyright by
designer/architect.*

Plan #391017

Dimensions: 77' W x 41'6" D
Levels: 2
Square Footage: 2,176
Main Level Sq. Ft.: 1,671
Upper Level Sq. Ft.: 505
Bedrooms: 3
Bathrooms: 2½
Foundation: Crawl space, slab, or basement
Materials List Available: Yes
Price Category: D

Quaint, complex pitched rooflines and long, light-filled windows make this house a proper Tudor-style home befitting today's lifestyles.

Features:

• Entry: This formal entry, with its double doors, opens on a sophisticated library on one side and a formal dining room on the other.

• Living Room: This living room is central to the layout, inviting folks to gather at the fireplace, hang out on the screened porch, join the hustle bustle in the kitchen, or take meals to the outdoor patio.

Images provided by designer/architect.

• Master Suite: This master suite, with its special ceiling and dreamy full bath (tub tucked beneath a corner of windows, plus a separate shower) enjoys main-floor access to the library and a front yard view.

• Bedrooms: Upstairs, a lavishly long hallway delivers two dramatic-looking bedrooms, built around a spacious bathroom. One bed room with picture window also features an expansive closet (cedar treatment optional). Another bedroom with wall-length closet enjoys a backyard view.

Rear View

Main Level Floor Plan

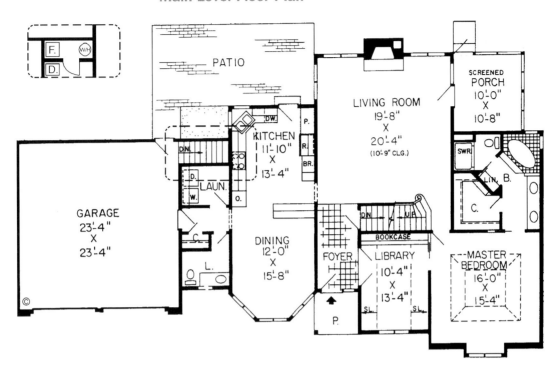

F.
D.
W/H

PATIO

LIVING ROOM
19'-8"
X
20'-4"
(10'-9" CLG.)

SCREENED
PORCH
10'-0"
X
10'-8"

KITCHEN
11'-10"
X
13'-4"

DW.
P.
R.
BR.

SWR

DN.

D.
W.
LAUN.
O.

LIN. B.

C.

GARAGE
23'-4"
X
23'-4"

C.

DINING
12'-0"
X
15'-8"

DN
W.I.R.

BOOKCASE

FOYER

LIBRARY
10'-4"
X
13'-4"

MASTER
BEDROOM
16'-0"
X
15'-4"

L.

SL
SL

P.

kitchen

Upper Level Floor Plan

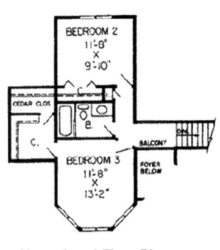

BEDROOM 2
11'-8"
X
9'-10"

CEDAR CLOS.

C.

B.

C.

BEDROOM 3
11'-8"
X
13'-2"

BALCONY

DN

FOYER
BELOW

Copyright by designer/architect.

Main Level Floor Plan

Three Car Garage
23'9" x 32'4"

Master Bedroom
15' x 15'

Porch

Breakfast
11'2" x 12'10"

Great Room
17' x 25'

Bath

Kitchen
11'2" x 11'6"

Bath

Laun.
8'6" x 7'6"

Bedroom
13' x 11'

Dining Room or Study
11'2" x 11'

Foyer

Bedroom
12'9" x 13'

Porch

First Floor Plan

80'-0"

74'-0"

Upper Level Floor Plan

Copyright by designer/architect.

Bonus Room
15' x 15'

Great Room Below

Kitchen Below

Plan #161072

Dimensions: 80' W x 74' D

Levels: 1

Square Footage: 2,183

Bedrooms: 3

Bathrooms: 3

Foundation: Basement

Materials List Available: Yes

Price Category: D

Images provided by designer/architect.

Plan #401042

Dimensions: 47' W x 48' D

Levels: 2

Square Footage: 2,239

Main Level Sq. Ft.: 1,092

Upper Level Sq. Ft.: 1,147

Bedrooms: 4

Bathrooms: 2½

Foundation: Basement

Materials List Available: Yes

Price Category: E

Images provided by designer/architect.

Main Level Floor Plan

din
10'x13'

brk
9'6"x13'8

fam
16'x13'

k 10'2x13'6

liv
12'x15'

UP ENTRY

garage
20'6x23'6

PORCH

Rear Elevation

Upper Level Floor Plan

Copyright by designer/architect.

br4
10'x10'2

br3
10'6x13'8

W.I.C.

mbr
12'x17'
VAULTED

COMPUTER CENTER

br2
13'5x11'10

Plan #371059

Dimensions: 77'8" W x 56'6" D

Levels: 1

Square Footage: 2,240

Bedrooms: 4

Bathrooms: 2½

Foundation: Slab

Materials List Available: No

Price Category: E

This beautiful brick home achieves one-of-a-kind styling with a unique roofline.

Features:

- **Dining Room:** Once inside you will find a tiled entry that steps into this elegant room with an 11-ft.-high ceiling.

- **Living Room:** This large gathering area has an 11-ft.-high ceiling, built-in bookcases, and a grand fireplace.

- **Kitchen:** This kitchen is open to the breakfast nook and meets the garage entrance.

- **Master Suite:** This suite, with stepped-up ceiling, features a private bathroom with his and her walk-in closets and double vanities.

- **Bedrooms:** Three secondary bedrooms have large closets and share a hall bathroom.

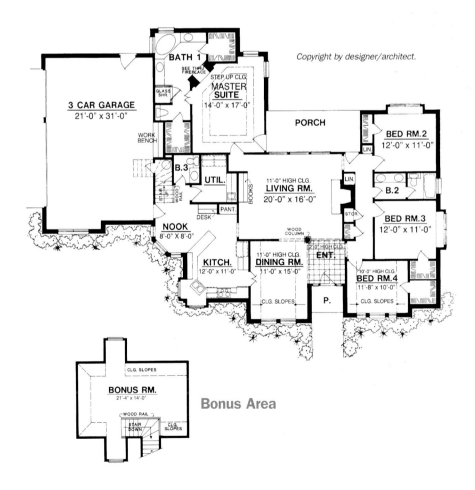

Bonus Area

Plan #371045

Dimensions: 56' W x 57'7" D
Levels: 2
Square Footage: 2,225
Main Level Sq. Ft.: 1,678
Upper Level Sq. Ft.: 547
Bedrooms: 3
Bathrooms: 2½
Foundation: Slab
Materials List Available: No
Price Category: E

Images provided by designer/architect.

With its spectacular brick gables and stunning windows, this French-style home will treat you to the lifestyle you deserve.

Features:

- **Living Room:** A 10-ft.-high ceiling, warm two-way fireplace, and generous windows give this large living room a touch of class.
- **Family Room:** French doors that provide access to the rear porch, a two-way fireplace with bookshelves on both sides, and a 10-ft.-high ceiling combine to create a warm and relaxing room the whole family will enjoy.
- **Dining Room:** This formal room has a 10-ft.-high ceiling and is open to the living room.
- **Kitchen:** In addition to easy access to the dining room, breakfast nook, and family room, this kitchen has a walk-in pantry and large central island.
- **Master Suite:** This large secluded retreat boasts an elegant bath with a marble tub and his and her walk-in closets.
- **Bedrooms:** Upstairs are two additional bedrooms with walk-in closets, and they share a hall bathroom with a dressing room.

Main Level Floor Plan

Upper Level Floor Plan

Copyright by designer/architect.

Plan #391023

Dimensions: 41'4" W x 47'4" D
Levels: 2
Square Footage: 2,244
Main Level Sq. Ft.: 1,115
Upper Level Sq. Ft.: 1,129
Bedrooms: 4
Bathrooms: 2½
Foundation: Crawl space, slab, or basement
Materials List Available: Yes
Price Category: E

Images provided by designer/architect.

This great four-bedroom home is perfect for your neighborhood.

Features:

• Living Room: Step down from the entry to this vaulted-ceiling gathering area.

• Dining Room: This special area has a 9-ft.-high ceiling and is open to the living room.

• Family Room: This casual, relaxing area has a fireplace and a sliding glass door to the patio.

• Master Suite: This oasis has a vaulted ceiling, his and her closets, and a private master bath.

• Bedrooms: The two secondary bedrooms share a hall bathroom. The loft can be converted to a fourth bedroom.

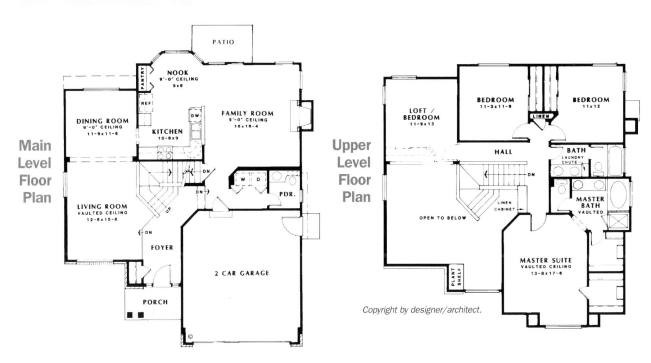

Main Level Floor Plan

Upper Level Floor Plan

Copyright by designer/architect.

Plan #401029

Dimensions: 37'6" W x 48'4" D
Levels: 2
Square Footage: 2,163
Main Level Sq. Ft.: 832
Upper Level Sq. Ft.: 1,331
Bedrooms: 3
Bathrooms: 2½
Foundation: Basement
Materials List Available: Yes
Price Category: D

Images provided by designer/architect.

This two-level plan has a bonus—a roof deck with hot tub! A variety of additional outdoor spaces makes this one wonderful plan.

Features:

- First Level: Family bedrooms, a full bath room, and a cozy den are on the first level, along with a two-car garage.

- Living Area: The living spaces are on the second floor and include a living/dining room combination with a deck and fireplace. The dining room has buffet space.

- Family Room: Featuring a fireplace and a built-in entertainment center, the gathering area is open to the breakfast room and sky lighted kitchen.

- Master Bedroom: This room features a private bath with a whirlpool tub and two-person shower, a walk-in closet, and access to still another deck.

Master Bathroom

Rear View

Rear Elevation

Upper Level Floor Plan

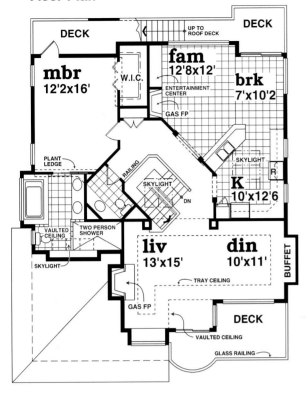

DECK

DECK

UP TO ROOF DECK

mbr
12'2x16'

W.I.C.

fam
12'8x12'

brk
7'x10'2

ENTERTAINMENT CENTER

GAS FP

PLANT LEDGE

RAILING

SKYLIGHT

SKYLIGHT

K
10'x12'6

R

DN

VAULTED CEILING

TWO PERSON SHOWER

SKYLIGHT

liv
13'x15'

din
10'x11'

BUFFET

TRAY CEILING

GAS FP

DECK

VAULTED CEILING

GLASS RAILING

Copyright by designer/architect.

Main Level Floor Plan

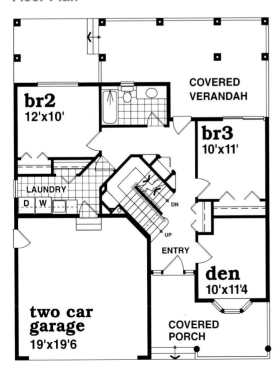

br2
12'x10'

COVERED VERANDAH

br3
10'x11'

LAUNDRY

D W

DN

UP

ENTRY

den
10'x11'4

two car garage
19'x19'6

COVERED PORCH

Dining Room/Kitchen

Family Room

Living Room

Plan #371023

Dimensions: 58'6" W x 49' D
Levels: 2
Square Footage: 2,444
Main Level Sq. Ft.: 1,524
Upper Level Sq. Ft.: 920
Bedrooms: 4
Bathrooms: 2½
Foundation: Slab
Materials List Available: No
Price Category: E

Images provided by designer/architect.

This stunning brick home, which has something for everyone, will be the envy of the neighborhood.

Features:

- Living Room: This large entertainment area has a sloped ceiling, media center and a cozy fireplace.

- Dining Room: You'll find wooden columns in this elegant formal room.

- Kitchen: With a raised bar and a walk-in pantry, this area is open to a cozy breakfast nook.

- Master Suite: This area is secluded downstairs with a luxurious master bathroom with two walk-in closets.

- Bedrooms: Upstairs are three additional bedrooms with walk-in closets; they share a convenient hall bathroom.

Main Level Floor Plan

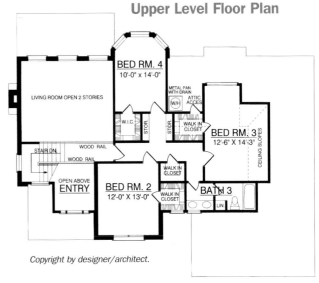

Upper Level Floor Plan

Copyright by designer/architect.

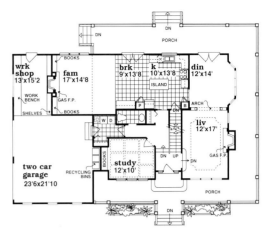

Main Level Floor Plan

PORCH

DN | DN

wrk shop 13'x15'2 | fam 17'x14'8 | brk 9'x13'8 | k 10'x13'8 | din 12'x14'

WORK BENCH | GAS F.P. | ISLAND

BOOKS | SHELVES | BOOKS

ARCH | liv 12'x17'

two car garage 23'6x21'10 | RECYCLING BINS | BOOKS | study 12'x10' | DN UP | GAS F.P.

PORCH

Images provided by designer/architect.

Upper Level Floor Plan

Copyright by designer/architect.

br3 10'x13'8 | br4 10'x10'2

ART NICHE | W.I.C.

SKYLIGHT | DN

SKYLIGHT | OPEN TO BELOW | VAULTED CEILING

W.I.C. | br2 12'x11'4 | mbr 12'x17'

Plan #401039

Dimensions: 69'8" W x 49' D
Levels: 2
Square Footage: 2,462
Main Level Sq. Ft.: 1,333
Upper Level Sq. Ft.: 1,129
Bedrooms: 4
Bathrooms: 2½
Foundation: Basement
Materials List Available: Yes
Price Category: E

Images provided by designer/architect.

Upper Level Floor Plan

Br 3 11 x 11 | skylt 10'-0" clg. ht.

Balcony | DN

Br 2 13-6 x 11 | MBr 1 21 x 15-6

slope | foyer below | Sitting Area 15 x 7-8

Deck

Breakfast Area | Kit 11-10 x 11 | Den / Office Br 4 12-4 x 13-4

Hearth Rm 18-4 x 13-4

Dining Rm 13 x 13-8 | DN | L'dry

1-1/2" clg. reveal | Garage 21-4 x 21-4

Living Rm 13 x 15-4 | UP Foyer

Main Level Floor Plan

Copyright by designer/architect.

Plan #391011

Dimensions: 46' W x 45' D
Levels: 2
Square Footage: 2,483
Main Level Sq. Ft.: 1,361
Upper Level Sq. Ft.: 1,122
Bedrooms: 4
Bathrooms: 2½
Foundation: Crawl space, slab, or basement
Materials List Available: Yes
Price Category: E

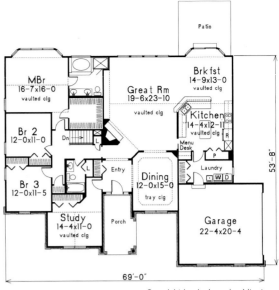

Images provided by designer/architect.

Copyright by designer/architect.

Plan #321005

Dimensions: 69' W x 53'8" D
Levels: 1
Square Footage: 2,483
Bedrooms: 3
Bathrooms: 2
Foundation: Basement
Materials List Available: Yes
Price Category: E

SMARTtip

Art in Pools

The tiled walls and floor of a pool make great canvases for art, so incorporate a serious or whimsical design. Also, make the stairs wide and shallow to form a wading area for kids.

Main Level Floor Plan

Upper Level Floor Plan

Images provided by designer/architect.

Copyright by designer/architect.

Plan #121074

Dimensions: 68'8" W x 47'8" D
Levels: 2
Square Footage: 2,486
Main Level Sq. Ft.: 1,829
Upper Level Sq. Ft.: 657
Bedrooms: 4
Bathrooms: 2½
Foundation: Basement
Materials List Available: Yes
Price Category: E

Plan #401013

Dimensions: 62' W x 47' D

Levels: 2

Square Footage: 2,381

Main Level Sq. Ft.: 1,193

Upper Level Sq. Ft.: 1,188

Bedrooms: 4

Bathrooms: 2½

Foundation: Basement

Materials List Available: Yes

Price Category: E

Images provided by designer/architect.

Graced by a wraparound veranda, multi-paned shutters, and decorative wood trim, this four-bedroom design is as attractive as it is comfortable. Large bay windows and high ceilings throughout the first level further enhance the charm.

Features:

• Living Room: This room features a masonry fireplace and extends to the bayed dining area.

• Kitchen: Eating or serving areas on the counter and the center food-preparation island make easy work of mealtimes here.

• Second Floor: Features on this floor include the bayed master suite and three additional family bedrooms.

Rear Elevation

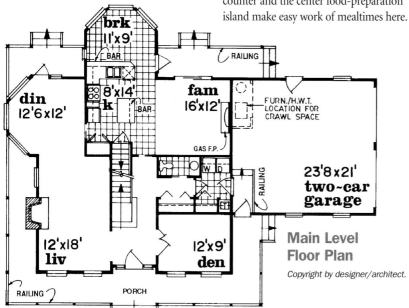

Main Level Floor Plan

Copyright by designer/architect.

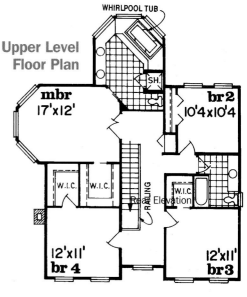

Upper Level Floor Plan

Plan #161074

Dimensions: 59'4" W x 67'10" D
Levels: 2
Square Footage: 2,427
Main Level Sq. Ft.: 1,949
Upper Level Sq. Ft.: 478
Bedrooms: 4
Bathrooms: 3½
Foundation: Basement
Materials List Available: No
Price Category: E

Images provided by designer/architect.

Brick, stone, and multiple gables decorate the exterior of this exciting home, creating curb appeal extraordinaire.

Features:

• Foyer: Along with an elegantly turned staircase, this entryway provides a view through the great room to a wall of windows on the rear wall.

• Master Suite: This suite will pamper you with a sloped ceiling, angled walls, and luxurious bathroom.

• Private Suite: A second bedroom on the first floor provides a suite for overnight guests.

• Second Floor: On the second floor a balcony overlooks the great room and foyer and leads to two additional bedrooms.

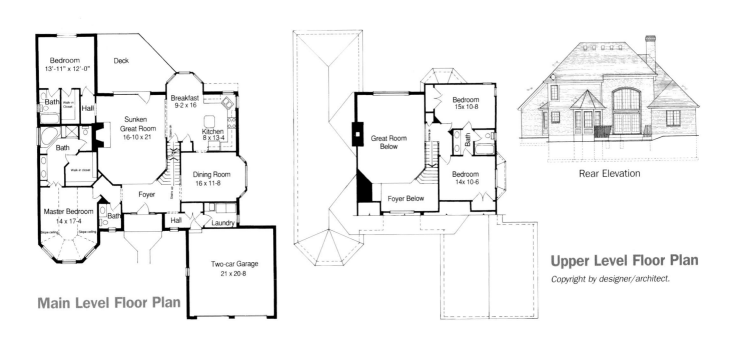

Main Level Floor Plan

Upper Level Floor Plan

Copyright by designer/architect.

Rear Elevation

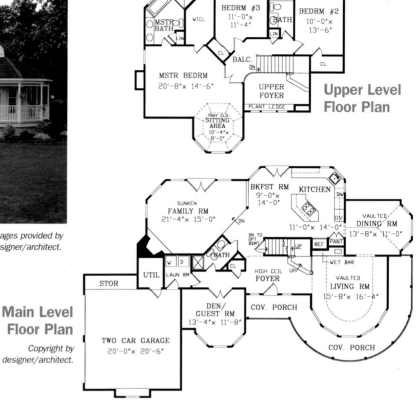

Upper Level Floor Plan

BEDRM #3
11'-0" x 11'-4"

BEDRM #2
10'-0" x 13'-6"

MSTR BATH

WICL

BATH

LIN

CL

LIN

BALC.

CL

MSTR BEDRM
20'-8" x 14'-6"

DN

UPPER FOYER

PLANT LEDGE

TRAY CLG.
SITTING AREA
10'-4" x 8'-0"

Plan #131032

Dimensions: 69'2" W x 46' D

Levels: 2

Square Footage: 2,455

Main Level Sq. Ft.: 1,499

Upper Level Sq. Ft.: 956

Bedrooms: 4

Bathrooms: 3

Foundation: Crawl space, slab, or basement

Materials List Available: Yes

Price Category: F

Images provided by designer/architect.

Main Level Floor Plan

Copyright by designer/architect.

BKFST RM
9'-0" x 14'-0"

KITCHEN
11'-0" x 14'-0"

DW

OV

SUNKEN
FAMILY RM
21'-4" x 15'-0"

DN

VAULTED
DINING RM
13'-8" x 11'-0"

DN TO OPT BSMT

UP

REF

PANT

WET BAR

BATH

W D

CL

HIGH CEIL
FOYER

UP

VAULTED
LIVING RM
15'-8" x 16'-4"

STOR

UTIL

LAUN RM

DEN/
GUEST RM
13'-4" x 11'-8"

COV. PORCH

TWO CAR GARAGE
20'-0" x 20'-6"

COV. PORCH

Plan #101012

Dimensions: 69'4" W x 62'9" D

Levels: 1

Square Footage: 2,288

Bedrooms: 3

Bathrooms: 2½

Foundation: Slab, crawl space, basement, or walkout

Materials List Available: No

Price Category: E

Images provided by designer/architect.

DECK
19'-8" x 15'-0"

DINING
15'10" x 11'-0"

VAULTS TO 13'5" PEAK

HEARTH ROOM
16'-7" x 13'-0"

12'-HIGH CEILING TV NICHE

13' HIGH CEILING

12' HIGH TRAY CEILING
UP 1'
UP 1'
14' HIGH

14' HIGH CEILING

MASTER BDRM
16'-0" x 15'-0"

HERS

HIS

FAMILY ROOM
16'-0" x 19'-0"

KITCHEN
16'-0" x 13'-0"

BRKFST
10'-0" x 10'-6"

PANTRY

LINEN

STAIRS TO BONUS ROOM

ENTRY
12' HIGH CEILING

UP

DN

62'-9"

BEDROOM 2
11'-0" x 14'-0"

13' HIGH CEILING

BEDROOM 3
11'-0" x 14'-0"

PORCH
12' HIGH CEILING

STAIRS TO BASEMENT

GARAGE
21'-0" x 23'-0"

BONUS ROOM ABOVE

69'-4"

Copyright by designer/architect.

Today's Fireplace Technology

Handsome and romantic, but drafty. Thirty years ago, you might have described a traditional fireplace in this way. But that was before technological advancements finally made fireplaces more efficient. Now, not only can you expect your fireplace to provide ambiance and warmth, you can relax knowing that your energy dollars aren't going up in smoke. Over the centuries, people had tried to improve the efficiency of the fireplace so that it would generate the maximum heat possible from the wood consumed. But real strides didn't come until the energy crisis of the early 1970s. That's when designers of fireplaces and stoves introduced some significant innovations. Today, fireplaces are not only more efficient, but cleaner and easier to use.

The traditional fireplace is an all-masonry construction, consisting of only bricks and mortar. However, new constructions and reconstructions of masonry fireplaces often include either a metal or a ceramic firebox. This type of firebox has double walls. The space between these walls is where cool air heats up after being drawn in through openings near the floor of the room. The warm air exits through openings near the top of the firebox. Although a metal firebox is more efficient than an all-masonry firebox, it doesn't radiate heat very effectively, and the heat from the fireplace is distributed by convection—that is, the circulation of warmed air. This im–provement in heating capacity comes from the warm air emitted by the upper openings. But that doesn't keep your feet toasty on a cold winter's night—remember, warm air rises.

A more recent development is the ceramic firebox, which is engineered from modern materials such as the type used in kilns. Fires in ceramic fireboxes burn hotter, cleaner, and more efficiently than in all-masonry or metal fireboxes. The main reason is that the back and the walls of a ceramic firebox absorb, retain, and reflect heat effectively. This means that during the time the fire is blazing, more heat radiates into the room than with the other fireboxes. Heat radiation is boosted by the fact that most ceramic units are made with

The warm glow of a realistic-looking modern zero-clearance gas fire, below, can make the hearth the heart of any room in the house.

Zero-Clearance Fireplace

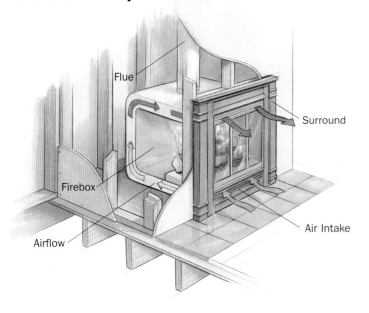

Flue

Surround

Firebox

Air Intake

Airflow

Traditional Masonry Fireplace

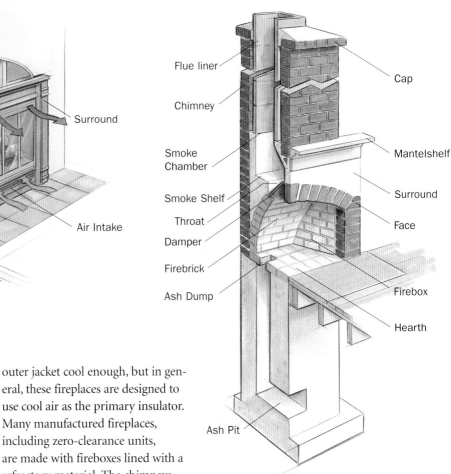

Flue liner

Chimney

Smoke Chamber

Smoke Shelf

Throat

Damper

Firebrick

Ash Dump

Ash Pit

Cap

Mantelshelf

Surround

Face

Firebox

Hearth

thick walls, and so the fire itself is not set as deeply into the hearth as it is with all-masonry or metal fireboxes. As a bonus, because heat is absorbed and retained by the material, the firebox actually radiates a significant amount of heat many hours after the fire has died down. By contrast, a metal firebox cools quickly once the heat source goes out.

In this type of efficient fireplace construction, a metal firebox is usually less expensive than a ceramic one, but the metal does break down over time, in a process professionals refer to as burnout. In addition, an air-circulating metal firebox can only be installed in masonry constructions that are built with ports for the intake of cool air and the discharge of warmed air, or in masonry fireplaces in which such ports can be added. On the other hand, ceramic fireboxes can be installed in any type of masonry fireplace and are not subject to burnout.

Manufactured Fireplaces

The metal fireplaces that are made today can be zero-clearance or freestanding. The zero-clearance units are so named because they can be installed safely against combustible surfaces such as wood. Any of a number of methods are used to keep the

outer jacket cool enough, but in general, these fireplaces are designed to use cool air as the primary insulator. Many manufactured fireplaces, including zero-clearance units, are made with fireboxes lined with a refractory material. The chimneys are also made of metal, and a variety of designs use noncombustible material or air as insulation to keep the outer surface at a safe temperature.

New-technology and traditional fireplaces are shown above. Woodstove-like inserts, below and opposite, make fireplaces more efficient.

The Advantages of a Manufactured Unit

There are some important pluses to choosing a zero-clearance manufactured fireplace. First is the price, which is relatively low, and second is the easy and quick installation. Also, these units are lightweight and can be installed over almost any type of flooring, including wood. This means they do not need elaborate foundations, which is another cost-saver. Manufactured fireplaces are also extremely efficient, and many are designed to provide both radiated heat from the firebox and convection heat from ducting.

Manufactured freestanding fireplaces are, in effect, stoves. They are available in an array of colors, finishes, shapes, and sizes. Like zero-clearance factory-built fireplaces, freestanding models are lightweight, offering the same advantages: no need for heavy masonry or additional reinforcement of flooring. And you have a choice of either a wood-burning or gas-powered unit. Heat efficiency is maximized because, in addition to the firebox, the chimney and all sides of the unit radiate heat into the room. Freestanding units may be the least expensive option because installation requires only a chimney hole and, depending on the type of flooring, a noncombustible pad. A major disadvantage is the space required for placement, because you cannot install most of these units near a combustible wall. Also, a freestanding fireplace is probably not the best choice for families with young children because so much heat is radiated from the exposed surfaces.

Hybrids

If you're looking for a way to get improved efficiency from a masonry fireplace, consider a gas insert (actually a prefabricated firebox equipped with gas logs). You can purchase either a venting insert or one that's nonventing. But be prepared to pay $1,500 to several thousand dollars for the unit in addition to the cost of installation. For a fraction of that amount you can simply replace real wood logs with ceramic logs powered by gas. Like inserts, these logs may or may not require venting. Consult an experienced plumber or heating contractor, and remember that once you convert to gas you cannot burn wood.

Improving a masonry fireplace on the inside by installing a metal firebox might also be an inspiration to think of the fireplace and mantel in a new design way. Pairing two or more finishing materials, such as metal and masonry, can make your fireplace a hybrid in more than one way. For example, combine a stone base with a metal hood and chimney to create a custom-designed fireplace that works as a room divider in a large space. The design options in terms of materials and technology are seemingly endless.

If you have plans for building an innovative custom design, carefully review them with an expert in fireplace construction and maintenance to make sure you're not doing something hazardous. Also, don't forget to check with your local building inspector so that you don't waste time and money on a project that may not comply with codes and regulations set forth where you live.

Enhancing the Basics

You can improve the efficiency of any manufactured fireplace, and of masonry and hybrid constructions as well, with a few extras. In a masonry fireplace, a device commonly referred to as a fresh-air intake accessory or an outside air kit may improve performance. A fresh-air accessory makes use of outside air instead of heated room air for combustion, thus improving the fireplace's efficiency. There is another way to make your fireplace more efficient that isn't high tech at all, however. Simply replace the traditional grate or firebasket with a superior design—one that provides greater air circulation and allows a better placement of logs. Another type, a heat-exchanger grate, works with a fan. The device draws in the room's air, reheats it quickly, and then forces it back into the room.

Capitalizing on Technology

Wood is the traditional fuel for a fireplace, and today's manufactured fireplaces offer designs that make the most of your cord of hardwood. However, wood is not the only fuel option. In fact, in some places, it's not an option at all. There are manufactured units that offer a choice of natural gas or propane as a fuel source, which heats ceramic logs designed to realistically simulate wood. The fire, complete with glowing embers, is often difficult to distinguish from one burning real wood.

In some areas of the country, fireplace emission regulations have become strict—in places such as much of Colorado and parts of Nevada and California so strict that new construction of wood-burning fireplaces has been outlawed. In these areas, manufactured units using alternative fuels allow homeowners all the benefits of a wood-burning fireplace without the adverse impact on air quality.

Most of the units available today also offer a variety of amenities, including built-in thermostatic control and remote-control devices for turning the fire on and off and regulating heat output.

The Importance of a Clean Sweep

Finally, one of the most important factors in the use of a fireplace or stove is the regular inspection and cleaning of the stovepipe, flue, and chimney. To understand why, remember that the burning of wood results in the combustion of solids as well as combustible gases. However, not everything that goes into the firebox is burned, no matter how efficient the appliance. One of the by-products of wood burning is the dark brown or black tar called creosote, a flammable substance that sticks to the linings of chimney flues.

Although the burning temperature of creosote is high, it can ignite and cause a chimney fire. It may be brief and without apparent damage, but a chimney fire may also be prolonged or intense and result in significant fire and smoke damage or, at worst, the loss of your home if the creosote buildup is great enough. Creosote causes other problems, too. It decreases the inside diameter of stovepipes and flues, causing slower burning. This makes burning less efficient and contributes to further deposits of creosote. In addition, because creosote is acidic, it corrodes mortar, metal, and eventually even stainless-steel and ceramic chimney liners.

To prevent costly and dangerous creosote buildup, have your chimney professionally cleaned by a qualified chimney sweep. How often depends on the amount of creosote deposited during the burning season, and this, in turn, depends largely on how and what kind of wood you burn. Professional sweeps usually recommend at least annual cleaning. Depending on where you live, you'll spend about $150, perhaps less, for a cleaning.

You'll enjoy a warm glow at the highest efficiency if you use a glass-front wood-burning or gas-fueled, right, fireplace insert.

Fireside Arrangements

Creating an attractive, comfortable setting around a fireplace should be easy. Who doesn't like the cozy ambiance of relaxing in front of a fire? But there are times when the presence of a fireplace in a room poses problems with the layout. A fireplace can take up considerable floor and wall space, and like any other permanent feature or built-in piece of furniture, its size or position can limit the design possibilities.

The Fireplace and the Space

What is the room's size and shape—large, small, square, long and narrow, L-shaped? Where is the fireplace located—in the center of a wall, to the side, or in a corner? What other permanent features, such as windows, doors, bookcases, or media units, will you have to work with in your arrangement? How much clearance can you allow around the furniture for easy passage? How close do you want to be to the fire? Think of these questions as you consider the design basics presented below.

Scale and Proportion. Remember the importance of spatial relationships. For example, a fireplace may seem large in a room with a low ceiling; conversely, it may appear small in a room with a vaulted ceil-ing. Size is relative. Applied to objects on the mantel or the wall above the fireplace, correct scale and proportion happen when the objects are the appropriate size for the wall or the fireplace.

Balance. Sometimes the architectural features of a mantel or surround are so strong, you'll have to match them with furnishings of equal visual weight. Or they may be so ornate or plain that you'll have to play them up or tone them down to make them work with the rest of the decor. That's balance. But balance also refers to arrangements: symmetrical, asymmetrical, and radial.

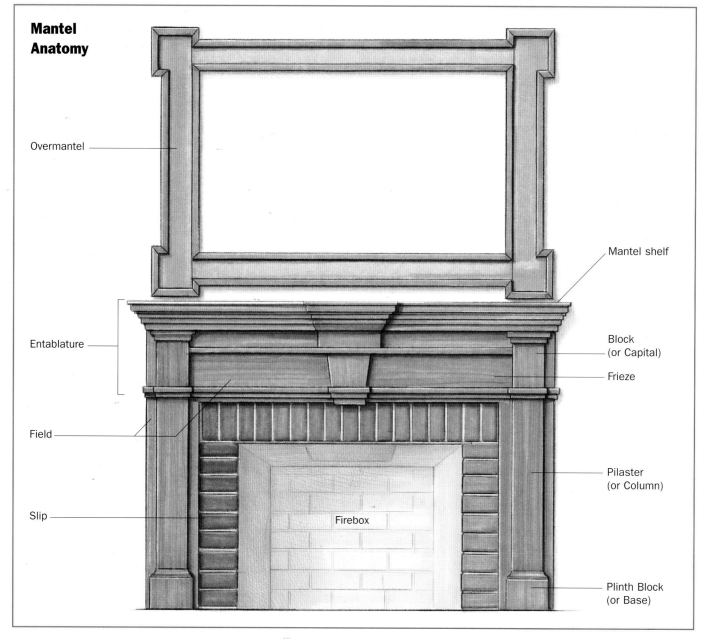

Mantel Anatomy

Overmantel

Mantel shelf

Entablature

Block (or Capital)

Frieze

Field

Pilaster (or Column)

Slip

Firebox

Plinth Block (or Base)

Line. Shape depends on line. Different types of lines suggest various qualities. Pay attention to the lines when you're creating arrangements and relationships among objects. Some lines are inherent in a room or an architectural feature, but you can modify them. For example: vertical lines are stately and dignified, which is just the look you want for your fireplace, but unfortunately, it's rather wide and squat instead. Solution? Create an arrangement above the fireplace that extends high on the wall, or hang a tall mirror or frame over than mantel.

What if the fireplace is too tall? Does it overwhelm the rest of the furniture? Add horizontal lines by moving seating pieces farther apart to the right and left of the hearth. Install wall art on the sides of the fireplace.

If the room is boxy, avoid grouping pieces at right angles to the fireplace and each other. Instead, de-emphasize the boxy shape by placing them on the diagonal to open the square. Use upholstered pieces with rounded arms or curvaceous cushions, legs, or frames. Create a radial arrangement. With the hearth as the central point, create a semicircular hub of furnishings that include seating and a small table or two.

Rhythm. Keep the eye moving at a measured pace by repeating motifs, colors, or shapes. For example, you might pick up the color from a tiled surround to use as an accent color in fabrics on upholstered pieces, curtains, pillows, throws, or other decorative accessories. Or repeat architectural features of the fireplace with other similar elements in the room, such as molding or other woodwork details.

Variety. Don't go overboard trying to match everything exactly. The most interesting rooms and arrangements mix objects of different sizes, shapes, lines, and sometimes even styles (as long as they are compatible).

Harmony. Create harmony among all of the parts of your design by connecting all of the elements either by color or motif. For example, in a display of family photos the frames may all be different shapes, styles, and heights, but because each one is made of brass, the overall appearance looks harmonious. Or you could assemble a wall vignette of frames over the fireplace, all different in finish but tied together by the subject matter of each one—all landscapes, for example, or all pink cabbage roses. Unifying diverse items in this way creates a finished-looking scheme.

How to Make a Hinged Fireboard

You'll need a hinged three-panel wooden fireplace screen, which you can buy or make. If you buy one, you'll have to sand and prime it thoroughly before applying the new finish over the existing one. Ideally, it's best to work on unfinished wood.

The screen used for this project features two 9 x 36-inch side panels and one 26 x 36-inch center panel that were cut from a ¾-inch-thick sheet of plywood. If you aren't handy with a circular saw or table saw, ask your local lumber supplier to cut the panels to your desired dimensions. Attach the side and center panels with two-way (piano) hinges, which are easy to install. Simply mark their location along the inside edges of the panel pieces, drill pilot holes, and then screw the hinges into place. To finish, prime the boards; then paint or stencil a design onto each panel. For Victorian authenticity, decoupage the panels with a motif cut out of a piece of fabric, wallpaper, old greeting cards, or postcards.

Symmetrical versus Asymmetrical Arrangements

If you like the symmetry of classic design, balance your arranged pieces accordingly. For example, position two sofas or love seats of the same size perpendicular to the fireplace and exactly opposite each other. Or place a single sofa parallel with the fireplace, with two chairs opposite one another and equidistant from both the sofa and the hearth. Try out a low coffee table or an oversize ottoman in the center of the arrangement. Leave the peripheral areas outside the main grouping for creating small impromptu conversation areas during parties and gatherings or to accommodate a modest dining area or home-office station.

If your design sense is less formal or contemporary, try an asymmetrical grouping in front of the fire. Turn seating pieces at a 45-degree angle from the hearth.

In a large open space, locate seating not directly in front of the hearth but slightly off to the side. Counterbalance the arrangement with a large table and chairs, a hutch, bookcases, or any element of relatively equal weight. This layout works especially well when the ceiling is vaulted (as most great rooms are) or when the hearth is massive. In many contemporary homes, especially where there is a zero-clearance unit, the fireplace is not on an outside wall, nor is it necessarily in a central location. This means you can put the fireplace almost anywhere.

Comfortable Arrangements

You may want an intimate environment in front of the fire, but the room is so large that it feels and looks impersonal. Large rooms afford lots of leeway for arranging, but people often make the mistake of pushing all of the furniture against the walls. If that's what you're doing, pull the major seating pieces closer together and near the fire, keeping a distance of only 4 to 10 feet between sofas and chairs. For the most comfortable result, create one or more small groupings that can accommodate up to four to six people in different areas of the room.

Modular Seating. Instead of a standard sofa and chairs, consider the convenience of modular seating, too, which comes in any number of armless and single-arm end pieces. The advantage of these separate upholstered units is that you can easily add, take away, or rearrange the modules to suit any of your layout or seating needs. Create an L or a U arrangement in front of the fire; subtract pieces, moving one or two outside of the area for an intimate

A raised hearth, above, reinforces the idea of a fireplace as a focal point, and it provides seating near the fire. Place other furniture to the sides of the hearth.

grouping. Use an area rug to further define the space. Or put the pieces together to make one large arrangement in any configuration. Versatile furnishings such as an ottoman with a hinged top or an antique trunk can double as seating, a low table, or storage.

A Quick Guide to Buying Firewood

How much wood you need to buy in a season depends on a number of factors, but there are three major variables: how often and how long you burn fires; the efficiency of your fireplace or stove; and the type of wood you burn. In general, hard, dense woods are ideal for fuel. As a rule of thumb, the wood from deciduous trees is best. (Deciduous trees are those that shed their leaves annually.) These include oak, maple, walnut, birch, beech, ash, and the wood from fruit trees such as cherry and apple.

Avoid burning wood from evergreens—those cone-bearing (coniferous) trees with needles instead of leaves. The wood of coniferous trees is soft and it will burn faster, so a greater volume of wood will be consumed per hour compared with hardwood. A greater problem with softwoods, however, is the resin content. Resin is the gummy substance that's used in the manufacture of some wood stains and shellacs, and when resin is burned it gives off a byproduct called creosote. Creosote, which is flammable, accumulates in flues and chimneys, and this buildup represents a potential fire hazard.

The wood you purchase should also be seasoned, which means that the tree should have been cut down at least six months or, preferably, a year prior to the burning of the wood. Ideally, the wood should be cut and split soon after the tree is felled, allowing for more effective drying. The moisture in unseasoned (or green) wood tends to have a cooling effect, preventing complete combustion and making it harder to keep a fire blazing. A low-burning fire also increases creosote. (It's okay to burn green wood occasionally, but make sure to use small logs or split sticks and add them to an already hot fire.)

Mantel Vignettes

A grouping of objects on your mantel can be as simple or complex as you like. To make your display lively, choose a variety of shapes and sizes. For dramatic impact, group related objects that you can link in theme or color.

Remember that a symmetrical arrangement has classical overtones and will reinforce the formality of traditional designs. Stick with similar objects: a pair of Chinese ginger jars or antique silver candlesticks arranged in mirror fashion on either side of the mantel equidistant from the center, for example. Or keep the look simple by placing a single but important object in the center; it could be a mantel clock, a floral arrangement, or some other objet d'art.

Asymmetry, on the other hand, brings a different dynamic to a mantel vignette with mismatched pieces. Try placing a large object to one side of the mantel, and then balance that piece by massing several small objects or a different type of object of similar scale on the opposite side. An example might be an arrangement of books of varying heights and sizes at one end of the mantel and a simple large vase at the other end. Or you might oppose tall thin candlesticks with one fat candle.

A simple brick wall, left, serves as a backdrop for a gleaming fireplace insert.

Plan #371021

Dimensions: 53' W x 48'10" D
Levels: 2
Square Footage: 2,384
Main Level Sq. Ft.: 1,542
Upper Level Sq. Ft.: 842
Bedrooms: 4
Bathrooms: 3½
Foundation: Slab
Materials List Available: No
Price Category: E

This beautiful brick-and-siding traditional home has an optional bonus room and will welcome you home for years to come.

Features:

• Living Room: You'll find three large windows, a cozy fireplace, and a built-in media center in this spacious room.

• Kitchen: This large gourmet kitchen has a charming morning room for quite Sunday brunches.

• Dining Room: An elegant space with wooden columns, this room is located off the tiled entryway.

• Master Suite: This large suite boasts a luxurious master bathroom with his and her vanities and walk-in closets.

• Bedrooms: Upstairs you will find three large additional bedrooms and two more bathrooms.

Main Level Floor Plan

Upper Level Floor Plan

Copyright by designer/architect.

Images provided by designer/architect.

Plan #391020

Dimensions: 54' W x 50' D
Levels: 1
Square Footage: 2,387
Bedrooms: 3
Bathrooms: 2½
Foundation: Basement
Materials List Available: Yes
Price Category: E

This bi-level home transforms 2,387 sq. ft. Vaulted ceilings soar above most rooms, including the living and sleeping rooms, so families can make the most of both formal and relaxed living.

Features:

- Kitchen: This room features a peninsula counter, which feeds into the dining and living rooms on one side. On the other side, it nurtures a breakfast nook with deck access.

- Bedrooms: Secondary bedrooms share a full bath and a front-yard view.

- Master Suite: A dreamy window seat in the bedroom overlooks the backyard, and a spa-style private bath features double vanity sinks. A U-shaped walk-in closet provides storage for two.

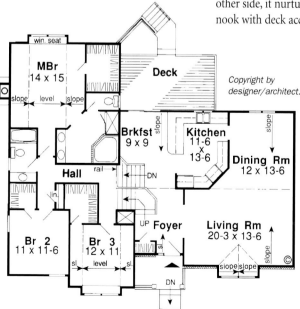

Copyright by designer/architect.

Optional Basement Level Floor Plan

Plan #371022

Dimensions: 76'10" W x 54'3" D

Levels: 1

Square Footage: 2,390

Bedrooms: 4

Bathrooms: 2

Foundation: Slab

Materials List Available: No

Price Category: E

Images provided by designer/architect.

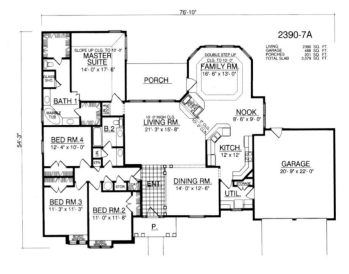

Copyright by designer/architect.

Plan #191012

Dimensions: 60' W x 76' D

Levels: 1

Square Footage: 2,123

Bedrooms: 3

Bathrooms: 2½

Foundation: Crawl space or slab

Materials List Available: No

Price Category: D

Images provided by designer/architect.

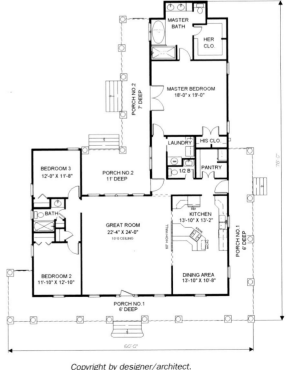

Copyright by designer/architect.

Plan #391015

Dimensions: 52' W x 43' D
Levels: 2
Square Footage: 2,411
Main Level Sq. Ft.: 1,241
Upper Level Sq. Ft.: 1,170
Bedrooms: 4
Bathrooms: 2½
Foundation: Crawl space, slab, or basement
Materials List Available: Yes
Price Category: E

Images provided by designer/architect.

Upper Level Floor Plan

Optional Kitchen

Main Level Floor Plan

Copyright by designer/architect.

Optional Retreat

Plan #151028

Dimensions: 36' W X 69' D
Levels: 2
Square Footage: 2,252
Main Level Sq. Ft.: 1,694
Upper Level Sq. Ft.: 558
Bedrooms: 3
Bathrooms: 3
Foundation: Crawl space, slab; optional basement plan available for extra fee
Materials List Available: No
Price Category: E

Images provided by designer/architect.

Main Level Floor Plan

Upper Level Floor Plan

Copyright by designer/architect.

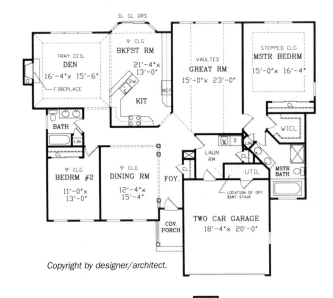

Copyright by designer/architect.

Images provided by designer/architect.

Plan #131006

Dimensions: 61' W x 53'6" D

Levels: 1

Square Footage: 2,193

Bedrooms: 3

Bathrooms: 2

Foundation: Crawl space, slab, or basement

Materials List Available: Yes

Price Category: E

Alternate Floor Plan

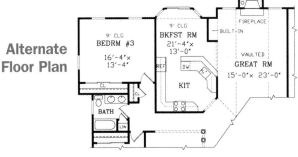

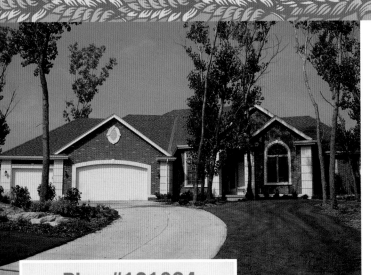

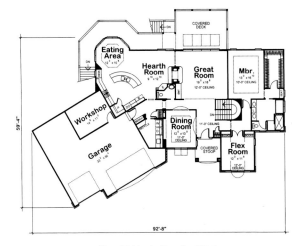

Copyright by designer/architect.

Images provided by designer/architect.

Plan #121034

Dimensions: 92'8" W x 59'4" D

Levels: 1

Square Footage: 2,223

Bedrooms: 1

Bathrooms: 1½

Foundation: Basement

Materials List Available: Yes

Price Category: E

Optional Basement Level Floor Plan

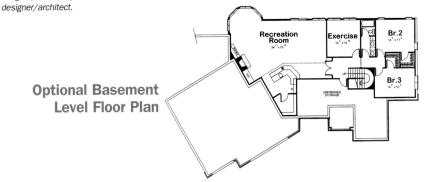

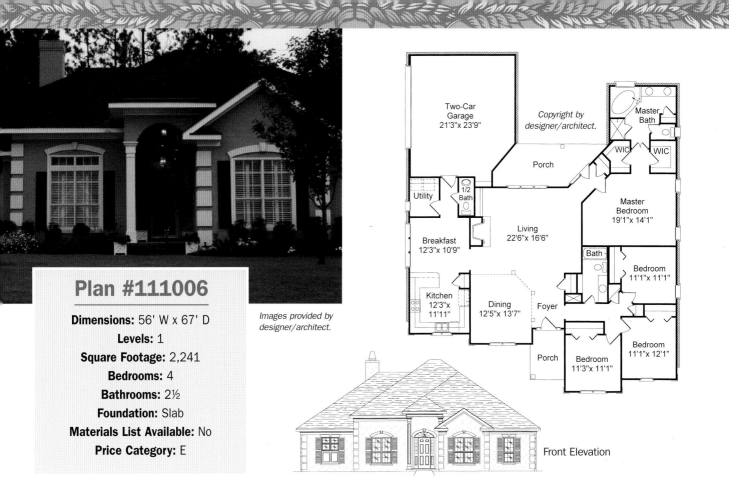

Plan #111006

Dimensions: 56' W x 67' D

Levels: 1

Square Footage: 2,241

Bedrooms: 4

Bathrooms: 2½

Foundation: Slab

Materials List Available: No

Price Category: E

Images provided by designer/architect.

Front Elevation

Plan #351007

Dimensions: 73'8" W x 53'2" D

Levels: 1

Square Footage: 2,251

Bedrooms: 3

Bathrooms: 2½

Foundation: Crawl space, slab, or basement

Materials List Available: Yes

Price Category: E

Images provided by designer/architect.

Bonus Room

Copyright by designer/architect.

Main Level Floor Plan

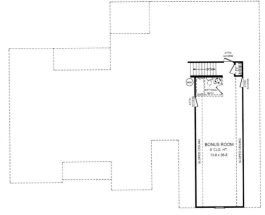

Bonus Area Floor Plan

Copyright by designer/architect.

Plan #351055

Dimensions: 73'8" W x 58'4" D

Levels: 1

Square Footage: 2,251

Bedrooms: 3

Bathrooms: 2½

Foundation: Crawl space, slab, or basement

Materials List Available: Yes

Price Category: E

Images provided by designer/architect.

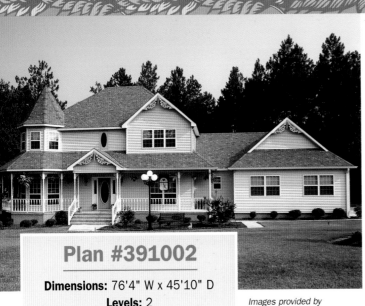

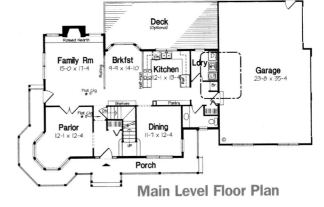

Main Level Floor Plan

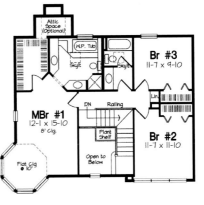

Upper Level Floor Plan

Copyright by designer/architect.

Plan #391002

Dimensions: 76'4" W x 45'10" D

Levels: 2

Square Footage: 2,281

Main Level Sq. Ft.: 1,260

Upper Level Sq. Ft.: 1,021

Bedrooms: 3

Bathrooms: 2½

Foundation: Crawl space, slab, or basement

Materials List Available: Yes

Price Category: E

Images provided by designer/architect.

Alternate Crawl Space/Slab

Plan #371060

Dimensions: 70'9" W x 59' D

Levels: 1

Square Footage: 2,296

Bedrooms: 4

Bathrooms: 2

Foundation: Basement

Materials List Available: No

Price Category: E

This stylish country home will be the talk of the neighborhood.

Features:

- **Front Porch:** The copper roof above this cozy covered porch welcomes you home.

- **Dining Room:** Enter the tiled foyer, and find wood posts that separate this elegant room from the spacious family room.

- **Family Room:** This room has a stepped-up ceiling, cozy fireplace, and built-in media center.

- **Kitchen:** This gourmet island kitchen, with its roomy breakfast nook and built-in desk, has a serving bar into the family room.

- **Master Suite:** This suite has a stepped-up ceiling. The master bath has his and her vanities, a marble tub, a separate shower, and two walk-in closets.

- **Bedrooms:** The three additional spacious bedrooms, each with its own walk-in closet, share a convenient hall bathroom with separate dressing room.

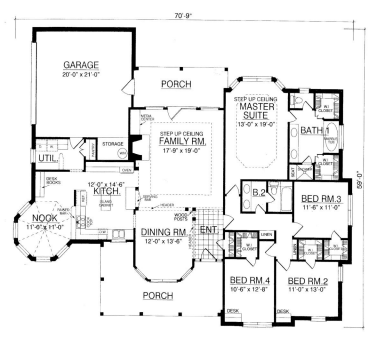

Plan #371003

Dimensions: 61' W x 57'4" D
Levels: 2
Square Footage: 2,297
Main Level Sq. Ft.: 1,752
Upper Level Sq. Ft.: 545
Bedrooms: 3
Bathrooms: 2½
Foundation: Crawl space, slab, or basement
Materials List Available: No
Price Category: E

Images provided by designer/architect.

This striking French-style home is set apart from all others. The beautiful front window treatments and stone accents will take your breath away.

Features:

• **Living Room:** The built-in bookcase, media center, and fireplace will bring the whole family together in this large gathering area.

• **Dining Room:** This formal dining room has easy access to the kitchen through a butler's pantry.

• **Kitchen:** Open to the cozy breakfast nook for informal meals, this island-equipped kitchen has all the gourmet touches.

• **Master Suite:** This secluded suite has a step-up ceiling and a luxurious bathroom with his and her vanities, a marble tub, a glass shower, and an extra-large walk-in closet.

• **Bedrooms:** Upstairs are two large additional bedrooms that share a convenient hall bath room with optional bonus room.

• **Office:** There is an office or optional fourth bedroom with a half-bath across the hall on the first level.

Rear Elevation

Upper Level Floor Plan

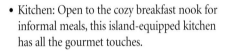

Main Level Floor Plan
Copyright by designer/architect.

Plan #401012

Dimensions: 48' W x 52'6" D
Levels: 2
Square Footage: 2,301
Main Level Sq. Ft.: 1,180
Upper Level Sq. Ft.: 1,121
Bedrooms: 3-4
Bathrooms: 2½
Foundation: Basement
Materials List Available: Yes
Price Category: E

A turret roof, prominent bay window, and wraparound veranda designate this four bedroom design as classic Victorian. The plans include two second-level layouts--one with four bedrooms or one with three bedrooms and a vaulted ceiling over the family room.

Features:

- Living Room: This formal room has windows that overlook the veranda.

- Family Room: This gathering space includes a fireplace for atmosphere.

- Kitchen: This U-shaped kitchen has a sunny breakfast bay; you'll find a half-bath and a laundry room in the service area that leads to the two-car garage.

- Master Suite: This lavish area has an octagonal tray ceiling in the sitting room, a walk-in closet, and a private bath with a colonnaded whirlpool spa and separate shower.

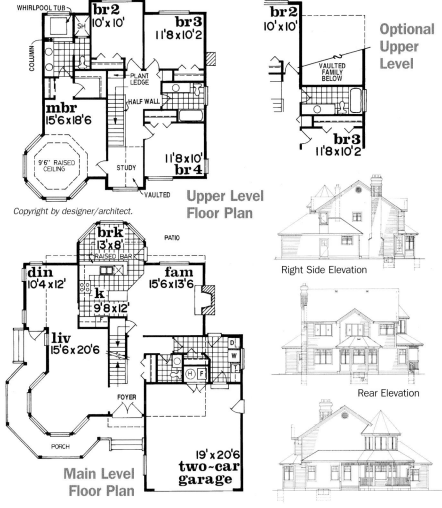

Images provided by designer/architect.

Copyright by designer/architect.

Upper Level Floor Plan

Optional Upper Level

Main Level Floor Plan

Right Side Elevation

Rear Elevation

Images provided by designer/architect.

Copyright by designer/architect.

Bonus Room

Plan #151168

Dimensions: 66' W x 65'2" D
Levels: 1
Square Footage: 2,261
Bedrooms: 4
Bathrooms: 2½
Foundation: Crawl space, slab, basement, or daylight basement
Materials List Available: No
Price Category: E

Main Level Floor Plan

Upper Level Floor Plan

Images provided by designer/architect.

Copyright by designer/architect.

Plan #151027

Dimensions: 37' W x 73' D
Levels: 2
Square Footage: 2,323
Main Level Sq. Ft.: 1,713
Upper Level Sq. Ft.: 619
Bedrooms: 3
Bathrooms: 3
Foundation: Crawl space, slab; optional basement plan available for extra fee
Materials List Available: No
Price Category: E

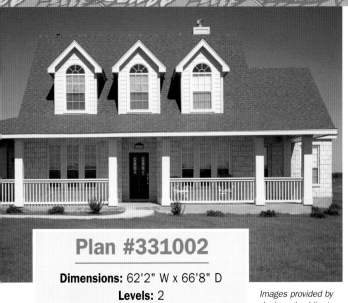

Plan #331002

Dimensions: 62'2" W x 66'8" D
Levels: 2
Square Footage: 2,299
Main Level Sq. Ft.: 1,517
Upper Level Sq. Ft.: 782
Bedrooms: 3
Bathrooms: 2½
Foundation: Crawl space, slab, or basement
Materials List Available: No
Price Category: E

Images provided by designer/architect.

Main Level Floor Plan

Upper Level Floor Plan
Copyright by designer/architect.

Plan #121088

Dimensions: 56'8" W x 48' D
Levels: 2
Square Footage: 2,340
Main Level Sq. Ft.: 1,701
Upper Level Sq. Ft.: 639
Bedrooms: 4
Bathrooms: 2½
Foundation: Basement
Materials List Available: Yes
Price Category: E

Images provided by designer/architect.

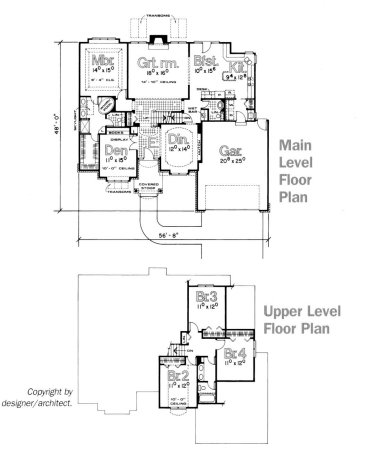

Main Level Floor Plan

Upper Level Floor Plan

Copyright by designer/architect.

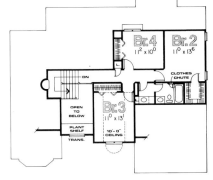

Main Level Floor Plan

Images provided by designer/architect.

Plan #121017

Dimensions: 54' W x 50' D

Levels: 2

Square Footage: 2,353

Main Level Sq. Ft.: 1,653

Upper Level Sq. Ft.: 700

Bedrooms: 4

Bathrooms: 2½

Foundation: Basement

Materials List Available: Yes

Price Category: E

Upper Level Floor Plan

Copyright by designer/architect.

Plan #151002

Dimensions: 67' W x 66' D

Levels: 1

Square Footage: 2,444

Bedrooms: 3

Bathrooms: 2½

Foundation: Crawl space, slab, or basement

Materials List Available: No

Price Category: E

Images provided by designer/architect.

Copyright by designer/architect.

Plan #371016

Dimensions: 81'8" W x 56'6" D

Levels: 1

Square Footage: 2,316

Bedrooms: 4

Bathrooms: 2½

Foundation: Slab

Materials List Available: No

Price Category: E

Large rooms and high ceilings give this French-style home an expansive feel, and the abundance of windows imparts atmosphere and grace.

Features:

- **Entry:** This tiled entry boasts a 12-foot-high ceiling and an arched transom to enter into the living room.

- **Living Room:** This massive room has a wet bar opposite a cozy fireplace.

- **Dining Room:** This elegant room has a ceiling that slopes gently to 11 feet.

- **Kitchen:** This large island kitchen opens into a cozy breakfast nook, which receives plenty of natural light from three tall windows.

- **Master Suite:** This secluded retreat boasts a double stepped-up ceiling and has a luxurious bath with his and her walk-in closets.

- **Bedrooms:** On the opposite side of the house from the master suite, the three large bedrooms share a convenient hall bathroom.

Images provided by designer/architect.

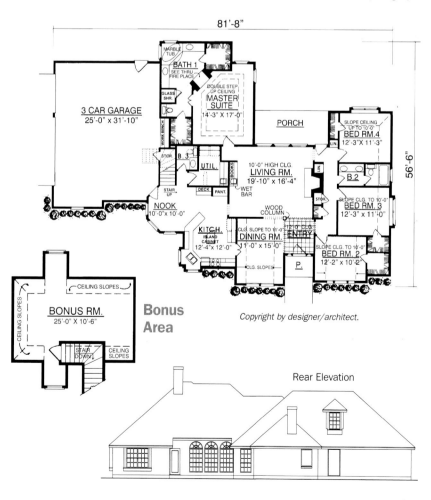

Copyright by designer/architect.

Bonus Area

Rear Elevation

Images provided by designer/architect.

Plan #391014

Dimensions: 64' W x 52' D
Levels: 2
Square Footage: 2,372
Main Level Sq. Ft.: 1,752
Upper Level Sq. Ft.: 620
Bedrooms: 3
Bathrooms: 2½
Foundation: Crawl space, slab, or basement
Materials List Available: Yes
Price Category: E

This home sets the imagination in motion, with its showcase vaulted ceilings, open entry, two-way fireplace, and more.

Features:

- Kitchen: In this kitchen and dinette area, a built-in desk lines up along a wall of shelving and cabinetry, and a pantry and half-bath line the back wall.

- Master Bedroom: The main-floor master bedroom is a treat for mom and dad who prefer not to climb stairs. And, a bright windowed master bath and roomy walk-in closet add the finishing touch.

- Loft: This area has a tremendous draw, with its overview of the fireplace and family room below.

- Bedrooms: Two secondary bedrooms with walk-in closets flank opposite ends of the upper level. Each bedroom also has a private vanity sink and a separate entrance to the shared toilet, tub, and linen closet.

Family Room

Main Level Floor Plan

Upper Level Floor Plan

Deck

Family Rm
15-6 x 19-2
vaulted

Dinette/Kitchen
22 x 13-8
bench

L

D
W

MBr 1
15 x 13-2
pan vault

Balcony above

spa

UP DN

desk

ov

pantry

Br 2
13-2 x 13-10
shelves

Loft
linen
DN

lin.

Living Rm
13 x 13-8
vaulted

Foyer
vaulted

Dining Rm
11 x 13-8

Garage
21-4 x 31-4

Br 3
12-6 x 10-8

Copyright by designer/architect.

©

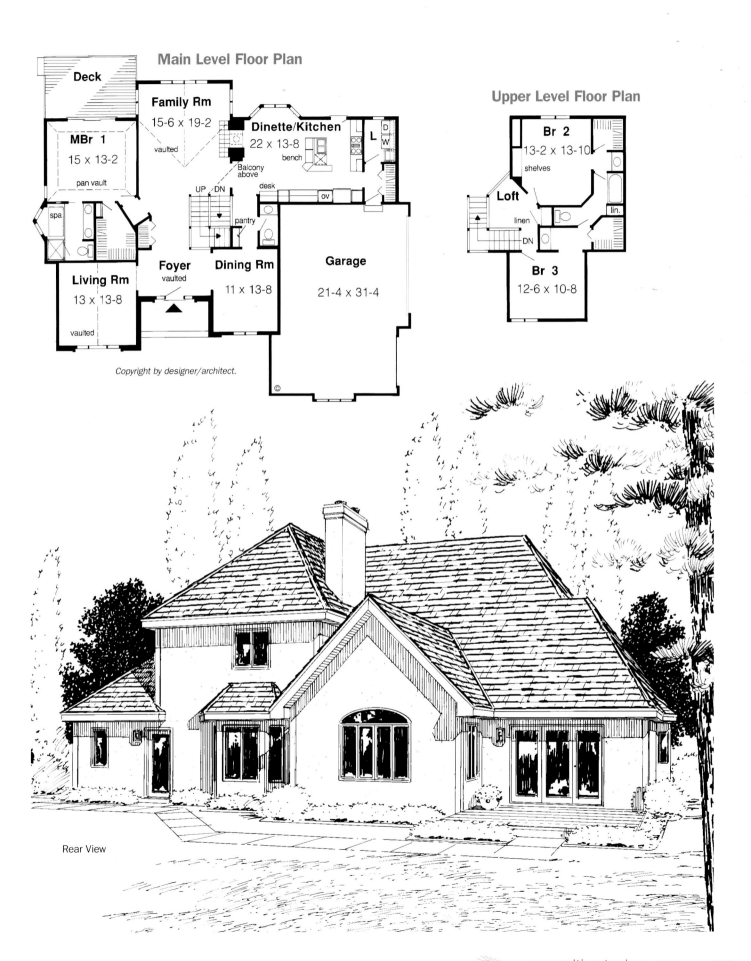

Rear View

Plan #371062

Dimensions: 81'8" W x 61' D
Levels: 1
Square Footage: 2,328
Bedrooms: 4
Bathrooms: 2½
Foundation: Slab
Materials List Available: *No*
Price Category: E

Images provided by designer/architect.

This stunning country home will impress you from the start with its beautiful windows, plus the stone, brick, and siding facade. There is an optional bonus room above the garage.

Features:

• Living Room: This entertaining area has a built-in bookcase and a cozy fireplace.

• Dining Room: Wooden columns adorn this large formal room, which opens into the living room and has easy access to the kitchen.

• Kitchen: This large island kitchen has a raised bar and pantry, and it's open to a cozy breakfast nook with a built-in desk.

• Master Suite: This getaway area boasts a luxurious bathroom with a marble tub, glass shower, see-through fireplace, and two walk-in closets.

• Bedrooms: The three additional bedrooms share a convenient hall bathroom.

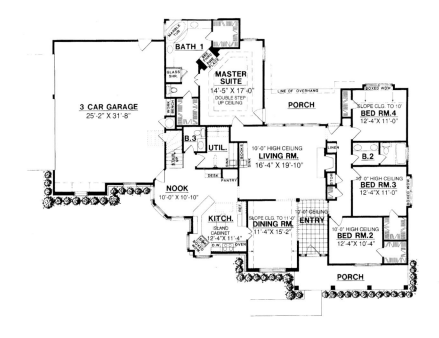

Bonus Area Floor Plan

Copyright by designer/architect.

Plan #371063

Dimensions: 81' W x 40'6" D
Levels: 2
Square Footage: 2,330
Main Level Sq. Ft.: 1,605
Upper Level Sq. Ft.: 725
Bedrooms: 3
Bathrooms: 2½
Foundation: Slab
Materials List Available: No
Price Category: E

From the striking dormers to the enclosed covered porch, this home defines country charm. There is an optional bonus room above the garage.

Features:

- **Living Room:** Enter to find this large room with fireplace and built-in media center.

- **Kitchen:** This massive country kitchen, with its raised bar, walk-in pantry, and built-in window seat, opens into a beautiful dining room with bay windows that look out onto a covered back porch.

- **Master Suite:** Secluded downstairs, this suite opens onto a private porch and has a luxurious master bathroom with his and her walk-in closets and vanities.

- **Bedrooms:** Upstairs you will find a loft that looks over the entry below and two additional bedrooms, each with its own walk-in closet, that share a bathroom equipped with a powder room.

Images provided by designer/architect.

Main Level Floor Plan

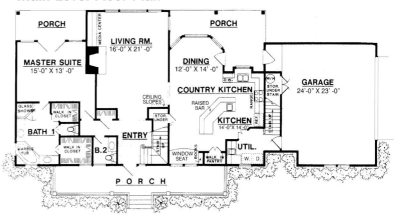

Copyright by designer/architect.

Upper Level Floor Plan

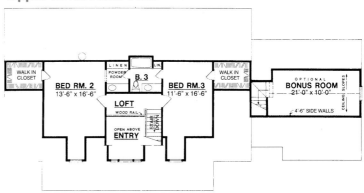

Creating a Media Room

A successor to the low-tech TV rooms of the 1950s and '60s, today's media room can offer a multimedia experience. It can be outfitted with everything from DVD and VHS players to sophisticated home-theater setups complete with speakers inconspicuously mounted into walls and ceilings.

However, creating a media room means more than hooking up electronics. You'll need proper housing for all of the components, such as a big-screen TV, as well as comfortable, attractive furnishings. You can go the custom route, or check out what's on the market. Cabinetry that's designed specifically for the equipment is readily available. So is movie-house-style row seating complete with cup holders and reclining chaises. You can also find floor-to-ceiling soundproofing systems that help hold and enhance the rich sound from digital equipment. It's your choice. It all depends on how much you want to spend.

A freestanding media cabinet, opposite, can be decorative and practical.

Semicustom kitchen cabinetry, above, can be outfitted and installed to suit your media-room needs.

Media-Wise Moves

No matter the size of your budget or the physical dimensions of your space, there are a full range of options that will make a media room look as good as it sounds.

Furniture

The focus here should be on functionality—enhancing your comfort and the entertainment experience. You can achieve both by furnishing the room with chairs, sectionals, and sofas that are upholstered in soft fabrics. Upholstery absorbs sound and can provide the comfort level you need when watching a two-hour movie. Add plush pillows to create an even cozier, more sound-friendly environment.

Leather furniture is always a fallback option. Although it does absorb sound better than hard materials, it can't compete with soft fabrics such as cotton, wool, and blended fabrics in terms of comfort or sound retention.

One smart option is a large upholstered storage ottoman, which can serve many purposes. It adds extra seating, serves as a coffee table, and provides a place for remote controls, DVDs, the television listings, and other media-room paraphernalia.

Cabinetry and Storage. Factor a lot of storage into your media-room plans. First, you need space for various components, such as a DVD player, VCR, receiver, CD player, and so forth. Next there's what will indeed be a growing collection of DVDs, videotapes, CDs, and remote controls. If you plan to order custom cabinetry for the space, buy your sound system and home-theater components first. Then have the cabinetmaker design the unit based on their specifications.

In terms of design, the cabinetry should accommodate components at eye level for easy operation. The topmost and lowest shelves can be reserved for lesser-used items. If you'll build the cabinet yourself, remember that there should be enough space around the components to "breathe;" built-in electronics need ventilation. Plus, you have to leave openings in the back to pull through any wires that have to be plugged into wall outlets.

In addition, be sure to include plenty of rollout drawers in the design to hold your library of favorite disks and tapes. Leave room for future purchases, too. Another option is to store tapes in a closet, a handsome trunk, or even a basket. Stockpiling tapes, CDs, and other clutter around the television screen can detract from the viewing experience.

When not in use, large TV monitors can look like big, ugly boxes. Hide smaller televisions—27- or 32-inch—behind the handsome doors of a semicustom TV cabinet. Very large screens should probably be housed behind pocket, tambour, or concealed doors. Large cabinet doors that swing out into the room can obstruct traffic or even your view of the screen.

Walls, Floors, Ceilings, and Doors

Light-colored walls will reflect sunlight and artificial light and increase glare. Both can wash out the TV screen. For the same reason, mirrors and other shiny materials or glossy finishes in a media room don't make sense. Choose deep neutrals for walls, or even try a darker tone. Walls lined with corkboard, upholstered in fabric, or outfitted with high-tech sound-absorbing glass-fiber panels covered in

fashionable fabrics are all good options.

Acoustical ceiling tiles are a simple and effective solution to prevent sound from leaking into other areas. They come in a range of styles, one of which is bound to fit in with your decor.

Carpeting is not only easy on the feet

One homeowner created a comfortable corner, above, for enjoying his collection of old recordings.

Stock cabinets, opposite, can be outfitted with optional features, such as drawers that neatly store CDs, DVDs, and VHS cassettes.

but also on the ear, preventing harsh echoes from bouncing around the room. Hard floor surfaces such as tile, stone, and marble can reflect and distort the sound coming from even the most expensive home-theater receiver and speakers. Cover the floor in a low-pile, low-maintenance Berber, sisal, or industrial carpet to keep sound true and pure.

Lighting

Indirect illumination that provides ambient light without on-screen glare is best for a media room. Lamps in a media room should have black or dark opaque lampshades that direct light up and down. Translucent shades radiate light in all directions. Rather than one or two bright-light sources, install several low-level lights. Dimmers will allow you to adjust lights for comfort. As a general rule, no light should be brighter than the TV screen. To avoid eyestrain and distraction, position light sources behind you and not between you and the screen.

If you want to create movie-house ambiance, install wall sconces like ones reminiscent of grand old theaters. Because you'll probably want to watch movies in a darkened room, make sure your plan includes aisle lighting, which you can plug into outlets. Wire them to one remote so you can dim them simultaneously.

Don't forget that you'll have to control natural light unless you plan to limit your home theater use to evenings. There are creative ways to reduce natural light as well. Shutters and blinds are easily adjustable window treatments. You can also check out the possibility of certain curtains that are made especially for home theaters.

Plugging into Your TV Options

Technology has clearly taken television to the next level. Even if you have an older standard model, you can improve the picture quality of broadcast viewing simply by adding cable, and even more by adding digital cable or digital satellite. But nothing beats DVDs for watching movies.

HDTV, or high-definition television, has twice the picture clarity of standard TV, whether you're watching network or cable TV broadcasts or viewing a DVD. Ironically, most HDTVs don't contain high-definition tuners. So, although the picture may be better, you're not getting true HDTV unless you buy the tuning box, which is sold separately and costs around $700. Still, it's an improvement over the old versions.

Plasma and LCD TV Screens.

Thin TV is also a trend that is here to stay. Slimmed down flat-screen plasma TVs and LCD screens provide brilliant colors, better contrast and resolution, and a greater viewing angle. Because the screen is flat, there is no problem with glare. Having the lights on or off does not affect the picture. LCDs are smaller; screens range from 15 to 30 inches diagonally. Plasma TVs start at 32

Plump upholstered seating, opposite, arranged at the proper distance from the screen, lets you view TV and movies comfortably.

Ready-to-assemble furniture, above, is an affordable alternative to custom or semicustom cabinets.

inches and go up to big-screen size from there. Most of them accept HDTV signals, but they are usually not powerful enough to display all of the high resolution.

Rear Projection. The screen size of a rear-projection TV is large—40 to 82 inches—and can be viewed in natural light without sacrificing picture quality. In general, the picture is often inferior, unless it is an HDTV format. Another drawback: rear projection TVs must be watched at eye-level and straight-on for optimal viewing.

Front Projection. This system has a separate screen, which can either drop down from the ceiling or remain fixed on the wall, and a projector that is mounted at ceiling height across the room from the screen. It's akin to a movie-theater system. Front projection is expensive and requires a professional to install it. Although even minor light can wash out the picture, the image quality is unbeatable when the room is dark.

More Tips

If you're thinking of creating a home theater in your new house, here are a few pointers.

- Most home-theater designers recommend televisions screens that are at least 27 inches wide.
- Seating distance can add or subtract from the viewing quality. For optimal viewing, there should be a distance between you and the TV that is 2 to 2½ times the width of the screen. That means placing sofa and chairs 54 to 68 inches from a 27-inch screen, for example. If your TV is a wide-screen high-definition model, place it a distance that is 1½ times the screen's diagonal width from your seating area.
- Five speakers will create a full-home theater sound. Place one speaker on each side of the TV screen, level with your ears when you are seated, and about 3 feet from the sidewalls. Place two speakers behind the sofa about 6 to 8 feet off the floor and at least as wide apart as the front speakers. Put the fifth speaker on top of the TV.
- Replace a collection of remote controls with a single universal model that can control everything from the DVD player to the lights (with a special receiver).

Plan #401023

Dimensions: 76' W x 63'4" D
Levels: 1
Square Footage: 2,806
Bedrooms: 3
Bathrooms: 2½
Foundation: Basement, walkout
Materials List Available: Yes
Price Category: F

The lower level of this magnificent home includes unfinished space that could have a future as a den and a family room with a fireplace. This level could also house extra bedrooms or an in-law suite.

Features:

- Foyer: On the main level, this foyer spills into a tray ceiling living room with a fireplace and an arched, floor-to-ceiling window wall.

- Family Room: Up from the foyer, a hall introduces this vaulted room with built-in media center and French doors that open to an expansive railed deck.

- Kitchen: Featured in this gourmet kitchen are a food-preparation island with a salad sink, double-door pantry, corner-window sink, and breakfast bay.

- Master Bedroom: The vaulted master bedroom opens to the deck, and the deluxe bath offers a raised whirlpool spa and a double-bowl vanity under a skylight.

- Bedroom: Two family bedrooms share a compartmented bathroom.

Images provided by designer/architect.

Foyer

Master Bathroom

Rear Elevation

Right Side Elevation

Left Side Elevation

Rear View

Front View

Master Bedroom

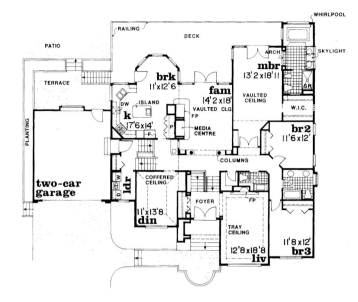

Copyright by designer/architect.

Optional Floor Plan

Kitchen

Kitchen

Plan #351068

Dimensions: 84' W x 54' D
Levels: 1
Square Footage: 2,501
Bedrooms: 4
Bathrooms: 3
Foundation: Crawl space or slab
Materials List Available: Yes
Price Category: D

This beautiful home includes an open floor plan with four spacious bedrooms, three baths, a split bedroom layout, and several other unique features.

Features:

- Porches: Large front and rear covered porches complement the livability of the home.

- Great Room: This expansive room features a vaulted ceiling and a gas log fireplace.

- Kitchen: Fully equipped with a wraparound raised bar, a walk-in pantry, and a large adjoining laundry, this kitchen is luxurious yet functional.

- Master Suite: This suite includes a raised ceiling in the master bedroom, two large walk-in closets, a jetted tub, and an oversized shower.

Images provided by designer/architect.

Main Level Floor Plan

Bonus Area Floor Plan

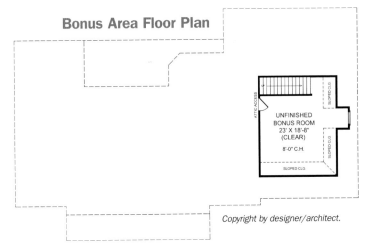

Copyright by designer/architect.

Plan #351057

Dimensions: 79'4" W x 53'6" D
Levels: 2
Square Footage: 2,505
Main Level Sq. Ft.: 2,100
Upper Level Sq. Ft.: 405
Bedrooms: 3
Bathrooms: 3
Foundation: Crawl space or slab
Materials List Available: Yes
Price Category: E

This brick-and-wood-sided farmhouse-style home with arched windows has a unique look.

Features:

• Great Room: A vaulted ceiling and a corner fireplace grace this gathering area, which is open to the kitchen.

• Master Suite: This large area has his and her private bathrooms and gigantic closets for all the "good stuff" you just cannot throw away.

• Bedrooms: The two secondary bedrooms are located just off the great room and share a hall bathroom.

• Garage: This large two-car garage has plenty of storage room or can be divided into an optional office just off the master suite.

Images provided by designer/architect.

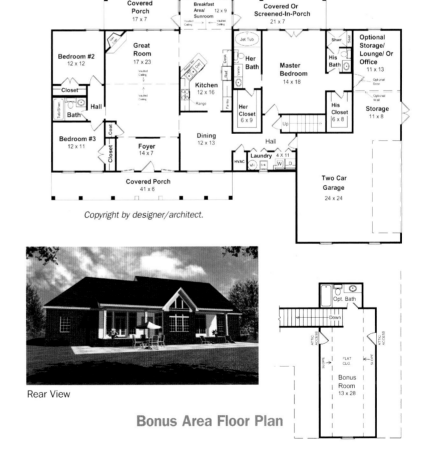

Copyright by designer/architect.

Rear View

Bonus Area Floor Plan

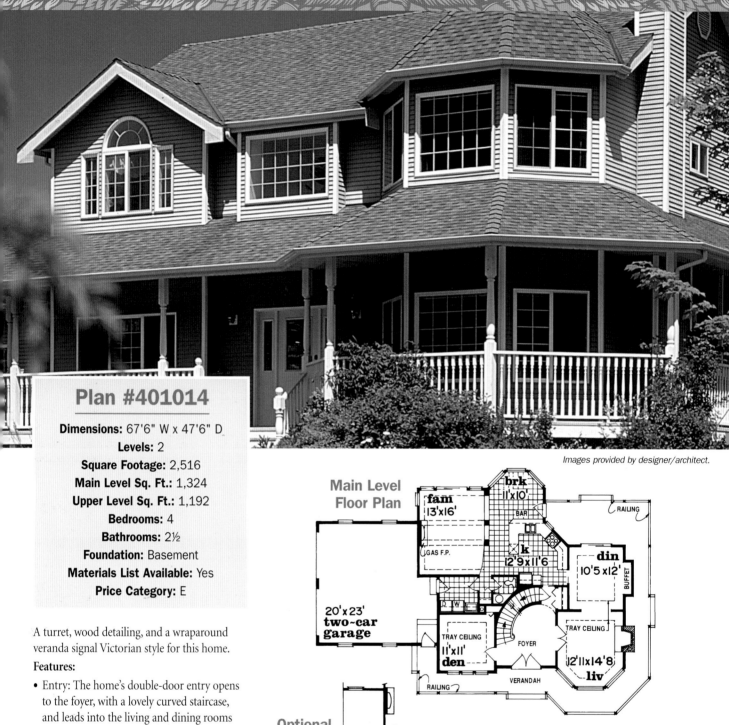

Plan #401014

Dimensions: 67'6" W x 47'6" D
Levels: 2
Square Footage: 2,516
Main Level Sq. Ft.: 1,324
Upper Level Sq. Ft.: 1,192
Bedrooms: 4
Bathrooms: 2½
Foundation: Basement
Materials List Available: Yes
Price Category: E

Images provided by designer/architect.

A turret, wood detailing, and a wraparound veranda signal Victorian style for this home.

Features:

- **Entry:** The home's double-door entry opens to the foyer, with a lovely curved staircase, and leads into the living and dining rooms on the right and the den on the left.

- **Living Room:** This formal room has a tray ceiling and a fireplace.

- **Formal Dining Room:** This room's features include a tray ceiling, a buffet alcove, and sliding glass doors that open to the veranda.

- **Master Suite:** A tray ceiling highlights the master suite. The private bath and walk-in closet give it a luxurious feel.

- **Bedroom 2:** This room sports a cozy window seat.

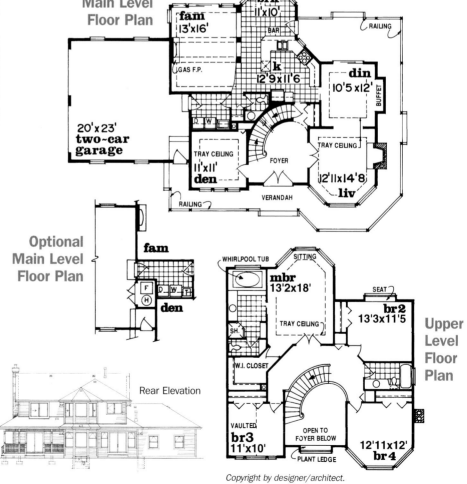

Copyright by designer/architect.

Plan #151232

Dimensions: 79'6" W x 71'4" D
Levels: 1.5
Square Footage: 3,901
Main Level Sq. Ft.: 3,185
Upper Level Sq. Ft.: 716
Bedrooms: 3
Bathrooms: 4
Foundation: Crawl space or slab
Materials List Available: No
Price Category: H

This elegant brick home has something for everyone

Features:

- Great Room: This large gathering area has a fireplace and access to the rear grilling porch.

- Hearth Room: Relaxing and casual, this cozy area has a fireplace and is open to the kitchen.

- Kitchen: This large island kitchen has a built-in pantry and is open to the breakfast nook.

- Master Suite: A private bathroom with a corner whirlpool tub and a large walk-in closet turn this area into a spacious retreat.

- Bonus Room: This large space located upstairs near the two secondary bedrooms can be turned into a media room.

Images provided by designer/architect.

Main Level Floor Plan

Copyright by designer/architect.

Upper Level Floor Plan

Kitchen

Great Room

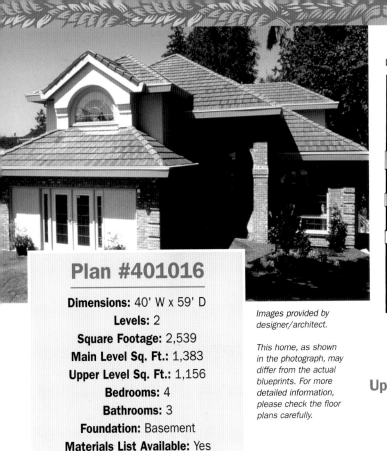

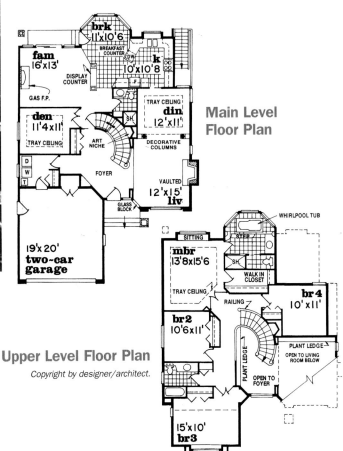

Plan #401016

Dimensions: 40' W x 59' D

Levels: 2

Square Footage: 2,539

Main Level Sq. Ft.: 1,383

Upper Level Sq. Ft.: 1,156

Bedrooms: 4

Bathrooms: 3

Foundation: Basement

Materials List Available: Yes

Price Category: E

Images provided by designer/architect.

This home, as shown in the photograph, may differ from the actual blueprints. For more detailed information, please check the floor plans carefully.

Main Level Floor Plan

Upper Level Floor Plan

Copyright by designer/architect.

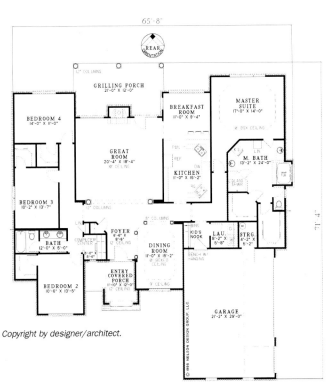

Plan #151216

Dimensions: 65'8" W x 71'4" D

Levels: 1

Square Footage: 2,545

Bedrooms: 4

Bathrooms: 2

Foundation: Crawl space or slab

Materials List Available: No

Price Category: E

Images provided by designer/architect.

Copyright by designer/architect.

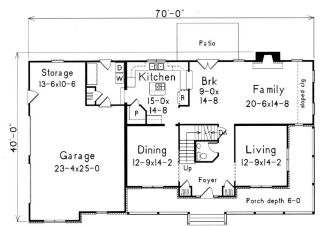

Main Level Floor Plan

70'-0"

Patio

Storage 13-6x10-6

Kitchen 15-0x 14-8

Brk 9-0x 14-8

Family 20-6x14-8

Garage 23-4x25-0

Dining 12-9x14-2

Living 12-9x14-2

Foyer

Up

Porch depth 6-0

40'-0"

Images provided by designer/architect.

Upper Level Floor Plan

Copyright by designer/architect.

Br 2 12-6x11-6

MBr 12-9x18-0

Br 3 12-9x12-0

Dn

open to below

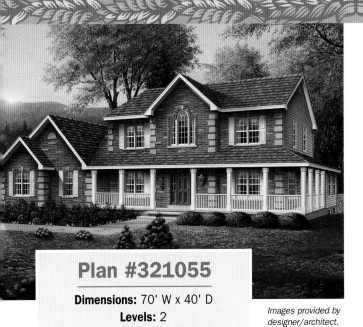

Plan #321055

Dimensions: 70' W x 40' D
Levels: 2
Square Footage: 2,505
Main Level Sq. Ft.: 1,436
Upper Level Sq. Ft.: 1,069
Bedrooms: 3
Bathrooms: 2½
Foundation: Basement
Materials List Available: Yes
Price Category: E

Plan #151023

Dimensions: 60' W x 96'6" D
Levels: 2
Square Footage: 3,203
Main Level Sq. Ft.: 2,328
Upper Level Sq. Ft.: 875
Bedrooms: 4
Bathrooms: 3½
Foundation: Crawl space, slab; optional full basement plan available for extra fee
Materials List Available: No
Price Category: G

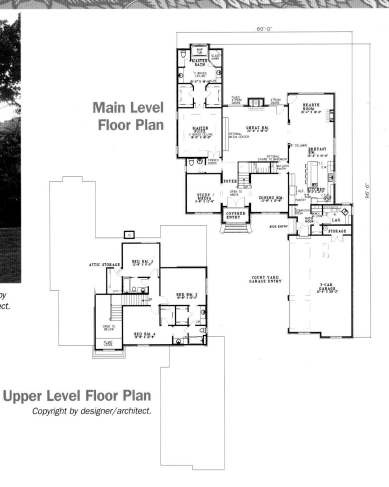

Photo provided by designer/architect.

Main Level Floor Plan

60'-0"

96'-6"

MASTER BATH

MASTER SUITE

GREAT RM.

HEARTH ROOM

BREAKFAST RM.

KITCHEN

FOYER

STUDY / MEDIA

DINING RM.

COVERED ENTRY

SIDE ENTRY

LAU

STORAGE

COURT YARD GARAGE ENTRY

3-CAR GARAGE

Upper Level Floor Plan

Copyright by designer/architect.

ATTIC STORAGE

BED RM. 2

BED RM. 3

BED RM. 4

OPEN TO BELOW

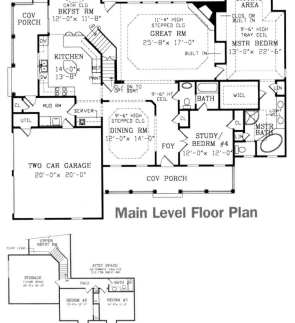

Main Level Floor Plan

Plan #131027

Dimensions: 62'4" W x 53'6" D

Levels: 2

Square Footage: 2,567

Main Level Sq. Ft.: 2,017

Upper Level Sq. Ft.: 550

Bedrooms: 4

Bathrooms: 3

Foundation: Crawl space, slab, or basement

Materials List Available: Yes

Price Category: F

Images provided by designer/architect.

Upper Level Floor Plan

Copyright by designer/architect.

Plan #321018

Dimensions: 88'4" W x 48'4" D

Levels: 1

Square Footage: 2,523

Bedrooms: 3

Bathrooms: 2

Foundation: Basement

Materials List Available: Yes

Price Category: E

Images provided by designer/architect.

Copyright by designer/architect.

SMARTtip

Tiebacks

You don't have to limit yourself to tiebacks made from matching or contrasting fabric. Achieve creative custom looks by making tiebacks from unexpected items. Some materials to consider are old cotton bandannas or silk scarves, strings of beads, lengths of leather, or old belts and chains.

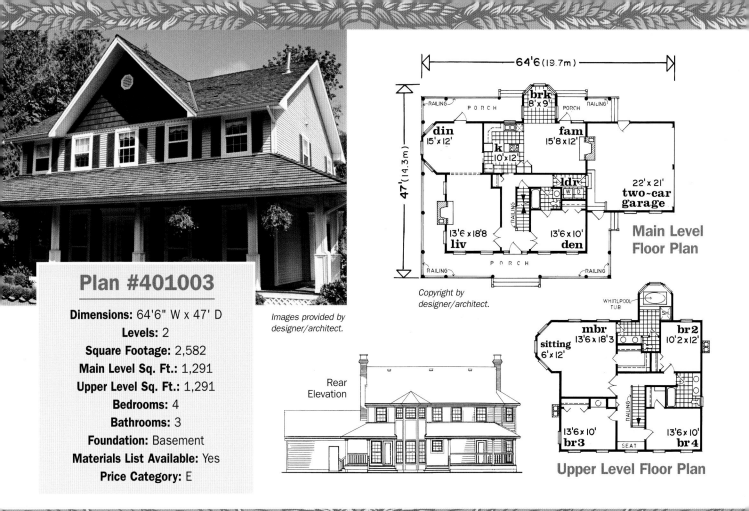

Plan #401003

Dimensions: 64'6" W x 47' D
Levels: 2
Square Footage: 2,582
Main Level Sq. Ft.: 1,291
Upper Level Sq. Ft.: 1,291
Bedrooms: 4
Bathrooms: 3
Foundation: Basement
Materials List Available: Yes
Price Category: E

Images provided by designer/architect.

Copyright by designer/architect.

Rear Elevation

Main Level Floor Plan

Upper Level Floor Plan

Plan #241008

Dimensions: 65' W x 56'8" D
Levels: 1
Square Footage: 2,526
Bedrooms: 4
Bathrooms: 3
Foundation: Slab
Materials List Available: No
Price Category: E

Images provided by designer/architect.

Copyright by designer/architect.

Optional Bonus Area Floor Plan

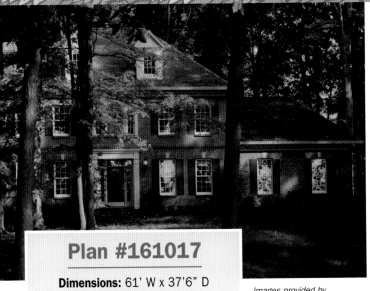

Plan #161017

Dimensions: 61' W x 37'6" D
Levels: 2
Square Footage: 2,653
Main Level Sq. Ft.: 1,365
Upper Level Sq. Ft.: 1,288
Bedrooms: 4
Bathrooms: 2½
Foundation: Basement
Materials List Available: Yes
Price Category: F

Main Level Floor Plan

Images provided by designer/architect.

Upper Level Floor Plan

Copyright by designer/architect.

Plan #151221

Dimensions: 64'6" W x 47'9" D
Levels: 2
Square Footage: 2,593
Main Level Sq. Ft.: 1,340
Upper Level Sq. Ft.: 1,253
Bedrooms: 4
Bathrooms: 2½
Foundation: Crawl space or slab
Materials List Available: No
Price Category: E

Images provided by designer/architect.

Main Level Floor Plan

Upper Level Floor Plan

Copyright by designer/architect.

Images provided by designer/architect.

Plan #401015

Dimensions: 56' W x 50'4" D
Levels: 2
Square Footage: 2,618
Main Level Sq. Ft.: 1,464
Upper Level Sq. Ft.: 1,154
Bedrooms: 3
Bathrooms: 3
Foundation: Basement
Materials List Available: Yes
Price Category: F

High vaulted ceilings and floor-to-ceiling windows enhance the spaciousness of this home. Decorative columns separate the living room from the tray-ceiling dining room.

Features:

- Kitchen: This gourmet kitchen offers a center food-preparation island, a pantry, and a pass-through to the family room and breakfast bay.

- Family Room: This spacious room boasts a fireplace and vaulted ceiling open to the second-level hallway.

- Den: This room has a wall closet and private access to a full bath. It can be used as extra guest space if needed.

- Master Suite: Located on the second floor, this area holds a bay-windowed sitting area, a walk-in closet, and a bath with a whirlpool tub and separate shower.

- Bedrooms: Family bedrooms are at the other end of the hall upstairs and share a full bath.

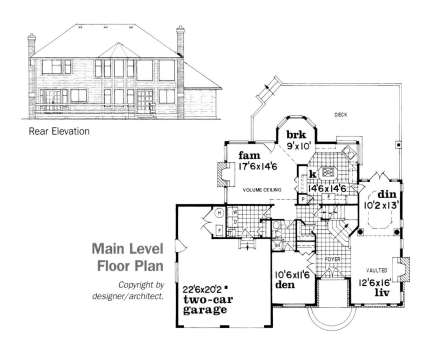

Rear Elevation

Main Level Floor Plan

Copyright by designer/architect.

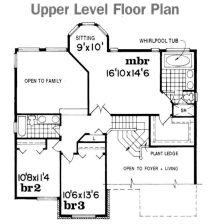

Upper Level Floor Plan

Plan #371087

Dimensions: 88'2" W x 62'10" D

Levels: 1

Square Footage: 2,643

Bedrooms: 3

Bathrooms: 2½

Foundation: Crawl space, slab, or basement

Materials List Available: No

Price Category: F

This beautiful country home has a warm look that is all its own.

Features:

- Dining Room: Once inside you will find a tiled entry that leads into this elegant room, with its 11-ft.-high ceiling.

- Living Room: This large gathering area has a 10-ft.-high ceiling, built-in bookcases, and a country fireplace.

- Kitchen: This island kitchen, with a raised bar, is open to the breakfast nook and meets the garage entrance.

- Master Suite: This suite, located in the rear of the home, features a private bathroom, large walk-in closet, marble tub, and double vanities.

- Bedrooms: Two secondary bedrooms have large closets and share a hall bathroom.

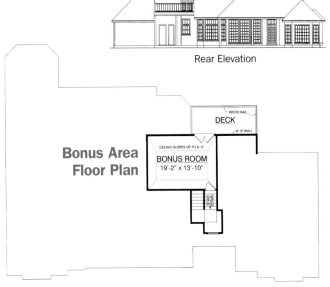

Rear Elevation

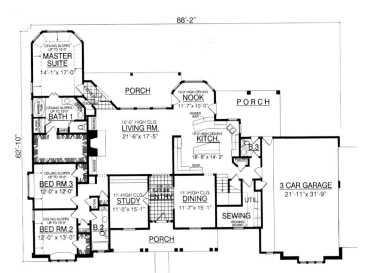

Bonus Area Floor Plan

Plan #391024

Dimensions: 71' W x 45' D
Levels: 2
Square Footage: 2,647
Main Level Sq. Ft.: 1,378
Upper Level Sq. Ft.: 1,269
Bedrooms: 4
Bathrooms: 2¾
Foundation: Crawl space, slab, or basement
Materials List Available: Yes
Price Category: F

The large wraparound porch adds a touch of country to this fine home.

Images provided by designer/architect.

Features:

- Foyer: Enter through the decorative front door, and you'll find this large foyer, with its attractive staircase to the second floor.

- Family Room: This room is expansive and includes a massive fireplace with built-in bookshelves.

- Kitchen: Built-in features continue in this kitchen, with its built-in pantry, and the breakfast room, with its built-in planning desk. The peninsula counter/eating bar separates the two rooms. Ample counter and storage space add to the kitchen's efficiency.

- Master Bedroom: This master bedroom is crowned by a cathedral ceiling and includes a lavish private bathroom with a walk-in closet.

- Study/Guest Room: To the left of the foyer is this dual-purpose room, which has convenient access to a full bathroom.

Rear View

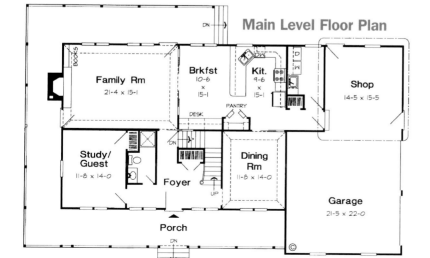

Main Level Floor Plan

Upper Level Floor Plan

Copyright by designer/architect.

Plan #371008

Dimensions: 86'4" W x 45'4" D

Levels: 2

Square Footage: 2,656

Main Level Sq. Ft: 1,969

Upper Level Sq. Ft.: 687

Bedrooms: 4

Bathrooms: 3

Foundation: Slab
(crawl space option for fee)

Materials List Available: No

Price Category: F

This lovely farmhouse-style home would be the perfect place to come home to.

Features:

• Entry: Dramatic, and with easy access to all areas of the home, this two-story entry welcomes you home in style.

• Master Suite: This large secluded area has a 10-ft.-high ceiling in the sleeping area. The luxurious private bath has his and her walk-in closets.

• Living Room: The voluminous two-story space, beautiful fireplace, and windows that provide a view of the backyard add up to gracious drama in this room.

• Kitchen: This large U-shaped kitchen with built-in pantry is open to the breakfast nook.

• Bedrooms: Bedroom 2 is located on the main level, while the other two remaining bedrooms are on the second level.

Images provided by designer/architect.

• Loft: This peaceful area has a view down into the living room on one side and down to the entry on the other.

Rear Elevation

Upper Level Floor Plan

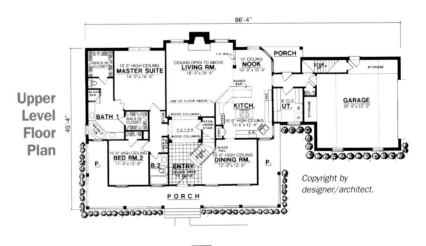

Copyright by designer/architect.

Main Level Floor Plan

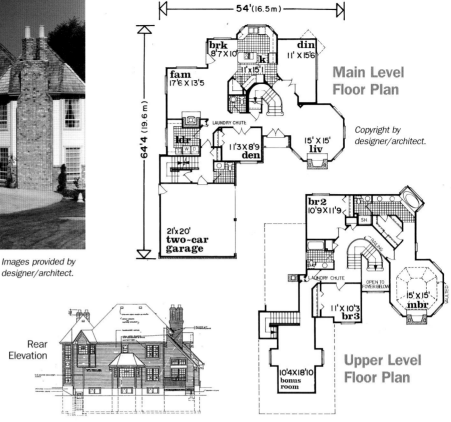

Main Level Floor Plan

brk 8'7 x 10'

din 11' x 15'6

k 11' x 15'

fam 17'6 X 13'5

ldr

11'3 X 8'9 den

15' X 15' liv

LAUNDRY CHUTE

21'x20' two-car garage

Copyright by designer/architect.

br2 10'9 x 11'9

SH

LAUNDRY CHUTE

OPEN TO FOYER BELOW

VAULTED CEILING

11' X 10'3 br3

15' X 15' mbr

10'4 X 18'10 bonus room

Upper Level Floor Plan

Images provided by designer/architect.

Rear Elevation

Plan #401004

Dimensions: 54' W x 64'4" D

Levels: 2

Square Footage: 2,684

Main Level Sq. Ft.: 1,620

Upper Level Sq. Ft.: 1,064

Bedrooms: 3

Bathrooms: 2 full, 2 half

Foundation: Basement

Materials List Available: Yes

Price Category: F

Plan #181241

Dimensions: 60' W x 44' D

Levels: 2

Square Footage: 2,687

Main Level Sq. Ft.: 1,297

Upper Level Sq. Ft.: 1,390

Bedrooms: 3

Bathrooms: 2½

Foundation: Basement

Materials List Available: Yes

Price Category: F

Images provided by designer/architect.

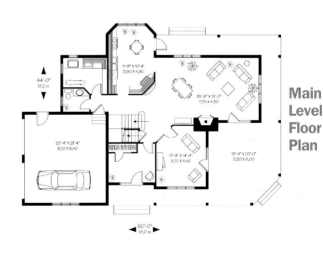

44'-0" 13.2 m

11'-8" X 16'-4" 3.50 X 4.90

25'-8" X 15'-0" 7.70 X 4.50

20'-4" X 21'-4" 6.10 X 6.40

12'-4" X 14'-6" 3.70 X 4.40

18'-4" X 20'-0" 5.50 X 6.20

60'-0" 18.0 m

Main Level Floor Plan

11'-0" X 10'-10" 3.50 X 3.25

16'-0" X 15'-0" 4.80 X 4.50

12'-4" X 13'-4" 3.70 X 4.00

12'-6" X 14'-2" 3.75 X 4.25

12'-0" X 14'-6" 3.60 X 4.35

11'-8" X 9'-8" 3.50 X 2.80

Upper Level Floor Plan

Copyright by designer/architect.

Plan #401049

Dimensions: 77'10" W x 55'8" D
Levels: 2
Square Footage: 4,087
Main Level Sq. Ft.: 2,403
Upper Level Sq. Ft.: 1,684
Bedrooms: 4
Bathrooms: 4½
Foundation: Basement
Materials List Available: Yes
Price Category: I

Images provided by designer/architect.

Finished in stucco, with an elegant entry, this dramatic two-story home is the essence of luxury.

Features:

- **Foyer:** Double doors open to this foyer, with a sunken living room on the right and a den on the left.

- **Dining Room:** An archway leads to this formal room, mirroring its own bow window and the curved window in the living room.

- **Den:** This den and the nearby computer room have use of a full bathroom--making them handy as extra guest rooms when needed.

- **Family Room:** This room, like the living room, is sunken and warmed by a hearth, but it also has built-in bookcases.

- **Kitchen:** A snack-bar counter separates this U-shaped kitchen from the light-filled break fast room.

- **Master Suite:** This gigantic space has his and her vanities, an oversized shower, a walk-in closet, and a sitting area.

Rear View

Living Room

Main Level Floor Plan

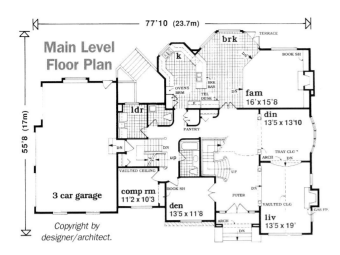

77'10 (23.7m)

55'8 (17m)

brk

k

BOOK SH

TERRACE

OVENS
BRM

BRK
BAR

TEL
DESK

DN

fam
16' x 15'8

DN

ldr

din
13'5 x 13'10

PANTRY

DN

up

DN

TRAY CLG

ARCH

DN

VAULTED CEILING

3 car garage

comp rm
11'2 x 10'3

BOOK SH

den
13'5 x 11'8

UP

FOYER

DN

ARCH

VAULTED CLG

GAS FP.

liv
13'5 x 19'

DN

Copyright by designer/architect.

Upper Level Floor Plan

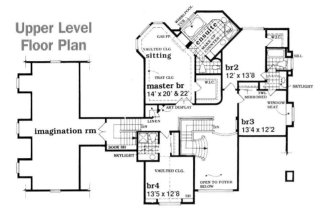

WHIRLPOOL TUB

GAS FP.

ensuite

MAKE-UP COUNTER

W.I.C.

SILL

VAULTED CLG

sitting

br2
12' x 13'8

TRAY CLG.

W.I.C.

SKYLIGHT

master br
14' x 20' & 22'

TWL
MIRRORED

WINDOW SEAT

ART DISPLAY

imagination rm

LINEN

DN

br3
13'4 x 12'2

BOOK SH

SKYLIGHT

VAULTED CLG.

DN

br4
13'5 x 12'8

OPEN TO FOYER BELOW

SH

Optional Upper Level Floor Plan

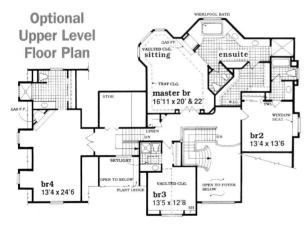

WHIRLPOOL BATH

GAS F.P.

GAS FP.

VAULTED CLG.

sitting

ensuite

STOR

TRAY CLG.

master br
16'11 x 20' & 22'

W.I.C.

TWL

WINDOW SEAT

LINEN

DN

br2
13'4 x 13'6

SKYLIGHT

br4
13'4 x 24'6

OPEN TO BELOW

PLANT LEDGE

VAULTED CLG.

br3
13'5 x 12'8

OPEN TO FOYER BELOW

DN

SH

Basement Level Floor Plan

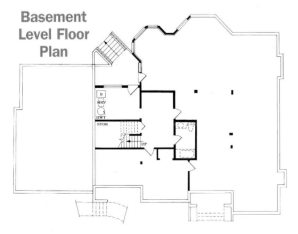

B

HRV

HWT

STOR

UP

Kitchen

Dining Room

Master Bathroom

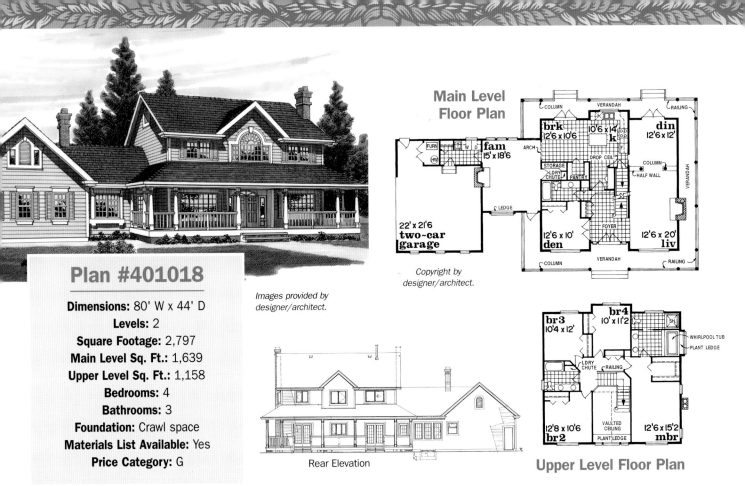

Main Level Floor Plan

Copyright by designer/architect.

Upper Level Floor Plan

Rear Elevation

Images provided by designer/architect.

Plan #401018

Dimensions: 80' W x 44' D
Levels: 2
Square Footage: 2,797
Main Level Sq. Ft.: 1,639
Upper Level Sq. Ft.: 1,158
Bedrooms: 4
Bathrooms: 3
Foundation: Crawl space
Materials List Available: Yes
Price Category: G

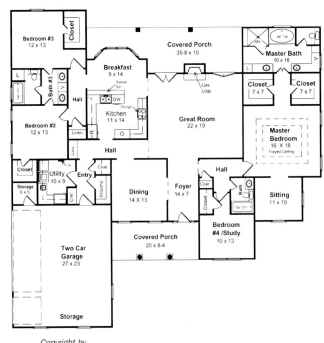

Copyright by designer/architect.

Plan #351059

Dimensions: 71'4" W x 70'2" D
Levels: 1
Square Footage: 2,805
Bedrooms: 4
Bathrooms: 3
Foundation: Crawl space, slab, or basement
Materials List Available: Yes
Price Category: F

Images provided by designer/architect.

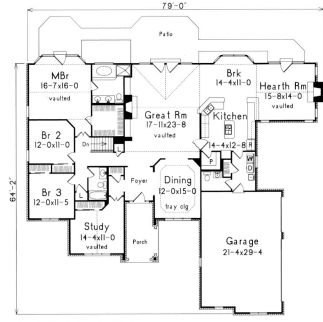

Plan #321028

Dimensions: 79' W x 64'2" D

Levels: 1

Square Footage: 2,723

Bedrooms: 3

Bathrooms: 2½

Foundation: Basement

Materials List Available: Yes

Price Category: F

Images provided by designer/architect.

Copyright by designer/architect.

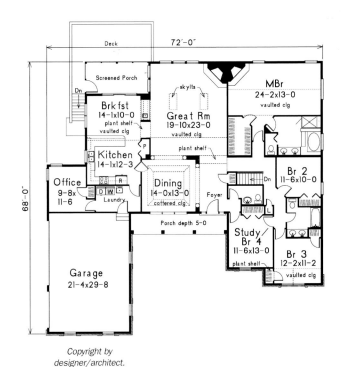

Plan #321027

Dimensions: 72' W x 68' D

Levels: 1

Square Footage: 2,758

Bedrooms: 4

Bathrooms: 2½

Foundation: Basement

Materials List Available: Yes

Price Category: F

Images provided by designer/architect.

Copyright by designer/architect.

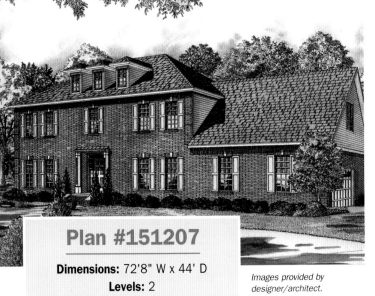

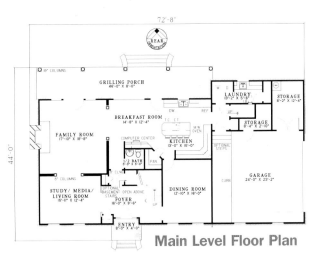

Main Level Floor Plan

Plan #151207

Dimensions: 72'8" W x 44' D
Levels: 2
Square Footage: 3,099
Main Level Sq. Ft.: 1,603
Upper Level Sq. Ft.: 1,496
Bedrooms: 4
Bathrooms: 3½
Foundation: Crawl space or slab
Materials List Available: No
Price Category: G

Images provided by designer/architect.

Upper Level Floor Plan

Copyright by designer/architect.

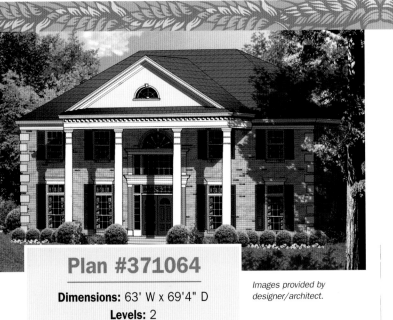

Plan #371064

Dimensions: 63' W x 69'4" D
Levels: 2
Square Footage: 3,140
Main Level Sq. Ft.: 1,965
Upper Level Sq. Ft.: 1,175
Bedrooms: 4
Bathrooms: 3½
Foundation: Slab
Materials List Available: No
Price Category: G

Images provided by designer/architect.

Main Level Floor Plan

Upper Level Floor Plan

Copyright by designer/architect.

**Main Level
Floor Plan**

sto   sto   sto

garage
22 x 22

porch 18 x 6

w d
14x9
util

built-in entertainment ctr and library

family rm
25 x 16

pan
books
desk

prm ref
ct

kit 14x13

china
ovns
dw

shr
bath 17 x 9

built-in entertainment ctr and library

sitting
14 x 12

mbr
16 x 13

foy

dining
16 x 12

eating
14 x 10

porch 34 x 8

*Images provided by
designer/architect.*

future space 28 x 12

sloped clg   sloped clg

dn

Upper Level Floor Plan

Copyright by designer/architect.

outline of lower level

br 4
11 x 12

sloped clg   sloped clg

bath   bath

attic space

balcony

attic space

br 2
13 x 13

hand
rail

open to
lower level

br 3
13 x 12

open to
lower level

Plan #211072

Dimensions: 62' W x 86' D

Levels: 2

Square Footage: 3,012

Main Level Sq. Ft.: 2,202

Upper Level Sq. Ft.: 810

Bedrooms: 4

Bathrooms: 3½

Foundation: Crawl space,
optional basement

Materials List Available: Yes

Price Category: G

Plan #121023

Dimensions: 85'5" W x 74'8" D

Levels: 2

Square Footage: 3,904

Main Level Sq. Ft.: 2,813

Upper Level Sq. Ft.: 1,091

Bedrooms: 4

Bathrooms: 3½

Foundation: Basement

Materials List Available: Yes

Price Category: H

**Main Level
Floor Plan**

Family
Room

Eating
Area

Living
Room

Garage

Mbr.

Dining
Room

Sitting
Area

Garage

STOOP

COVERED
STOOP

Den

85'-5"

74'-8"

©dbi

*Images provided by
designer/architect.*

Br.4

Br.2

Br.3

OPEN TO
BELOW

**Upper Level
Floor Plan**

Copyright by designer/architect.

Plan #371089

Dimensions: 85' W x 46' D
Levels: 2
Square Footage: 2,704
Main Level Sq. Ft.: 1,850
Upper Level Sq. Ft.: 854
Bedrooms: 3
Bathrooms: 2½
Foundation: Slab
Materials List Available: No
Price Category: F

Images provided by designer/architect.

Main Level Floor Plan

Copyright by designer/architect.

Upper Level Floor Plan

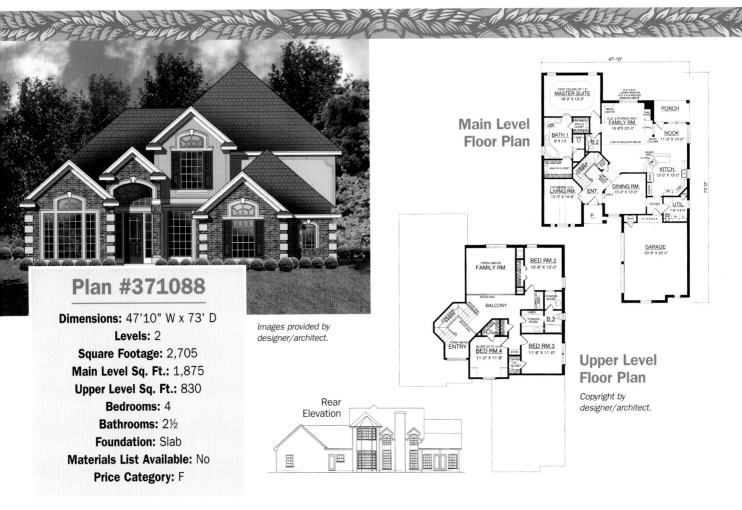

Plan #371088

Dimensions: 47'10" W x 73' D
Levels: 2
Square Footage: 2,705
Main Level Sq. Ft.: 1,875
Upper Level Sq. Ft.: 830
Bedrooms: 4
Bathrooms: 2½
Foundation: Slab
Materials List Available: No
Price Category: F

Images provided by designer/architect.

Main Level Floor Plan

Upper Level Floor Plan

Copyright by designer/architect.

Rear Elevation

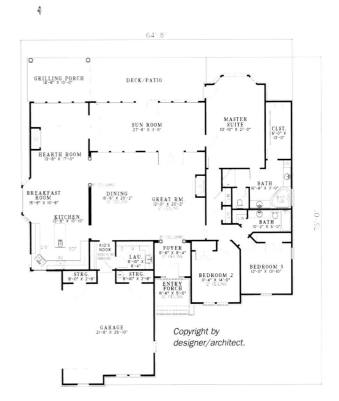

Plan #151222

Dimensions: 64'8" W x 75' D

Levels: 1

Square Footage: 2,707

Bedrooms: 3

Bathrooms: 2

Foundation: Crawl space or slab

Materials List Available: No

Price Category: F

Images provided by designer/architect.

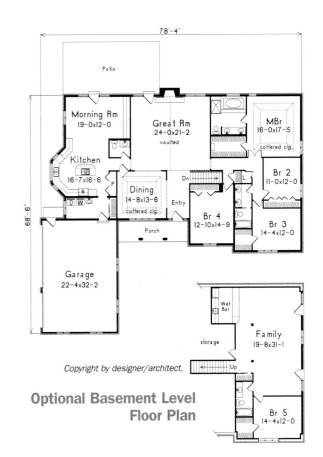

Plan #321036

Dimensions: 78'4" W x 68'6" D

Levels: 1

Square Footage: 2,900

Bedrooms: 4

Bathrooms: 2½

Foundation: Basement

Materials List Available: No

Price Category: F

Images provided by designer/architect.

Optional Basement Level Floor Plan

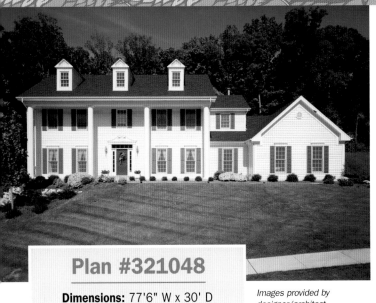

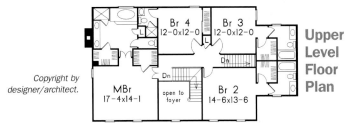

Main Level Floor Plan

Deck

Hearth
12-5x10-0
vaulted

Family
20-8x15-6

Bar

Brk
12-5x12-0

Kitchen
11-2x12-0

Garage
21-1x31-5

Living
17-4x13-3

Foyer

Up

Dining
14-6x13-3

W D

30'-0"

Porch
45-0x6-0

77'-6"

Images provided by designer/architect.

Upper Level Floor Plan

Br 4
12-0x12-0

Br 3
12-0x12-0

MBr
17-4x14-1

open to foyer

Br 2
14-6x13-6

Dn

Dn

Copyright by designer/architect.

Plan #321048

Dimensions: 77'6" W x 30' D
Levels: 2
Square Footage: 3,216
Main Level Sq. Ft.: 1,834
Upper Level Sq. Ft.: 1,382
Bedrooms: 4
Bathrooms: 4½
Foundation: Basement
Materials List Available: Yes
Price Category: G

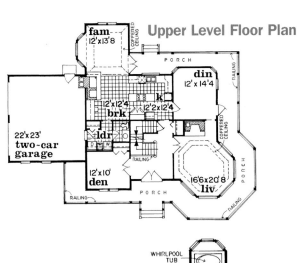

Upper Level Floor Plan

fam
12'x13'8

COFFERED CEILING

PORCH

din
12'x14'4

RAILING

12'x12'4

k
2'x12'4

brk

COFFERED CEILING

22'x23'
two-car
garage

ldr

RAILING

16'6x20'8
liv

PORCH

12'x10'
den

PORCH

RAILING

WHIRLPOOL TUB

SH

br3
12'x10'

br 4
12'x9'

RAILING

COFFERED CEILING

Main Level Floor Plan

Copyright by designer/architect.

12'x10'
br2

16'6 x 19'8
mbr

Plan #401009

Dimensions: 70'8" W x 54' D
Levels: 2
Square Footage: 2,750
Main Level Sq. Ft.: 1,462
Upper Level Sq. Ft.: 1,288
Bedrooms: 4
Bathrooms: 2½
Foundation: Basement
Materials List Available: Yes
Price Category: F

Images provided by designer/architect.

This home, as shown in the photograph, may differ from the actual blueprints. For more detailed information, please check the floor plans carefully.

Main Level Floor Plan

Bath
Laun.
Hall
CLOSET
DESK
Breakfast
11 x 14'6"
Family Room
19' x 15'3"
Garage
22' x 22'11"
Kitchen
10'4" x 11'5"
DOWN
ALCOVE
BUILT-IN
Dining Room
11'10" x 13'8"
Foyer
Study
11'10" x 11'5"
Porch

Copyright by designer/architect.

Images provided by designer/architect.

Upper Level Floor Plan

Master
Bedroom
13'11" x 18'1"
Master
Bath
Bedroom
12' x 11'7"
WALK IN
CLOSET
Hall
WOOD RAIL
DN 15 R.
Bedroom
11'10" x 12'
Open
Below
Bedroom
11'10" x 12'7"
Bath

Plan #161075

Dimensions: 63' W x 38'2" D
Levels: 2
Square Footage: 2,773
Main Level Sq. Ft.: 1,498
Upper Level Sq. Ft.: 1,275
Bedrooms: 4
Bathrooms: 2½
Foundation: Basement
Materials List Available: No
Price Category: F

Rear Elevation

Main Level Floor Plan

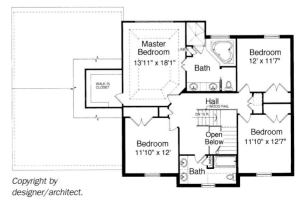

Bath
Laun.
Hall
CLOSET
DESK
Covered
Porch
Breakfast
11' x 14'6"
Family Room
19' x 15'3"
Garage
22' x 22'11"
Kitchen
10'4' 11'5"
PANTRY
ENT CENTER
BUILT-INS
Dining Room
11'10" x 13'8"
Foyer
Study
11'10" x 11'5"
CLOSET
CLOSET
Porch

Upper Level Floor Plan

Master
Bedroom
13'11" x 18'1"
Bath
Bedroom
12' x 11'7"
WALK IN
CLOSET
Hall
WOOD RAIL
DN 15 R.
Bedroom
11'10" x 12'
Open
Below
Bedroom
11'10" x 12'7"
Bath

Copyright by designer/architect.

Plan #161077

Dimensions: 63' W x 41'2" D
Levels: 2
Square Footage: 2,773
Main Level Sq. Ft.: 1,498
Upper Level Sq. Ft.: 1,275
Bedrooms: 4
Bathrooms: 2½
Foundation: Basement
Materials List Available: Yes
Price Category: F

Images provided by designer/architect.

Rear Elevation

The Right Light

Lighting is one of the most important design elements in any home. Coordinating all of your artificial lighting sources—lamps, recessed or track lighting, sconces, ceiling-mounted fixtures, even pendants—can make the difference between a place that is warm and welcoming or one that is dark and depressing. In addition, light can be used in more focused ways—whether that be illuminating your desk in a home office or minimizing reflection as you watch a DVD on your big-screen television.

Light even has the power to visually reconfigure space, making rooms seem larger or smaller than they are. Lastly, the smart use of lighting can shine attention on architectural high points while obscuring less desirable details.

Lighting Plans

The rooms in your new home will combine the three types of lighting: ambient, task, and accent light. How you plan to use the room will determine the amount and type of lighting you will need. Although there are some general rules and an actual formula to determine how many watts of light to use for every square foot of space in your house, you must be the ultimate judge of your lighting needs.

General Lighting

Ambient Light. Because this is the soft diffused overall light that fills a room, ambient lighting is also called general lighting. Obviously, it is critical to the mood of a room. Aside from natural light, there are numerous artificial sources of ambient light. You can use all or some of them for your home.

Ceiling Fixtures. Standard ceiling-mounted fixtures, such as pendants and chandeliers, and recessed canisters are good sources of general lighting.

Sconces and Torcheres. Wall fixtures usually direct light upward, where it washes the wall and is reflected back into the room. Other possible sources of good general lighting are lamps with opaque shades. But the important thing to remember is that ambient light is inconspicuous. Although you know the source of the light, the glow is diffused. Of course, never use an exposed bulb, which is much too harsh.

How bright you should make the rooms in your new home depends on the way and the time of day the room will be used. To create the precise level of light, wire ambient light sources to dimmer switches. This puts you in control and allows you to easily

Recessed accent lighting highlights the painting and the shelves of collectibles.

adjust the light level. For example, in a family room you may want subdued lighting for watching a movie, and stronger, more cheerful lighting when you're hosting a kid's birthday party.

Task Lighting

Task lighting focuses on a specific area. It illuminates the work surface—whether it be the kitchen counter or the top of your desk in a home office. Metal architects' lamps, under-cabinet lights, reading lamps, and desk lamps are all excellent examples

of task lighting. Optimally, task lights should be angled between you and the work. A reading lamp functions best, after all, when it is positioned behind you and over your shoulder. Aiming light directly on a surface creates glare, which causes eye strain.

In bathrooms, include task lights for grooming. Sconces on either side of the mirror are preferable to a strip of light above the mirror because the latter will cast shadows. If the room is small, the sconces may serve as general lighting as well.

Accent Lighting

Designers like to use accent lighting because it is decorative and often dramatic. Accent lighting draws attention to a favorite work of art, a recessed niche on a stairway landing, or a tall plant at the end of a long room, for example. Designers agree that when you want to highlight something special, be sure the light source is concealed in order not to detract from the object you are spotlighting.

Wall sconces, above left, placed on both sides of a bathroom mirror are good sources of light for applying makeup and general grooming.

Track-mounted spotlights, above right, serve a number of lighting needs. Here some provide general lighting while others accentuate the wall of art.

Use light to set off a collection, right, of personal objects. Here the items alone draw attention, but the lighting makes this area a focal point of the room.

Room-by-Room Guide to Lighting

With lighting, one size doesn't fit all. Each room presents its own lighting challenges and solutions. Think outside of the box. Recessed lighting, for example, can be tucked away under bookshelves, not just in the ceiling; track lighting can be installed in a circular pattern to mirror a room with sweeping curves rather than in straight strips. Here are some other strategies for lighting each of your new rooms.

Family/Play Room. Pendants or chandeliers are obvious choices here if headroom is not an issue. Add recessed lighting in the corners or near doors and windows. Or if the room is designed for active play, install recessed lighting throughout. Use lamps or track lighting for areas that will be used for reading or hobbies. And don't forget about accent lighting to highlight wall-hung photographs or paintings.

Media/TV Room. No light should be brighter than the TV screen. Instead of one bright light source, try several low-level lights—recessed lighting, lamps, and lighting under shelves. Three-way bulbs or dimmers are often the best solution. Remember: light should be behind you, not between you and the screen.

Home Office. A good lighting arrangement combines indirect overhead illumination with table lamps. Indirect light means that the light is softy diffused throughout the home office, not shining down on you. Use a desktop lamp, preferably an adjustable fixture, to focus light on the task at hand and to deflect glare from the computer screen. Install unobtrusive light fixtures in a hutch above the work surface or create a light bridge, a horizontal strip of wood with a light built into it, fastened to the underside of two upper cabinets.

In media room, try to keep the lighting levels below that of the TV.

Bedrooms. Any number of lighting combinations could work in this room, but generally an overhead fixture that you flip on when you first enter the room is practical and, depending on your choice of fixture, stylish. For a more intimate mood, wiring bedside lamps to a light switch will also work. A must-have is a swing-arm reading lamp with a narrow beam of light that enables you to finish your novel while your spouse gets some shuteye. These types of reading lamps are responsible for saving more than one marriage.

Bathrooms. As with a home office, you need ambient (general) light (to help you find your way to the toilet or shower without tripping) and task lighting (for personal grooming). The ideal task lighting should come from both sides of the mirror at eye level.

Kitchens. Team up general illumination—recessed or ceiling-mounted fixtures installed about 12 to 15 inches from the front of the upper cabinets is a good choice and a fixture or two over the sink—with under-the-cabinet task lighting for food preparation. Install decorative wood trim to hide the light strips.

Home Workshop. A workable solution that has stood the test of time is fluorescent fixtures at regular intervals along the ceiling and work lights for specific tasks. Installing a strip of outlets along the length of a worktable and plugging in lights, either portable ones or those attached to the underside of the cabinet, provides illumination on demand.

Staircase. Sufficient light is critical around staircases, where one false step can lead to injury. As a rule, figure you will need at least one 60-watt fixture per 10 feet of running stairs. Try recessed lighting in the ceiling, or for a more dramatic look, install lighting in several recessed niches along the staircase wall that won't invade the stair area.

Light home offices, right, using indirect general lighting combined with desk-mounted task lighting.

Kitchens, below, require overhead ambient lighting and concentrated task lighting over work surfaces.

For workshops, bottom, install overhead lights that won't cast shadows on the work.

Plan #391031

Dimensions: 78' W x 64' D

Levels: 2

Square Footage: 3,176

Main Level Sq. Ft.: 2,310

Upper Level Sq. Ft.: 866

Bedrooms: 3

Bathrooms: 3½

Foundation: Crawl space, slab, or basement

Materials List Available: Yes

Price Category: G

You can almost feel this home's architectural philosophy of only the best will do the moment you enter its two-story gallery.

Features:

- Family Room: This room is a showstopper, with its three large windows, fireplace, and vaulted ceilings.

- Kitchen: This G-Shaped kitchen glides to the breakfast nook, which in turn drifts to the outdoor patio.

- Utility Area: The laundry room and sewing workroom meet the garage entrance.

- Dining Room: This room with floor-to-ceiling windows maintains formality and aligns with an exterior porch.

- Living Room: This highly formal room is along the opposite side of the house from the family room.

- Study: This impressive study features atrium doors and clerestory windows.

- Master Suite: The first-floor master suite boasts a sit-down vanity, enormous closet, and spa-style tub.

Images provided by designer/architect.

Main Level Floor Plan

Copyright by designer/architect.

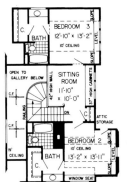

Upper Level Floor Plan

Rear View

Master Bedroom

Plan #391018

Dimensions: 93' W x 54' D
Levels: 2
Square Footage: 3,746
Main Level Sq. Ft.: 1,978
Upper Level Sq. Ft.: 1,768
Bedrooms: 4
Bathrooms: 3½
Foundation: Basement
Materials List Available: Yes
Price Category: H

Images provided by designer/architect.

While the facade of this house suggests the level of detail within, it gives no hint of the home's uniquely designed rooms.

Features:

- **Kitchen:** This L-shape kitchen, with its large, angled island, provides plenty of workspace and storage.

- **Built-ins:** Shelving, bookcases, and a built-in desk add extra usefulness throughout the home.

- **Porch:** This three-season porch is an ideal place to relax and enjoy the outdoors when the weather doesn't permit use of either of the two decks.

- **Garage:** This garage holds up to three vehicles, though the third bay can be used as storage or shop space.

- **Fireplaces:** The master suite, great room, and kitchen/breakfast area are all warmed by fireplaces.

Main Level Floor Plan

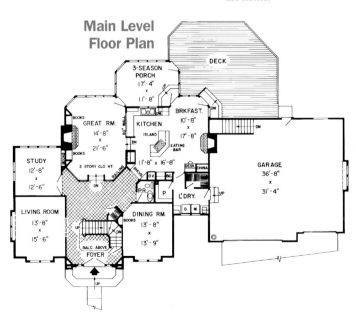

Upper Level Floor Plan

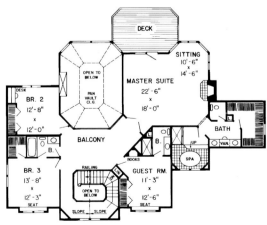

Copyright by designer/architect.

Plan #151209

Dimensions: 85'2" W x 57'6" D
Levels: 2
Square Footage: 4,468
Main Level Sq. Ft.: 2,733
Upper Level Sq. Ft.: 1,735
Bedrooms: 4
Bathrooms: 4½
Foundation: Crawl space or slab
Materials List Available: No
Price Category: I

Images provided by designer/architect.

You're sure to find all the amenities you could ever want in this two-story brick home.

Features:

• **Great Room:** This enormous room, with its fireplace and media center, is perfect for entertaining.

• **Home Theater:** Family movie night has never been better than in this personal space.

• **Master Suite:** This large area has an office/sitting room and a luxurious private bath.

• **Guest Room:** The bedroom and bathroom combination downstairs can serve as a guest or in-law suite.

• **Bedrooms:** Two additional bedrooms are located upstairs near the master suite.

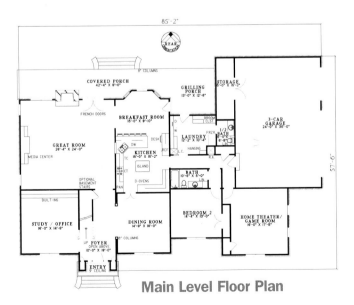

Main Level Floor Plan

Copyright by designer/architect.

Upper Level Floor Plan

Plan #121029

Dimensions: 58'8" W x 54' D

Levels: 2

Square Footage: 2,576

Main Level Sq. Ft.: 1,735

Upper Level Sq. Ft.: 841

Bedrooms: 4

Bathrooms: 2½

Foundation: Basement

Materials List Available: Yes

Price Category: E

Images provided by designer/architect.

This gracious home is designed with the contemporary lifestyle in mind.

Features:

- Ceiling Height: 8 ft. unless otherwise noted.

- Great Room: This room features a fireplace and entertainment center. It's equally suited for family gatherings and formal entertaining.

- Breakfast Area: The fireplace is two-sided so it shares its warmth with this breakfast area — the perfect spot for informal family meals.

- Master Suite: Halfway up the staircase you'll find double-doors into this truly distinctive suite featuring a barrel-vault ceiling, built-in bookcases, and his and her walk-in closets. Unwind at the end of the day by stretching out in the oval whirlpool tub.

- Computer Loft: This loft overlooks the great room. It is designed as a home office with a built-in desk for your computer.

- Garage: Two bays provide plenty of storage in addition to parking space.

Main Level Floor Plan

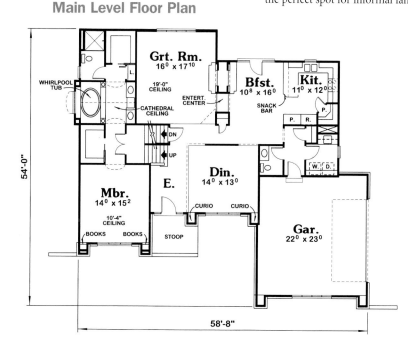

Upper Level Floor Plan

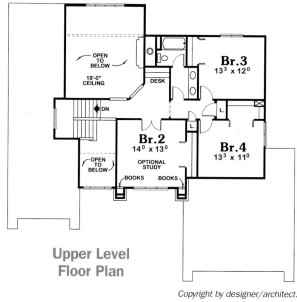

Copyright by designer/architect.

Plan #401048

Dimensions: 57'8" W x 103'6" D
Levels: 2
Square Footage: 5,159
Main Level Sq. Ft.: 2,473
Upper Level Sq. Ft.: 2,686
Bedrooms: 4
Bathrooms: 4½
Foundation: Basement
Materials List Available: Yes
Price Category: I

Images provided by designer/architect.

- Hearth Room: Attached to the kitchen, this hearth room has the requisite fireplace and three sets of French doors that lead to the covered porch.

- Family Room: This room features a coffered ceiling and a fireplace flanked by French doors.

- Master Suite: This area includes a tray ceiling, covered deck, and lavish bath.

- Bedrooms: All bedrooms are located on the second floor. Two full bathrooms serve the family bedrooms and a bonus room that might be used as an additional bedroom or hobby space.

This unusual stucco-and-siding design opens with a grand portico to a foyer that extends to the living room with fireplace.

Features:

- Dining Room: Step up a few steps to this dining room, with its coffered ceiling and butler's pantry, which connects to the gourmet kitchen.

Main Level Floor Plan

Copyright by designer/architect.

Upper Level Floor Plan

Rear Elevation

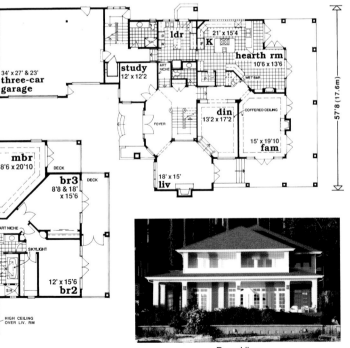

Rear View

Great Room

Foyer

Living Room

Kitchen

Plan #121073

Dimensions: 70' W x 52' D
Levels: 2
Square Footage: 2,579
Main Level Sq. Ft.: 1,933
Upper Level Sq. Ft.: 646
Bedrooms: 4
Bathrooms: 2½
Foundation: Basement
Materials List Available: Yes
Price Category: E

Images provided by designer/architect.

Luxury will surround you in this home with contemporary styling and up-to-date amenities at every turn.

Features:

• Great Room: This large room shares both a see-through fireplace and a wet bar with the adjacent hearth room. Transom-topped windows add both light and architectural interest to this room.

• Den: Transom-topped windows add visual interest to this private area.

• Kitchen: A center island and corner pantry add convenience to this well-planned kitchen, and a lovely ceiling treatment adds beauty to the bayed breakfast area.

• Master Suite: A built-in bookcase adds to the ambiance of this luxury-filled area, where you're sure to find a retreat at the end of the day.

Main Level Floor Plan

Upper Level Floor Plan

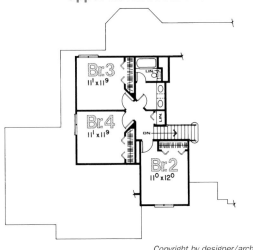

Copyright by designer/architect.

Plan #171013

Dimensions: 74' W x 72' D
Levels: 1
Square Footage: 3,084
Bedrooms: 4
Bathrooms: 3½
Foundation: Crawl space or slab
Materials List Available: Yes
Price Category: G

Images provided by designer/architect.

Impressive porch columns add to the country charm of this amenity-filled family home.

Features:

- Ceiling Height: 10 ft.

- Foyer: The sense of style continues from the front porch into this foyer, which opens to the formal dining room and the living room.

- Dining Room: Two handsome support columns accentuate the elegance of this dining room.

- Living Room: This living room features a cozy corner fireplace and plenty of room for the entire family to gather and relax.

- Kitchen: You'll be inspired to new culinary heights in this kitchen, which offers plenty of counter space, a snack bar, a built-in pantry, and a china closet.

- Master Suite: The bedroom of this master suite has a fireplace and overlooks a rear courtyard. The bath has two vanities a large walk-in closet, a deluxe tub, a walk-in shower, and a skylight.

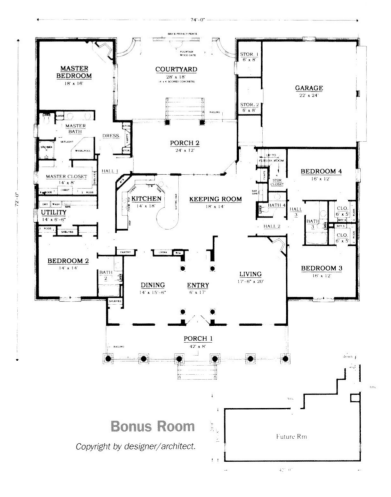

Bonus Room

Copyright by designer/architect.

Plan #121062

Dimensions: 70' W x 62' D
Levels: 2
Square Footage: 3,448
Main Level Sq. Ft.: 2,375
Upper Level Sq. Ft.: 1,073
Bedrooms: 4
Bathrooms: 3½
Foundation: Basement
Materials List Available: Yes
Price Category: G

Images provided by designer/architect.

You'll love this design if you're looking for a comfortable home with dimensions and details that create a sense of grandeur.

Features:

- Entry: A soaring ceiling, curved staircase, and balcony that overlooks a tall plant shelf combine to create your first impression of grandeur in this home.

- Great Room: A transom-topped bowed window highlights this room, with its 11-ft., beamed ceiling, built-in wet bar, and see-through fireplace.

- Kitchen: Designed for the gourmet cook, this kitchen has every amenity you could desire.

- Breakfast Room: Adjacent to the great room and the kitchen, this gazebo-shaped breakfast area lights both the kitchen and hearth room.

Main Level Floor Plan

Upper Level Floor Plan

Copyright by designer/architect.

Plan #151217

Dimensions: 88' W x 90'6" D
Levels: 1
Square Footage: 2,864
Bedrooms: 3
Bathrooms: 3
Foundation: Crawl space or slab
Materials List Available: No
Price Category: F

Images provided by designer/architect.

The planters on either side of this traditional design's entry porch are certain to be the topic of conversation when guests arrive.

Features:

- Great Room: This large gathering room, with a cozy fireplace, has access to the rear porch.

- Dining Room: This room has a view of the backyard and is open to the great room.

- Kitchen: This island kitchen boasts an abundant amount of cabinets, and counter space is open to the breakfast room.

- Master Suite: This suite features a private bathroom with double vanities, a whirlpool tub, and a large walk-in closet.

- Garage: This large attached three-car garage has a storage area.

Copyright by designer/architect.

Plan #151225

Dimensions: 81'10" W x 67'2" D
Levels: 1
Square Footage: 2,875
Bedrooms: 5
Bathrooms: 4
Foundation: Crawl space or slab
Materials List Available: No
Price Category: F

This brick home with columns has an elegant look.

Images provided by designer/architect.

Features:

- Front Porch: This entry area has beautiful columns and an 11-ft.-high ceiling.
- Great Room: A 10-ft.-high ceiling, a fireplace, a built-in media center, and French doors to the rear porch distinguish this gathering area.
- Kitchen: This kitchen, which has an island and a walk-in pantry, is open to the hearth room and the breakfast room.

- Breakfast Room: A bay window and access to the rear grilling porch make this area attractive and functional.
- Master Suite: This oasis has a sitting room with a bay window. The master bathroom has a walk-in closet, corner whirlpool bath, corner glass shower, and split vanities.
- In-Law Suite: A private bathroom with a whirlpool tub, shower, and walk-in closet makes this space perfect for guests or in-laws.

Main Level Floor Plan

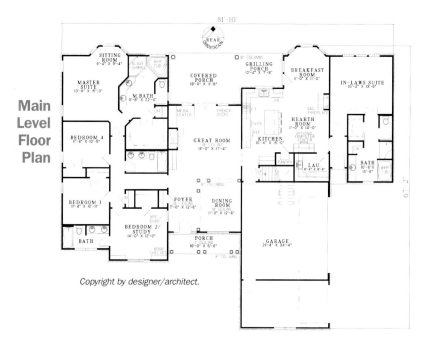

Copyright by designer/architect.

Bonus Area Floor Plan

Main Level Floor Plan

Upper Level Floor Plan

Images provided by designer/architect.

Copyright by designer/architect.

Plan #151029

Dimensions: 59'4" W x 74'2" D

Levels: 1½

Square Footage: 2,777

Main Level Sq. Ft.: 2,082

Upper Level Sq. Ft.: 695

Bedrooms: 4

Bathrooms: 2½

Foundation: Crawl space, slab; optional basement plan available for extra fee

Materials List Available: No

Price Category: F

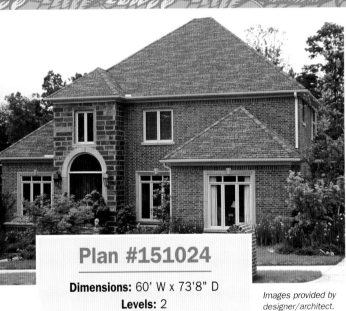

Main Level Floor Plan

Upper Level Floor Plan

Images provided by designer/architect.

Copyright by designer/architect.

Plan #151024

Dimensions: 60' W x 73'8" D

Levels: 2

Square Footage: 3,623

Main Level Sq. Ft.: 2,391

Upper Level Sq. Ft.: 1,232

Bedrooms: 3

Bathrooms: 3½

Foundation: Crawl space, slab; optional full basement plan available for extra fee

Materials List Available: No

Price Category: H

Images provided by designer/architect.

Plan #401050

Dimensions: 81' W x 61' D
Levels: 2
Square Footage: 6,841
Main Level Sq. Ft.: 2,596
Upper Level Sq. Ft.: 2,233
Finished Basement Sq. Ft.: 2,012
Bedrooms: 4
Bathrooms: 3 full, 2 half
Foundation: Basement
Materials List Available: Yes
Price Category: I

This grand two-story European home is adorned with a facade of stucco and brick, meticulously appointed with details for gracious living.

Features:

• Foyer: Guests enter through a portico to find this stately two-story foyer.

• Living Room: This formal area features a tray ceiling and a fireplace and is joined by a charming dining room with a large bay window.

• Kitchen: A butler's pantry joins the dining room to this gourmet kitchen, which holds a separate wok kitchen, an island work center, and a breakfast room with double doors that lead to the rear patio.

• Family Room: Located near the kitchen, this room enjoys a built-in aquarium, media center, and fireplace.

• Den: This room with a tray ceiling, window seat, and built-in computer center is tucked in a corner for privacy.

• Master Suite: The second floor features this spectacular space, which has a separate sitting room, an oversized closet, and a bath with a spa tub.

Right Side Elevation

Kitchen

Rear Elevation

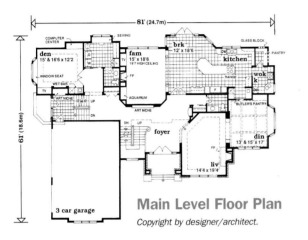

Main Level Floor Plan

Copyright by designer/architect.

Upper Level
Floor Plan

Basement Level
Floor Plan

Master Bedroom

Great Room

Master Bathroom

Main Level Floor Plan
Copyright by designer/architect.

Three-car Garage 21' x 31'10"
Hearth Room 16'4" x 14'
Terrace
Dressing
Hall
Laun. 11' x 14'
Bath
Breakfast 24' x 26' Irr
Kitchen
Great Room 18'9" x 15'6"
Master Bedroom 17' x 28'
Gallery
Bath
Dining Room 16' x 15'2"
Foyer
Library 16' x 14'
Porch

Plan #161029

Dimensions: 87' W x 82' D
Levels: 2
Square Footage: 4,470
Main Level Sq. Ft.: 3,300
Upper Level Sq. Ft.: 1,170
Bedrooms: 4
Bathrooms: 3 Full; 2 Half
Foundation: Basement
Materials List Available: Yes
Price Category: I

Images provided by designer/architect.

Bedroom 12'8" x 15'6"
walk-in closet
Bath
walk-in closet
stairs dn
wood rail
Hall
Bedroom 15' x 15'2"

Upper Level Floor Plan

Bedroom 12' x 13'6"
Balcony
walk-in closet

Rear View

Plan #161025

Dimensions: 63'4" W x 48' D
Levels: 2
Square Footage: 2,738
Main Level Sq. Ft.: 1,915
Upper Level Sq. Ft.: 823
Bedrooms: 4
Bathrooms: 3½
Foundation: Basement
Materials List Available: No
Price Category: F

Images provided by designer/architect.

This home, as shown in the photograph, may differ from the actual blueprints. For more detailed information, please check the floor plans carefully.

Dressing
walk-in closet
Great Room 16' x 19'6"
Breakfast 14' x 11'2"
Hearth Room 17' x 14'10"
Kitchen
Laun.
Master Bedroom 14' x 14'1"
Foyer
Porch
Dining Room 12' x 13'10"
Two-car Garage 21' x 20'4"
Sitting Area 11'2" x 9'4"

Main Level Floor Plan

Great Room Below
Balcony
Bedroom 17' x 12'6"
Bedroom 10' x 13'10"
Bath
Bedroom 12' x 10'6"
slope ceiling
slope ceiling

Upper Level Floor Plan

Copyright by designer/architect.

Copyright by designer/architect.

Plan #321007

Dimensions: 76' W x 55'2" D

Levels: 1

Square Footage: 2,695

Bedrooms: 3

Bathrooms: 2½

Foundation: Basement

Materials List Available: Yes

Price Category: F

Images provided by designer/architect.

Decorative Poles

Drapery poles are supported by the brackets fastened to the window frame or wall. The brackets that are provided with the poles generally coordinate and blend in with the pole finish. Brackets can be simple but also decorative. If you opt for a spectacular, attention-grabbing bracket, consider choosing less showy finials for the ends of the pole.

Plan #121090

Dimensions: 60' W x 58' D

Levels: 2

Square Footage: 2,645

Main Level Sq. Ft.: 1,972

Upper Level Sq. Ft.: 673

Bedrooms: 4

Bathrooms: 2½

Foundation: Basement

Materials List Available: Yes

Price Category: F

Images provided by designer/architect.

Main Level Floor Plan

Upper Level Floor Plan

Copyright by designer/architect.

**Main Level
Floor Plan**

*Images provided by
designer/architect.*

Plan #121081

Dimensions: 76'8" W x 68' D
Levels: 2
Square Footage: 3,623
Main Level Sq. Ft.: 2,603
Upper Level Sq. Ft.: 1,020
Bedrooms: 4
Bathrooms: 4½
Foundation: Basement
Materials List Available: Yes
Price Category: G

**Upper Level
Floor Plan**

Copyright by designer/architect.

Copyright by designer/architect.

Plan #321034

Dimensions: 75'8" W x 52'6" D
Levels: 1
Square Footage: 3,508
Bedrooms: 4
Bathrooms: 3
Foundation: Basement, walkout
Materials List Available: Yes
Price Category: H

*Images provided by
designer/architect.*

**Optional
Basement Level
Floor Plan**

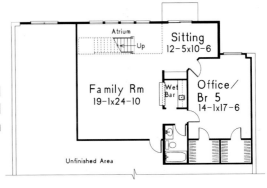

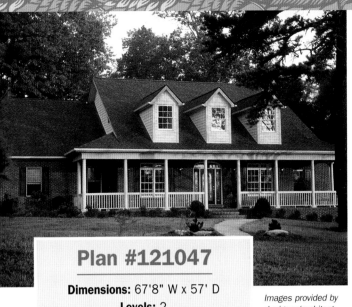

Main Level Floor Plan

Plan #121047

Dimensions: 67'8" W x 57' D

Levels: 2

Square Footage: 3,072

Main Level Sq. Ft.: 2,116

Upper Level Sq. Ft.: 956

Bedrooms: 4

Bathrooms: 3½

Foundation: Slab

Materials List Available: Yes

Price Category: G

Images provided by designer/architect.

Upper Level Floor Plan

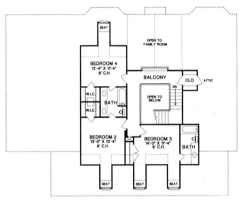

Copyright by designer/architect.

Main Level Floor Plan

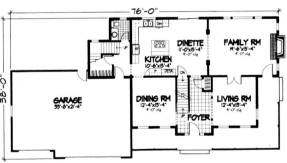

Plan #271072

Dimensions: 76' W x 38' D

Levels: 2

Square Footage: 3,081

Main Level Sq. Ft.: 1,358

Upper Level Sq. Ft.: 1,723

Bedrooms: 3

Bathrooms: 2½

Foundation: Crawl space or basement

Materials List Available: No

Price Category: G

Images provided by designer/architect.

Upper Level Floor Plan

Copyright by designer/architect.

Plan #371024

Dimensions: 54'4" W x 47'8" D

Levels: 2

Square Footage: 2,843

Main Level Sq. Ft.: 1,810

Upper Level Sq. Ft.: 1,033

Bedrooms: 5

Bathrooms: 3½

Foundation: Slab

Materials List Available: No

Price Category: F

Images provided by designer/architect.

You're sure to find all the room you could ever want in this five-bedroom two-story home.

Features:

- Family Room: The fireplace and built-in bookshelves in this enormous room make it perfect for entertaining.
- Living Room: This large formal room has a bay window looking onto the front yard.
- Kitchen: Cabinet- and counter-filled, this kitchen has a raised bar and is open to the family room and the breakfast nook.
- Master Suite: This large area, located on the first floor, has two walk-in closets and a luxurious private bath.
- Bedrooms: Four additional bedrooms are located upstairs and share two full bathrooms.

Main Level Floor Plan

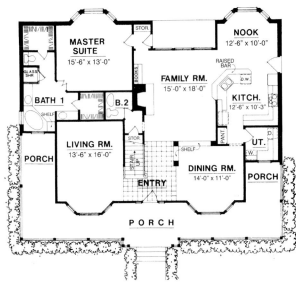

Upper Level Floor Plan

Copyright by designer/architect.

Plan #401032

Dimensions: 56' W x 53'6" D
Levels: 2
Square Footage: 2,851
Main Level Sq. Ft.: 1,592
Upper Level Sq. Ft.: 1,259
Bedrooms: 4
Bathrooms: 3
Foundation: Basement
Materials List Available: Yes
Price Category: F

A combination of architectural details makes this home elegant: keystone arches, shuttered windows, a two-story bay with a copper roof, and a recessed entry.

Features:

- Foyer: A formal living room with a fireplace and a dining room with a bay window flank this vaulted foyer.

- Family Room: This hearth-warmed family room sits at the rear of the house near the island kitchen and breakfast bay; double doors lead from the bay to a deck.

- Den: This den—or guest room—with a tray ceiling has the use of a full bath.

- Master Suite: Located on the second floor, just off a skylighted hall, this suite features a walk-in closet and private bathroom with a separate tub and shower.

- Bedrooms: The other three bedrooms share the use of a hall bathroom.

Images provided by designer/architect.

Main Level Floor Plan

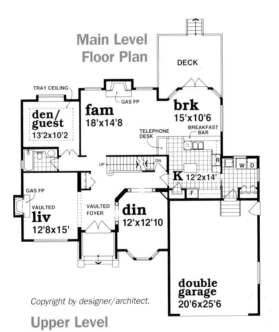

Copyright by designer/architect.

Upper Level Floor Plan

Rear Elevation

Right Side Elevation

Left Side Elevation

Plan #121069

Dimensions: 58' W x 59'4" D

Levels: 2

Square Footage: 2,914

Main Level Sq. Ft.: 1,583

Upper Level Sq. Ft.: 1,331

Bedrooms: 4

Bathrooms: 3½

Foundation: Basement

Materials List Available: Yes

Price Category: F

Images provided by designer/architect.

You'll love this design if you're looking for a home to complement a site with a lovely rear view.

Features:

- **Great Room:** A trio of lovely windows looks out to the front entry of this home. The French doors in this room open to the breakfast area for everyone's convenience.

- **Kitchen:** Designed to suit a gourmet cook, this kitchen includes a roomy pantry and an island with a snack bar.

- **Breakfast Area:** The boxed window here is perfect for houseplants or a collection of culinary herbs. A door leads to the rear porch, where you'll love to dine in good weather.

- **Master Suite:** On the upper level, the bedroom features a cathedral ceiling, two walk-in closets, and a window seat. The bath also has a cathedral ceiling and includes dual lavatories, a large dressing area, and a sunlit whirlpool tub.

Main Level Floor Plan

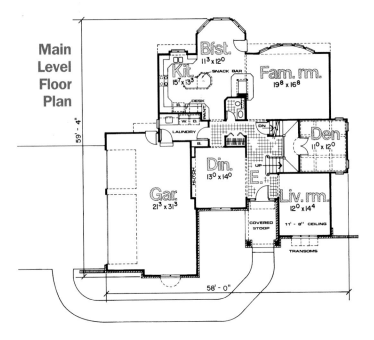

Upper Level Floor Plan

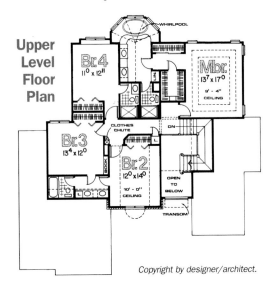

Copyright by designer/architect.

Plan #151011

Dimensions: 59'6" W x 74'4" D
Levels: 2
Square Footage: 3,437
Main Level Sq. Ft.: 2,184
Upper Level Sq. Ft.: 1,253
Bedrooms: 5
Bathrooms: 4
Foundation: Crawl space or slab; basement or daylight basement for fee
Materials List: No
Price Category: G

Images provided by designer/architect.

Beauty, comfort, and convenience are yours in this luxurious, split-level home.

Features:

- Ceiling Height: 10 ft. unless otherwise noted.

- Master Suite: The 11-ft. pan ceiling sets the tone for this secluded area, with a lovely bay window that opens onto a rear porch, a pass-through fireplace to the great room, and a sitting room.

- Great Room: The pass-through fireplace makes this spacious room a cozy spot,

while the French doors leading to a rear porch make it a perfect spot for entertaining.

- Dining Room: Gracious 8-in. columns set off the entrance to this room.

- Kitchen: An island bar provides an efficient work area that's fitted with a sink.

- Breakfast Room: Open to the kitchen, this room is defined by a bay window and a spiral staircase to the second floor.

- Laundry Room: Large enough to accommodate a folding table, this room can also be fitted with a swinging pet door.

- Play Room: French doors in the children's playroom open onto a balcony where they can continue their games.

- Bedrooms: The 9-ft. ceilings on the second story make the rooms feel bright and airy.

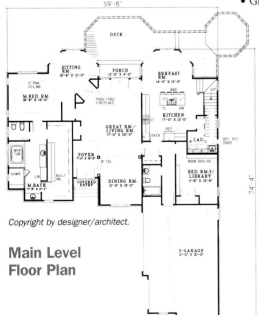

Copyright by designer/architect.

**Main Level
Floor Plan**

**Upper Level
Floor Plan**

Let Us Help You
Plan Your
Dream Home

Whether you've always dreamed of building your own home or you can't find the right house from among the dozens you've toured, our collection of Midwestern-inspired home plans can help you achieve the home of your dreams. You could have an architect create a one-of-a-kind home for you, but the design services alone could end up costing up to 15 percent of the cost of construction—a hefty premium for any building project. Isn't it a better idea to select from among the hundreds of unique designs shown in our collection for a fraction of the cost?

What does Creative Homeowner Offer?

In this book, Creative Homeowner provides hundreds of home plans from the country's best architects and designers. Our designs are among the most popular available. Whether your taste runs from traditional to contemporary, Victorian to early American, you are sure to find the best house design for you and your family. Our plans packages include detailed drawings to help you or your builder construct your dream house. (See page 281.)

Can I Make Changes to the Plans?

Creative Homeowner offers three ways to help you achieve a truly unique home design. Our customizing service allows for extensive changes to our designs. (See page 282.) We also provide reverse images of our plans, or we can give you and your builder the tools for making minor changes on your own. (See page 283.)

Can You Help Me Stay on Budget?

Building a house is a large financial investment. To help you stay within your budget, Creative Homeowner can provide you with general construction costs based on your zip code. (See page 283.) Also, many of our plans come with the option of buying detailed materials lists to help you price out construction costs.

Is There Anything I Missed?

A typical construction crew consists of a number of skilled professionals. If you plan on doing all or part of the work yourself, or you want to keep tabs on your builder, we offer best-selling building and design books at attractive prices. (See our company Web site at www.creativehomeowner.com.) Our home-building books cover all phases of home construction. For more home plans, choose from our best-selling library of home plans books. (See page 288.)

Our Plans Packages Offer:

All of our home plans are the result of many hours of work by leading architects and professional designers. Most of our home plans include each of the following.

Frontal Sheet
This artist's rendering of the front of the house gives you an idea of how the house will look once it is completed and the property landscaped.

Detailed Floor Plans
These plans show the size and layout of the rooms. They also provide the locations of doors, windows, fireplaces, closets, stairs, and electrical outlets and switches.

Foundation Plan
A foundation plan gives the dimensions of basements, walk-out basements, crawl spaces, pier foundations, and slab construction. Each house design lists the type of foundation included. If the plan you choose does not have the foundation type you require, our customer service department can help you customize the plan to meet your needs.

Roof Plan
In addition to providing the pitch of the roof, these plans also show the locations of dormers, skylights, and other elements.

Exterior Elevations
These drawings show the front, rear, and sides of the house as if you were looking at it head on. Elevations also provide information about architectural features and finish materials.

Interior Elevations and Details
Interior elevations show specific details of such elements as fireplaces, kitchen and bathroom cabinets, built-ins, and other unique features of the design.

Cross Sections
These show the structure as if it were sliced to reveal construction requirements, such as insulation, flooring, and roofing details.

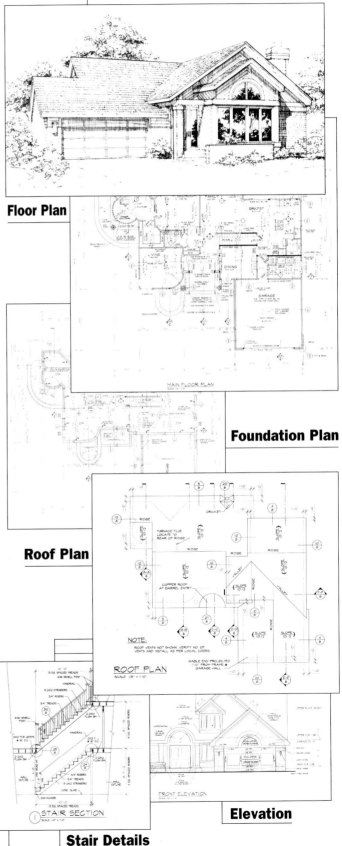

Frontal Sheet

Floor Plan

Foundation Plan

Roof Plan

Cross Sections

Stair Details

Elevation

Customize Your Plans in 4 Easy Steps

1 Select the home plan that most closely meets your needs. Purchase of a reproducible master is necessary in order to make changes to a plan.

2 Call 1-800-523-6789 to place your order. Tell our sales representative you are interested in customizing your plan. To receive your customization cost estimate, we will send you a checklist (via fax or email) for you to complete indicating the changes you would like to make to your plan. There is a $50 nonrefundable consultation fee for this service. If you decide to continue with the custom changes, the $50 fee is credited to the total amount charged.

3 Fax the completed checklist to 1-201-760-2431 or email it to us at customize@creativehomeowner.com. Within three business days of receipt of your checklist, a detailed cost estimate will be provided to you.

4 Once you approve the estimate, a 75% retainer fee is collected and customization work begins. Preliminary drawings typically take 10 to 15 business days. After approval, we will collect the balance of your customization order cost before shipping the completed plans. You will receive five sets of blueprints or a reproducible master, plus a customized materials list if desired.

Modification Pricing Guide

Categories	Average Cost For Modification
Add or remove living space	Quote required
Bathroom layout redesign	Starting at $120
Kitchen layout redesign	Starting at $120
Garage: add or remove	Starting at $400
Garage: front entry to side load or vice versa	Starting at $300
Foundation changes	Starting at $220
Exterior building materials change	Starting at $200
Exterior openings: add, move, or remove	$65 per opening
Roof line changes	Starting at $360
Ceiling height adjustments	Starting at $280
Fireplace: add or remove	Starting at $90
Screened porch: add	Starting at $280
Wall framing change from 2x4 to 2x6	Starting at $200
Bearing and/or exterior walls changes	Quote required
Non-bearing wall or room changes	$65 per room
Metric conversion of home plan	Starting at $400
Adjust plan for handicapped accessibility	Quote required
Adapt plans for local building code requirements	Quote required
Engineering stamping only	Quote required
Any other engineering services	Quote required
Interactive illustrations (choices of exterior materials)	Quote required

Note: *Any home plan can be customized to accommodate your desired changes. The average prices above are provided only as examples of the most commonly requested changes, and are subject to change without notice. Prices for changes will vary according to the number of modifications requested, plan size, style, and method of design used by the original designer. To obtain a detailed cost estimate, please contact us.*

Terms & Copyright

These home plans are protected under the terms of United States Copyright Law and may not be copied or reproduced in any way, by any means, unless you have purchased reproducible masters, which clearly indicate your right to copy or reproduce. We authorize the use of your chosen home plan as an aid in the construction of one single-family home only. You may not use this home plan to build a second or multiple dwellings without purchasing another blueprint or blueprints, or paying additional home plan fees.

Architectural Seals

Because of differences in building codes, some cities and states now require an architect or engineer licensed in that state to review and "seal" a blueprint, or officially approve it, prior to construction. Delaware, Nevada, New Jersey, and New York require that all plans for houses built in those states be redrawn by an architect licensed in the state in which the home will be built. We strongly advise you to consult with your local building official for information regarding architectural seals.

Before Customization

After

Decide What Type of Plan Package You Need

How many Plans Should You Order?

Standard 8-Set Package. We've found that our 8-set package is the best value for someone who is ready to start building. Once the process begins, a number of people will require their own set of blueprints. The 8-set package provides plans for you, your builder, the subcontractors, mortgage lender, and the building department.

Minimum 4-Set Package. If you are in the bidding process, you may want to order only four sets for the bidding round and reorder additional sets as needed.

1-Set Study Package. The 1-set package allows you to review your home plan in detail. The plan will be marked as a study print, and it is illegal to build a house from a study print alone. It is a violation of copyright law to reproduce a blueprint without permission.

Buying Additional Sets

If you require additional copies of blueprints for your home construction, you can order additional sets within 60 days of the original order date at a reduced price. The cost is $45.00 for each additional set. For more information, contact customer service.

Reproducible Masters

If you plan to make minor changes to one of our home plans, you can purchase reproducible masters. Printed on vellum paper, an erasable paper that you can reproduce in a copying machine, reproducible masters allow an architect, designer, or builder to alter our plans to give you a customized home design. This package also allows you to print as many copies of the modified plans as you need for construction.

Mirror-Reverse Sets

Plans can be printed in mirror-reverse—we can "flip" plans to create a mirror image of the design. This is useful when the house would fit your site or personal preferences if all the rooms were on the opposite side than shown. As the image is reversed, the lettering and dimensions will also be reversed, meaning they will read backwards. Therefore, when ordering mirror-reverse drawings, you must order at least one set of right-reading plans. A $50.00 fee per order will be charged for mirror-reverse (regardless of the number of mirror-reverse sets ordered).

EZ Quote: Home Cost Estimator

EZ Quote is our response to one of the most frequently asked questions we hear from customers: "How much will the house cost me to build?" EZ Quote: Home Cost Estimator will enable you to obtain a calculated building cost to construct your new home, based on labor rates and building material costs within your zip code area. This summary is useful for those who want to know the total construction costs before purchasing sets of home plans. It will also provide a level of comfort when you begin soliciting bids from builders. The cost is $29.95 for the first EZ Quote and $14.95 for each additional one. Available only in the U.S. and Canada.

CompleteCost Estimator

CompleteCost Estimator is a valuable tool for use in planning and constructing your new home. It combines the detail of a materials list with line-by-line cost estimating. The result is a complete, detailed estimate—similar to a bid—that will act as a checklist for all the items you will need to select or coordinate during our building process. CompleteCost Estimator is only available for certain plans (please see Plan Index) and may only be ordered with the purchase of a set of home plans. The cost is $125 for CompleteCost Estimator.

Materials List

Available for most of our plans, the Materials List provides you an invaluable resource in planning and estimating the cost of your home. Each Materials List outlines the quantity, dimensions, and type of materials needed to build your home (with the exception of mechanical systems). You will get faster, more-accurate bids from your contractors and building suppliers—and avoid paying for unused materials. A Materials List may only be ordered with the purchase of a set of home plans.

Order Toll Free by Phone
1-800-523-6789
By Fax: 201-760-2431

Regular office hours are
8:30AM–7:00PM ET, Mon–Fri

Orders received 3PM ET, will be
processed and shipped within two
business days.

Order Online
www.ultimateplans.com

Mail Your Order
Creative Homeowner
Attn: Home Plans
24 Park Way
Upper Saddle River, NJ 07458

Canadian Customers
Order Toll Free 1-800-393-1883

Mail Your Order (Canada)
Creative Homeowner Canada
Attn: Home Plans
113-437 Martin St., Ste. 215
Penticton, BC V2A 5L1

Before You Order

Our Exchange Policy

Blueprints are nonrefundable. However, should you find that the plan you have purchased does not fit your needs, you may exchange that plan for another plan in our collection within 60 days from the date of your original order. The entire content of your original order must be returned before an exchange will be processed. You will be charged a processing fee of 20% of the amount of the original plan set, the cost difference between the new plan set and the original plan set (if applicable), and shipping costs for the new plans. Contact our customer service department for more information. Please note: reproducible masters may only be exchanged if the package is unopened.

Building Codes and Requirements

At the time of creation, our plans meet the building code requirements published by the Building Officials and Code Administrators International, the Southern Building Code Congress International, the International Conference of Building Officials, or the Council of American Building Officials. Because building codes vary from area to area, some drawing modifications and/or the assistance of a professional designer or architect may be necessary to comply with your local codes or to accommodate specific building site conditions. We strongly advise you to consult with your local building official for information regarding codes governing your area.

Blueprint Price Schedule

Price Code	1 Set	4 Sets	8 Sets	Reproducible Masters	Materials List
A	$290	$330	$380	$510	$60
B	$360	$410	$460	$580	$60
C	$420	$460	$510	$610	$60
D	$470	$510	$560	$660	$70
E	$520	$560	$610	$700	$70
F	$570	$610	$670	$750	$70
G	$620	$670	$720	$850	$70
H	$700	$740	$800	$900	$70
I	$810	$850	$900	$940	$80

Note: Prices subject to change

Shipping & Handling

	1-4 Sets	5-7 Sets	8+ Sets or Reproducibles
US Regular (7–10 business days)	$15	$20	$25
US Priority (3–5 business days)	$25	$30	$35
US Express (1–2 business days)	$40	$45	$50
Canada Regular (8–12 business days)	$35	$40	$45
Canada Express (1–2 business days)	$60	$70	$80
Worldwide Express (2–5 business days)	$80	$80	$80

Note: *All delivery times are from date the blueprint package is shipped (typically within 1-2 days of placing order).*

Order Form

Please send me the following:

Plan Number: _____

Price Code: _____ (see Plan Index)

Indicate Foundation Type: (Select ONE. See plan page for availability.)
❏ Slab ❏ Crawl space ❏ Basement ❏ Walk-out basement

Basic Blueprint Package

	Cost
❏ Reproducible Masters	$_____
❏ 8-Set Plan Package	$_____
❏ 4-Set Plan Package	$_____
❏ 1-Set Study Package	$_____
❏ Additional plan sets: __ sets at $45.00 per set	$_____
❏ Print in mirror-reverse: $50.00 per order __ sets printed in mirror-reverse	$_____

Important Extras

❏ Materials List	$_____
❏ CompleteCost Materials Report at $125	$_____
❏ Zip Code of Home/Building Site_____	
❏ EZ Quote for Plan #_____at $29.95	$_____
❏ Additional EZ Quotes for Plan #s_____ at $14.95 each	$_____
Shipping (see chart above)	$_____
SUBTOTAL	$_____
Sales Tax (NJ residents only add 6%)	$_____
TOTAL	$_____

Order Toll Free: 1-800-523-6789 By Fax: 201-760-2431
Creative Homeowner
24 Park Way
Upper Saddle River, NJ 07458

Name _____
(Please print or type)

Street _____
(Please do not use a P.O. Box)

City _____ State _____

Country _____ Zip _____

Daytime telephone ( )_____

Fax ( )_____
(Required for reproducible orders)

E-Mail _____

Payment ❏ Check/money order *Make checks payable to Creative Homeowner*

❏ VISA ❏ MasterCard ❏ American Express Cards ❏ DISCOVER

Credit card number _____

Expiration date (mm/yy) _____

Signature _____

Please check the appropriate box:
❏ Licensed builder/contractor ❏ Homeowner ❏ Renter

SOURCE CODE	CA750

Copyright Notice

Index

Plan #	Price Code	Page	Total Finished Area Square Feet	Materials List	CompleteCost
101005	D	163	1,992	Yes	No
101012	E	195	2,288	No	No
101026	B	24	1,420	No	No
101027	C	87	1,695	No	No
101028	D	137	1,963	No	No
101029	D	126	1,897	No	No
101036	B	40	1,343	No	No
111006	E	209	2,241	No	No
121001	D	138	1,911	Yes	No
121002	B	33	1,347	Yes	No
121004	C	79	1,666	Yes	No
121005	B	34	1,496	Yes	No
121015	D	142	1,999	Yes	No
121017	E	216	2,353	Yes	No
121023	H	249	3,904	Yes	No
121029	E	261	2,576	Yes	No
121034	E	208	2,223	Yes	No
121044	D	122	1,923	Yes	No
121047	G	275	3,072	Yes	No
121050	D	157	1,996	Yes	No
121060	B	27	1,339	Yes	No
121062	G	266	3,448	Yes	No
121064	D	123	1,846	Yes	No
121069	F	278	2,914	Yes	No
121073	E	264	2,579	Yes	No
121074	E	192	2,486	Yes	No
121081	G	274	3,623	Yes	No
121088	E	215	2,340	Yes	No
121090	F	273	2,645	Yes	No
131003	B	32	1,466	Yes	No
131005	C	84	1,595	Yes	No
131005	C	85	1,595	Yes	No
131006	E	208	2,193	Yes	No
131007	D	60	1,595	Yes	No
131007	D	61	1,595	Yes	No
131009	D	143	2,018	Yes	No
131014	B	35	1,380	Yes	No
131017	C	32	1,480	Yes	No
131027	F	236	2,567	Yes	No
131032	F	195	2,455	Yes	No
131047	C	101	1,793	Yes	No
151002	E	216	2,444	No	Yes
151004	D	178	2,107	No	Yes
151007	C	79	1,787	No	Yes
151008	D	124	1,892	No	Yes
151009	C	67	1,601	No	Yes
151010	B	33	1,379	No	Yes
151011	G	279	3,437	No	Yes
151023	G	235	3,203	No	Yes
151024	H	269	3,623	No	Yes
151026	C	66	1,574	No	Yes
151027	E	214	2,323	No	Yes
151028	E	207	2,252	No	Yes
151029	F	269	2,777	No	Yes
151034	D	179	2,133	No	Yes
151050	D	163	2,096	No	Yes
151168	E	214	2,261	No	Yes
151205	C	152	1,969	No	Yes
151206	D	173	2,151	No	Yes
151207	G	248	3,099	No	Yes
151209	I	260	4,468	No	Yes
151210	C	82	1,716	No	Yes
151211	C	98	1,797	No	Yes
151212	B	37	1,462	No	Yes
151213	B	8	1,231	No	Yes
151215	C	63	1,519	No	Yes
151216	E	234	2,545	No	Yes
151217	F	267	2,864	No	Yes
151218	B	17	1,008	No	Yes
151219	C	81	1,712	No	Yes
151220	B	16	1,325	No	Yes
151221	E	238	2,593	No	Yes
151222	F	251	2,707	No	Yes
151225	F	268	2,875	No	Yes
151232	H	233	3,901	No	Yes
151243	D	120	1,923	No	Yes
151244	D	133	1,923	No	Yes
151245	D	165	1,923	No	Yes
161002	D	124	1,860	Yes	No
161007	C	93	1,611	Yes	No
161008	D	143	1,860	No	No
161016	D	178	2,101	Yes	No
161017	F	238	2,653	Yes	No
161020	D	139	2,082	Yes	No
161024	C	96	1,698	No	No
161025	F	272	2,738	No	No
161029	I	272	4,470	Yes	No
161034	D	180	2,156	No	No
161072	D	184	2,183	Yes	No
161074	E	194	2,427	No	No
161075	F	253	2,773	No	No
161077	F	253	2,773	Yes	No
161082	D	160	2,049	Yes	No
171013	G	265	3,084	Yes	No
181151	E	181	2,283	Yes	No
181215	A	14	929	Yes	No
181216	A	23	910	Yes	No
181219	B	13	1,311	Yes	No
181223	B	38	1,440	Yes	No
181225	C	90	1,746	Yes	No
181226	B	31	1,485	Yes	No
181227	B	45	1,248	Yes	No
181230	D	136	1,943	Yes	No
181233	B	30	1,482	Yes	No
181235	B	20	1,077	Yes	No
181239	D	181	2,181	Yes	No
181241	F	243	2,687	Yes	No
181242	D	132	1,826	Yes	No
191012	D	206	2,123	No	No
211001	C	96	1,655	Yes	No
211006	D	180	2,177	Yes	No
211069	C	93	1,600	Yes	No
211072	G	249	3,012	Yes	No
241008	E	237	2,526	No	No
271001	B	34	1,400	Yes	No
271002	B	35	1,252	Yes	No
271072	G	275	3,081	No	No
271077	C	103	1,786	No	No
291005	A	23	896	No	No
311001	D	157	2,085	No	No
311011	D	138	1,955	Yes	No
311018	C	142	1,867	Yes	No
321001	C	92	1,721	Yes	No
321003	C	92	1,791	Yes	No
321005	E	192	2,483	Yes	No
321006	D	123	1,977	Yes	No
321007	F	273	2,695	Yes	No
321008	C	102	1,761	Yes	No
321014	C	66	1,676	Yes	No
321018	E	236	2,523	Yes	No
321021	C	67	1,708	Yes	No
321024	B	27	1,403	Yes	No
321025	A	11	914	Yes	No
321027	F	247	2,758	Yes	No
321028	F	247	2,723	Yes	No
321030	D	139	2,029	Yes	No
321034	H	274	3,508	Yes	No
321036	F	251	2,900	No	No
321037	E	179	2,397	Yes	No
321048	G	252	3,216	Yes	No
321055	E	235	2,505	Yes	No
331002	E	215	2,299	No	No
351001	D	121	1,855	Yes	No
351002	C	91	1,751	Yes	No

Index

Plan #	Price Code	Page	Total Finished Area Square Feet	Materials List	CompleteCost
351003	C	83	1,751	Yes	No
351004	D	121	1,852	Yes	No
351005	C	62	1,501	Yes	No
351007	E	209	2,251	Yes	No
351018	B	22	1,251	Yes	No
351021	C	36	1,500	Yes	No
351023	C	72	1,600	Yes	No
351026	C	80	1,603	Yes	No
351032	C	75	1,650	Yes	No
351033	C	77	1,654	Yes	No
351040	D	99	1,800	Yes	No
351044	E	155	2,000	Yes	No
351045	E	155	2,000	Yes	No
351049	E	156	2,004	Yes	No
351055	E	210	2,251	Yes	No
351057	E	231	2,505	Yes	No
351059	F	246	2,805	Yes	No
351068	D	230	2,501	Yes	No
371003	E	212	2,297	No	No
371004	D	162	1,815	No	No
371005	B	46	1,250	No	No
371006	B	41	1,374	No	No
371008	F	242	2,656	No	No
371009	B	22	1,223	No	No
371010	B	25	1,429	No	No
371011	C	87	1,681	No	No
371012	C	83	1,720	No	No
371013	C	100	1,791	No	No
371014	D	130	1,908	No	No
371016	E	217	2,316	No	No
371021	E	204	2,384	No	No
371022	E	206	2,390	No	No
371023	E	190	2,444	No	No
371024	F	276	2,843	No	No
371028	B	42	1,376	No	No
371030	B	26	1,434	No	No
371031	C	71	1,599	No	No
371032	C	78	1,659	No	No
371033	C	89	1,724	No	No
371034	C	86	1,753	No	No
371036	C	94	1,764	No	No
371037	C	95	1,774	No	No
371038	D	126	1,896	No	No
371039	D	127	1,898	No	No
371040	D	137	1,913	No	No
371042	D	154	1,999	No	No
371043	E	158	2,013	No	No
371044	D	164	2,094	No	No
371045	E	186	2,225	No	No
371049	B	29	1,440	No	No
371053	C	76	1,654	No	No
371059	E	185	2,240	No	No
371060	E	211	2,296	No	No
371062	E	220	2,328	No	No
371063	E	221	2,330	No	No
371064	G	248	3,140	No	No
371069	B	31	1,484	No	No
371071	C	90	1,729	No	No
371072	C	94	1,772	No	No
371075	E	128	1,904	No	No
371079	D	162	2,089	No	No
371081	D	176	2,143	No	No
371087	F	240	2,643	No	No
371088	F	250	2,705	No	No
371089	F	250	2,704	No	No
391001	D	159	2,015	Yes	No
391002	E	210	2,281	Yes	No
391003	D	129	1,907	Yes	No
391004	C	91	1,750	Yes	No
391005	C	88	1,575	Yes	No
391006	B	39	1,456	Yes	No
391007	D	140	2,083	Yes	No
391007	D	141	2,083	Yes	No
391008	B	15	1,312	Yes	No
391011	E	191	2,483	Yes	No
391012	D	174	2,157	Yes	No
391012	D	175	2,157	Yes	No
391013	D	125	1,894	Yes	No
391014	E	218	2,372	Yes	No
391014	E	219	2,372	Yes	No
391015	E	207	2,411	Yes	No
391016	C	95	1,785	Yes	No
391017	D	182	2,176	Yes	No
391017	D	183	2,176	Yes	No
391018	H	259	3,746	Yes	No
391020	E	205	2,387	Yes	No
391021	C	70	1,568	Yes	No
391022	D	131	1,908	Yes	No
391023	E	187	2,244	Yes	No
391024	F	241	2,647	Yes	No
391026	B	9	1,470	Yes	No
391031	G	258	3,176	Yes	No
391033	D	156	2,007	Yes	No
391036	B	12	1,301	Yes	No
391038	C	74	1,642	Yes	No
391039	C	64	1,539	Yes	No
391043	D	173	2,143	Yes	No
391046	D	153	1,978	Yes	No
391060	B	28	1,359	Yes	No
391064	A	43	988	Yes	No
401001	D	161	2,071	Yes	No
401002	D	136	1,938	Yes	No
401003	E	237	2,582	Yes	No
401004	F	243	2,684	Yes	No
401005	B	19	1,073	Yes	No
401006	C	86	1,670	Yes	No
401007	B	44	1,286	Yes	No
401008	C	65	1,541	Yes	No
401009	F	252	2,750	Yes	No
401010	D	164	2,094	Yes	No
401011	D	134	2,097	Yes	No
401012	E	213	2,301	Yes	No
401013	E	193	2,381	Yes	No
401014	E	232	2,516	Yes	No
401015	F	239	2,618	Yes	No
401016	E	234	2,539	Yes	No
401018	G	246	2,797	Yes	No
401019	B	47	1,256	Yes	No
401021	C	68	1,543	Yes	No
401023	F	228	2,806	Yes	No
401023	F	229	2,806	Yes	No
401027	C	73	1,634	Yes	No
401028	E	177	2,219	Yes	No
401029	D	188	2,163	Yes	No
401029	D	189	2,163	Yes	No
401030	C	97	1,795	Yes	No
401032	F	277	2,851	Yes	No
401036	C	88	1,583	Yes	No
401037	D	135	1,924	Yes	No
401038	D	172	2,142	Yes	No
401039	E	191	2,462	Yes	No
401041	B	21	1,108	Yes	No
401042	E	184	2,239	Yes	No
401043	A	10	988	Yes	No
401044	C	69	1,568	Yes	No
401046	D	154	1,990	Yes	No
401047	B	18	1,064	Yes	No
401048	I	262	5,159	Yes	No
401048	I	263	5,159	Yes	No
401049	I	244	4,087	Yes	No
401049	I	245	4,087	Yes	No
401050	I	270	6,841	Yes	No
401050	I	271	6,841	Yes	No

Complete Your Home Plans Library with these Great Books from Creative Homeowner

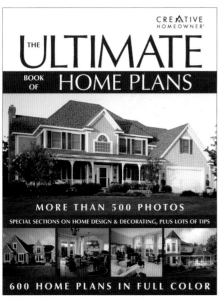

528 pages
Book # 277039

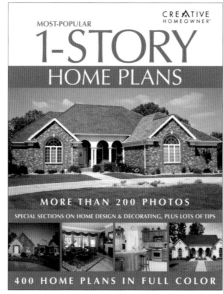

352 pages
Book # 277020

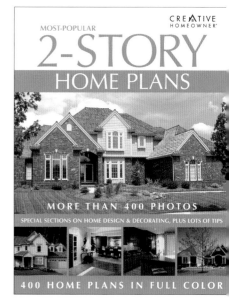

352 pages
Book # 277028

320 pages
Book # 277027

320 pages
Book # 277005

The Best Home Plan Books You Can Find

- Hundreds of home designs from top residential architects and designers

- Hundreds of full-color photographs of actual home that have been built. Many of the homes also include beautiful interior photographs

- Up to 1,000 or more drawings of floor plans, side views and rear views

- Dozens of informative pages containing design and decorating ideas and tips, from working with builders to designing kitchens and installing trimwork and landscaping

Books To Help You Build

Creative Homeowner offers an extensive selection of leading how-to books.

Home Building Package

Build and repair your home—inside and out—with these essential titles.

Retail Price: $74.80
Your Price: $65.95
Order #: 267095

Wiring: Complete Projects for the Home
Provides comprehensive information about the home electrical system. Over 750 color photos and 75 illustrations. 288 pages.

Plumbing: Basic, Intermediate & Advanced Projects
An overview of the plumbing system with code-compliant, step-by-step projects. Over 750 full-color photos, illustrations. 272 pages.

House Framing
Walks you through the framing basics, from assembling simple partitions to cutting compound angles for dormers. 650 full-color illustrations and photos. 240 pages.

Drywall: Pro Tips for Hanging and Finishing
Covers tools and materials, estimating, cutting, hanging, and finishing gypsum wallboard. 250 color photos and illustrations. 144 pages.

Look for these and other fine Creative Homeowner books wherever books are sold
For more information and to place an order, go to **www.creativehomeowner.com**